CREATIVE COOKING

Collection

Publications International, Ltd.

Photography on page 177 by Vuksanovich, Chicago.
Remaining photography by Sacco Productions Limited, Chicago.
Pictured on the front cover: Walnut Chicken *(page 184)*.
Pictured on the back cover: Belgian Tuile Cookies *(page 284)*.

ISBN: 0-7853-1423-7

Library of Congress Catalog Card Number: 95-68526

Manufactured in U.S.A.

8   7   6   5   4   3   2   1

Microwave Cooking: Microwave ovens vary in wattage. The microwave cooking times given in this publication are approximate. Use the cooking times as guidelines and check for doneness before adding more time. Consult manufacturer's instructions for suitable microwave-safe cooking dishes.

The publisher would like to thank the following organizations for the use of their recipes in this publication: A-OK Cook Off, American Lamb Council, California State Fair, Christopher Ranch Garlic, Delmarva Poultry Industry, Inc., Essex Agricultural Society, The Hartford Courant, Illinois State Fair, Michigan Apple Committee, Michigan State Fair, National Broiler Council, Nebraska State Fair, New Mexico State Fair, New York Cherry Growers Association, North Dakota Beef Commission, North Dakota Cattlewomen, North Dakota Wheat Commission and Southeast United Dairy Industry Association, Inc.

Contents

Introduction

Creative Cooking Collection is designed to teach all skill levels of cooks—from the novice to the very experienced—how to prepare fabulous, eye-catching recipes using fresh ingredients. This gourmet collection of over 160 recipes combines sensational tastes with contemporary cooking techniques and terms.

Each delectable recipe has been carefully developed to ensure the best possible results. To guide you through preparation and cooking, the instructions are written with precise step-by-step directions. As you read through the recipes, many of the techniques are illustrated in the helpful how-to photographs. To further tantalize your creativity, each recipe is featured in a mouthwatering full-page photograph.

In addition to the wonderful recipes, the following introduction is full of informative tips, hints and guidelines. Detailed instructions and illustrations—from carving a roast and deboning a chicken breast to cookie baking tips—direct you through cooking techniques with ease, ensuring success in the kitchen. This wealth of culinary information is waiting for you to explore.

APPETIZERS
General Guidelines

When serving appetizers before a meal, keep in mind they are meant to tease the appetite, not satisfy it. One or two selections should be ample, allowing for a total of five to seven servings per person. Prepare recipes that contrast in texture, temperature and flavor with the meal that follows. Many people prefer to serve first-course appetizers before the guests are seated at the dinner table, as this allows the cook time to make last-minute meal preparations.

Cold appetizers, such as dips and marinated vegetables, should be made at least several hours to one day ahead since their flavors actually improve with time. Some hot appetizers can be cooked ahead and simply reheated just before serving, while others must be prepared at the last moment.

If the appetizers will be sitting out for several hours, it is important to maintain serving temperatures. Cold appetizers, such as shrimp cocktail, should be served on a platter set over cracked ice. Hot appetizers, such as meatballs, should be served in a warming device, such as a chafing dish or fondue pot.

MEATS
General Guidelines

A stand time of 10 to 20 minutes is recommended for large cuts of meat, such as roasts, turkeys and whole chickens to allow the meat to finish cooking. The internal temperature given for removing meat and poultry from the oven is 5° to 10°F lower than the expected final temperature because it continues to rise during the stand time. Meat is also easier to carve after standing. If meat is carved immediately out of the oven, it loses more of its flavorful juices.

Carving Techniques

Unless you are planning to carve at the table, place the meat on a large cutting board with a well at one end to hold the juice. (Or, place a cutting board inside a baking sheet where the juice will collect.) Use a long-handled meat fork to steady the meat and a long, sharp carving knife to slice it.

Boneless Roasts

Boneless beef, pork and lamb roasts are easy to carve. Hold the roast steady with a long-handled meat fork. With the knife blade held so that it is perpendicular to the cutting board, cut across the grain into thin uniform slices about ¼ to ½ inch thick.

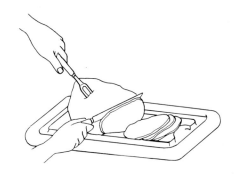

A beef brisket is a thinner cut of meat. Follow the preceding directions, but slice the meat diagonally rather than straight across the grain. This will give you a slice of meat with a larger surface area.

POULTRY

General Guidelines

When handling raw poultry, you must keep everything that comes into contact with it clean. Raw poultry should be rinsed and patted dry with paper towels before cooking; cutting boards and knives must be washed in hot, sudsy water after using and hands must be scrubbed thoroughly before and after handling. Why? Raw poultry can harbor harmful salmonella bacteria. If bacteria are transferred to work surfaces, utensils or hands, they could contaminate other foods and may cause food poisoning. With careful handling and proper cooking, this is easily prevented.

Poultry should always be cooked completely before eating. You should never cook poultry partially, then store it to be finished later, since this promotes bacterial growth as well.

Storing & Freezing

Fresh, raw poultry can be stored in its original wrap for up to two days in the coldest part of the refrigerator. However, freeze poultry immediately if you do not plan to use it within two days after purchasing. You can freeze most poultry in its original packaging safely for up to two months; if you plan to freeze it longer, consider double-wrapping or rewrapping with freezer paper, aluminum foil or plastic wrap. Airtight packaging is the key to freezing poultry successfully.

When freezing whole chickens, turkeys, ducks and Cornish hens, remove and rinse giblets (if any) and pat dry with paper towels. Trim away any excess fat.

Tightly wrap, label, date and freeze in freezer-strength plastic or foil wraps.

Thaw frozen poultry, wrapped, in the refrigerator for best results. Thawing times vary depending on how thoroughly frozen the poultry is and whether it is whole or cut up. A general guideline is to allow 24 hours thawing time for 5 pounds; allow about 5 hours per pound for thawing pieces. *Never* thaw chicken on the kitchen counter as this promotes bacterial growth.

Doneness Tests

There are a number of ways to determine if poultry is thoroughly cooked and ready to eat. For whole chickens and turkeys, a meat thermometer inserted into the thickest part of the thigh, but not near bone or fat, should register 180° to 185°F before removing from the oven. If a whole chicken or turkey is stuffed, insert the thermometer into the center of the body cavity; when the stuffing registers 160°F, it should be done. (Chickens and turkeys should only be stuffed just before roasting; never stuff ahead of time.) Roasted whole chicken breasts are done when they register 170°F on a meat thermometer.

To test bone-in chicken pieces, you should be able to insert a fork into the chicken with ease and the juices should run clear; however, the meat and juices nearest the bones might still be a little pink even though the chicken is cooked thoroughly. Boneless chicken pieces are done when the centers are no longer pink; you can determine this by simply cutting into the chicken with a knife.

Preparation Techniques

Flattening Uncooked Boneless Chicken Breasts

Place one chicken breast half between two sheets of waxed paper. Using the flat side of a meat mallet or rolling pin, gently pound chicken from center to outside of breast to desired thickness.

Skinning and Deboning a Whole Chicken Breast

1. Freeze chicken breast until firm, but not hard. (However, do not refreeze thawed chicken.) Grasp skin with clean cotton kitchen towel or paper towel and pull away from meat; discard skin. When finished skinning chicken breast, launder kitchen towel before using again.

2. Place breast, meaty side down, on cutting board. Cut small slit through membrane and cartilage at the V of the neck end.

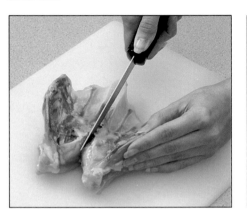

3. Grasp breast with both hands and gently bend both sides backward to snap breastbone.

4. With fingers, work along both sides of breastbone to loosen meat from triangular keel bone; carefully pull out keel bone.

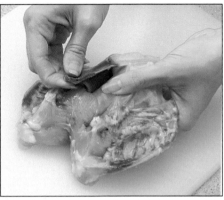

5. With tip of sharp knife, cut along both sides of cartilage at end of breastbone. Remove cartilage.

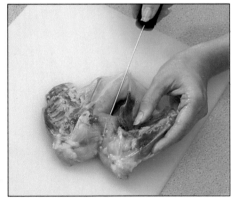

6. Slip point of knife under long rib bone on one side of breast. Cut and scrape meat from rib bones, pulling bones away from meat.

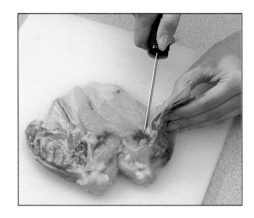

7. Cut meat away from collarbone. Remove bones. Repeat procedure to debone other side of breast.

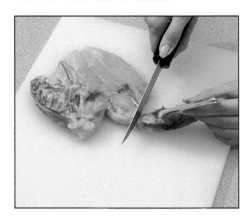

8. Remove wishbones of chicken breasts that have been cut from whole chickens in your home kitchen. Cut meat away from wishbone at neck end of breast. Grasp wishbone and pull it out of breast.

9. To remove white tendon from each side of breast, cut enough meat away from each tendon so you can grasp it. (Use paper towel for firmer grasp.) Remove tendon.

10. Flip breast to meaty side up. If desired, remove chicken tenders from thickest edge of each breast half and reserve for another use. Trim any loosened remaining connective tissue, if needed. Cut whole chicken breast into halves lengthwise, if desired.

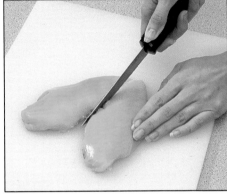

FISH

General Guidelines

Fish comes in various forms. Fillets are sold boneless and may or may not be skinless. Steaks are the cross sections from large round fish (fish with rounded bodies and eyes on both sides of the head). They vary from ¾ to 1 inch in thickness. Steaks contain part of the backbone and the outside edge is covered with skin.

When purchasing fillets and steaks, look for cuts with moist flesh that is free from discoloration and skin that is shiny and resilient. The odor is a sure sign of freshness. If the fish has an off odor, do not buy it.

When purchasing frozen fish, the package should still have its original shape with the wrapper intact. There should be no ice crystals, visible blood or discoloration on the skin and flesh.

Cooking Methods & Doneness Tests

The most common methods of cooking fish are pan-frying, deep-fat frying, poaching, broiling, grilling and baking. Before cooking, rinse fish under cold, running water and pat it dry with paper towels. Fish cooks quickly! Be careful not to overcook it as this makes the fish tough and destroys the flavor. Fish is done cooking when the flesh turns opaque and flakes easily when tested with a fork. Cooking times vary with each fish and cut. The following is a guideline for cooking times: 10 minutes per inch of thickness; 15 minutes per inch when cooked in a sauce; 20 minutes per inch when frozen.

SHELLFISH

General Guidelines

All fresh shellfish should have a fresh, mild, sea-breeze odor. Fresh lobsters and crabs should be purchased live as close to the time of cooking as possible. Both should actively move their claws; lobsters should flap their tails tightly against their chests or, when picked up, curl their tails under their shells. However, if the lobsters and crabs have been refrigerated, they will be less active. Do not purchase any lobsters or crabs that do not show these signs of life. Shrimp should feel firm to the touch.

Clams can be purchased live in their shells or freshly shucked in their liquor. Hard-shelled clams, mussels and oysters should have tightly closed shells or snap tightly closed when tapped. If they do not close when tapped, they are dead and should be discarded. The soft-shell clam is unable to close its shell completely. To determine if it is alive, gently touch the protruding neck of the clam to see if it will retract. If the neck does not retract slightly, discard the clam. Discard any clams, mussels or oysters that have cracked or broken shells.

Freshly shucked clams should be plump, moist and shiny. The color varies from grayish green to beige to light or dark orange depending on the variety.

Freshly shucked oysters should be surrounded by a clear, slightly milky white or light gray liquid. Oysters are usually creamy white but the color varies depending on the variety.

Freshly shucked scallops vary in color from creamy white to tan to a light pink color. Bay scallops, generally found on the East Coast, are about ½ inch in diameter. Sea scallops are larger, about 1½ inches in diameter.

Doneness Tests

The main point to remember when cooking shellfish is not to overcook it. If shellfish is cooked too long, it becomes tough and dry and loses much of its flavor. Heat precooked shellfish until heated through. Raw shellfish, shucked or in the shell, only takes a short time to cook. The following are guidelines for judging when shellfish is cooked.

Shucked shellfish, such as clams, mussels and oysters, become opaque. The edges of the oysters start to curl. Be careful not to overcook because this causes them to shrink.

Clams, mussels and oysters in the shell should open. Remove them as they open and continue cooking until all are opened. Discard any that do not open.

Lobsters are cooked according to weight. Even though they turn bright red almost immediately, this is not an indication of doneness. When boiling, the cooking time begins once the water has returned to a boil. Boil lobsters for the time recommended on page 242.

Scallops turn milky white or opaque and firm. Depending on the size of the scallop, it takes 3 to 4 minutes to cook.

Shrimp turn pink and opaque. Timing varies depending on size. For example, it takes 3 to 5 minutes to boil or steam 1 pound of medium shrimp in the shell, while it takes 5 to 8 minutes for jumbo shrimp.

COOKIES

General Guidelines

There are five basic types of cookies: bar, drop, refrigerator, rolled and shaped. These types are determined by the consistency of the dough and how it is formed into cookies.

Bar Cookies: Always use the pan size called for in the recipe. Using a different size will affect the cookies' baking time and texture. A smaller pan will result in a more cakelike texture while a larger pan will produce a drier texture.

Drop Cookies: Cookies that are uniform in size and shape finish baking at the same time. To easily shape drop cookies into a uniform size, use an ice cream scoop with a release bar. The bar usually has a number on it indicating the number of scoops that can be made from one quart of ice cream. Choose a #80 or #90 for standard-size cookies. Either of these will yield about one rounded teaspoonful of dough for each cookie.

Refrigerator Cookies: Always shape the dough into rolls before chilling. Shaping is easier if you first place the dough on a piece of waxed paper or plastic wrap. Before chilling, wrap the rolls securely in plastic wrap because exposure to air can cause the dough to dry out.

Use gentle pressure and a back-and-forth sawing motion with a sharp knife when slicing the rolls; this ensures that the cookies will keep a nice round shape. Rotating the roll while slicing also keeps one side from flattening.

Rolled Cookies: Chill the cookie dough before rolling for easier handling. Remove only enough dough from the refrigerator to work with at one time. Save any trimmings and reroll them all at once to prevent the dough from becoming tough.

Shaped Cookies: These cookies can be simply hand-shaped into balls or crescents or forced through a cookie press into more complex shapes.

If the recipe calls for a cookie press, do not shape the cookies by hand unless the recipe states that you may do so. The consistency of the dough was created to work in a cookie press. When using a cookie press, if your first efforts are not successful, just return the dough to the cookie press and try again.

Baking

The best cookie sheets to use are those with no sides or one or two short sides. These sheets allow the heat to circulate easily during baking and promote even browning.

For optimum baking and browning, place only one cookie sheet at a time in the center of the oven. If the cookies appear to be browning unevenly, rotate the cookie sheet from front to back halfway through the baking time.

If you need to bake more than one sheet of cookies at a time, rotate them from top to bottom halfway through the baking time.

For best results, use shortening or a nonstick cooking spray to grease cookie sheets. Or, just line the cookie sheets with parchment paper; it significantly reduces cleanup, allows the cookies to bake more evenly and the cookies can cool right on the paper instead of on wire racks.

Cookie sheets should cool between batches, as the dough spreads if placed on a hot cookie sheet.

To avoid overbaking cookies, check them at the minimum baking time. If more time is needed, watch carefully to make sure they don't burn. It is usually better to slightly underbake than to overbake cookies.

Many cookies should be removed from cookie sheets immediately after baking and placed in a single layer on wire racks to cool. Fragile cookies may need to cool slightly on the cookie sheet before removing to wire racks to cool completely. Bar cookies may be cooled and stored right in the baking pan.

Storing & Freezing

Store soft and crisp cookies separately at room temperature to prevent changes in texture and flavor. Keep soft cookies in airtight containers. If they begin to dry, add a piece of apple or bread to the container to help the cookies retain moisture. If crisp cookies become soggy, heat undecorated cookies in a 300°F oven for 3 to 5 minutes.

Store cookies with sticky glazes, fragile decorations and icings in single layers between sheets of waxed paper. Bar cookies may be stored in their baking pan. Cover with foil or plastic wrap when cooled.

As a rule, crisp cookies freeze better than soft, moist cookies. Rich, buttery bar cookies and brownies are an exception to this rule since they freeze extremely well. Baked cookies can be frozen in airtight containers or freezer bags for up to three months. Meringue-based cookies do not freeze well and chocolate-dipped cookies may discolor if frozen. Thaw unwrapped cookies and brownies at room temperature.

CAKES

Baking

Place the filled cake pan(s) in the center of a preheated oven. Oven racks may need to be set lower for cakes baked in tube pans. If two racks are used, arrange them so they divide the oven into thirds and then stagger the pans so they are not directly over each other. Avoid opening the oven door during the first half of the baking time. The oven temperature must remain constant in order for the cake to rise properly.

A butter cake is done when it begins to pull away from the side of the pan, the top springs back when lightly touched and a cake tester or wooden toothpick inserted in the center comes out clean and dry. A sponge cake is done when it is delicately browned and the top springs back when lightly touched.

Cooling

After removing butter cakes from the oven, let them stand in their pans on wire racks for 10 minutes, or as the recipe directs. Run a knife around the edge of the cake to loosen it from the side of the pan. Place a wire rack over the pan. Flip the rack and the pan over together; the cake should drop out onto the rack. If it doesn't, tap the bottom of the pan. Lift the pan and remove the paper liner from the cake if one was used. Place a second wire rack over the cake and flip both racks and the cake back over so the cake can cool top side up. Remove the top rack.

Invert an angel food cake baked in a tube pan onto a heatproof funnel or bottle immediately after removing it from the oven. If it is cooled top side up, it will fall. Do not remove from the pan until it is completely cool.

SPECIAL TECHNIQUES

Stir-Frying

Stir-frying—a rapid-cooking method invented by the Chinese—is the brisk cooking of small pieces of ingredients in hot oil over intense heat for a short time. While cooking, the ingredients must be kept in constant motion by stirring or tossing vigorously. Once cooking is completed, remove from heat immediately.

When stir-frying, organize and prepare all ingredients *before beginning to cook*. They should be measured or weighed, cleaned, chopped, sliced and combined because there is not enough time to prepare while cooking. Meat, poultry, fish and vegetables should be cut into pieces of about the same size to ensure even cooking.

The intensity of the heat used for wok cooking is important. In most cases, easily controlled high heat is necessary. For this reason, a gas range with its ability for instant heat control is generally more efficient than an electric range or electric wok.

Making a Pie Crust

Cut the shortening into the combined dry ingredients with a pastry blender or 2 knives until the mixture forms pea-sized pieces.

Sprinkle with ice water, stirring with a fork just until mixture holds together. If making a double crust pie, divide the dough in half and form each half into a disc. For a single crust pie, form a single disc with the dough. Roll out the dough on a floured surface with a floured rolling pin into a ⅛-inch-thick circle about 1 inch larger than the pie plate, sprinkling with additional flour

as necessary. Transfer to the pie plate by placing a rolling pin over one edge of the circle. Gently roll the dough over the rolling pin and lift.

Carefully unroll the dough over the pie plate, easing the dough into it.

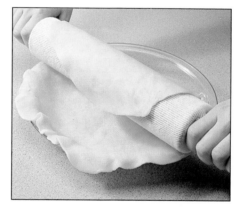

Roasting Fresh Chilies

Roast fresh chilies over an open gas flame or in the broiler. For a gas flame, hold the chili with tongs and place it directly in the medium flame. Roast, turning chili until evenly blistered and charred. Immediately place the chili into a bag; close the bag. For the broiler,

place the chilies on a foil-lined broiler rack; roast them 2 to 3 inches from the heat source until they are evenly blistered and charred, turning as needed. Place the chilies in a bag and close.

Let the chilies stand in the closed bag 20 minutes. Peel under cold running water, rubbing and pulling off the skin.

Slit the chili open lengthwise using scissors or a knife. Carefully pull out and discard the seeds and veins.

Rinse the chilies well and drain; pat them dry with paper towels.

GLOSSARY

Capers: The flower buds of a bush native to the Mediterranean that are sun-dried, then pickled in a vinegar brine. Capers should be drained and rinsed before using to remove excess salt.

Cardamom: An aromatic spice that's a member of the ginger family and is native to India. It is available whole or ground. Whole cardamom has a more intense flavor than ground. Its seeds are removed from the pods before being used in cooking.

Chorizo: An orange- or red-colored, coarse-textured pork sausage sold bulk-style or in casings. The flavor ranges from highly seasoned to quite hot. Always remove the casing before using.

Cilantro (also called fresh coriander or Chinese parsley): A pungent herb with green delicate leaves, similar in appearance, but not flavor, to flat-leaf parsley. Used extensively in Mexican cooking, there is no substitute. Store it in the refrigerator for up to one week with the stems in a glass of water, covering the leaves with a plastic bag.

De árbol chili: A very small, slender, almost needle-shaped chili with smooth, bright red skin and a very hot flavor.

Fish sauce (also called nam pla): An extract of fermented fish. It is used as a condiment and flavoring ingredient in the cuisine of Southeast Asia.

Five-spice powder, Chinese: A cocoa-colored, ready-mixed blend of five ground spices, usually anise seed, fennel, clove, cinnamon and ginger or pepper. It has a slightly sweet, pungent flavor and should be used sparingly.

Hoisin sauce: A thick, dark brown sauce made of soybeans, flour, sugar, spices, garlic, chili and salt. It has a sweet, spicy flavor and is called for in numerous Chinese recipes.

Jalapeño chili: A small, dark green chili, normally 2 to 3 inches long and about ¾ inch wide with a blunt or slightly tapered end. Its flavor varies from hot to very hot. Jalapeños are also sold canned or pickled. Serranos or any other small, hot, fresh chilies can be substituted.

Lemongrass: A stiff, pale green, grassy plant with a sour lemon flavor and aroma that is an essential part of Southeast Asian cuisine. It is available fresh or dried in Oriental markets.

Oyster sauce: A thick, brown, concentrated sauce made of ground oysters, soy sauce and brine. It imparts very little fish flavor and is used as a seasoning to intensify other flavors.

Poblano chili: A very dark green, large triangular-shaped chili with a pointed end. Poblanos are usually 3½ to 5 inches long. Their flavor ranges from mild to quite hot. For a milder flavor, Anaheim chilies can be substituted.

Prosciutto: The Italian word for "ham," prosciutto is seasoned, salt-cured and air-dried (not smoked). It is usually sold in very thin slices and eaten as a first course with melon slices and figs or stirred into pasta and vegetable dishes. Wrap tightly and refrigerate for up to 3 days or freeze for up to 1 month.

Rice wine (also called mirin): This low-alcohol wine is made from glutinous rice. It is a staple of Japanese cooking, used to add flavor and sweetness to sauces and glazes. A "cooking rice wine" is best used only for cooking. Dry sherry can be used as a substitute.

Sake: A Japanese wine made from fermented rice. It is traditionally served warm as a beverage but is also used in marinades and sauces. Dry sherry can be used as a substitute.

Satay sauce: A hot and spicy sauce made of soy sauce, ground shrimp, chili peppers, sugar, garlic, oil and spices. It is also called Chinese barbecue sauce.

Serrano chili: A medium green, very small chili with a very hot flavor. It usually ranges from 1 to 1½ inches in length and is about ⅜ inch wide with a pointed end. Serranos are also available pickled. Jalapeños or any other small, hot, fresh chilies can be substituted.

Sesame oil: An amber-colored oil made from pressed, toasted sesame seeds. It is often used as a flavoring in Asian cuisine. Because it has a low smoke point and burns easily, it is seldom used as a cooking oil.

Shiitake mushroom: A large, dark brown mushroom with a meaty cap and full-bodied flavor. It is originally from Japan and Korea and can be purchased fresh or dried.

Tomatillo (also called tomate verde or Mexican tomato): A small, hard, green fruit with a papery outer husk that is pulled off before using. Tomatillos have a distinct acidic flavor and are used extensively in cooked sauces. They are available fresh or canned (often labeled tomatillo entero). There is no substitute.

Wood ear (also called tree ear or cloud ear): A dried mushroom that will expand five to six times its size when soaked in warm water. It has a crunchy texture and delicate flavor that often assumes the flavor of other ingredients with which it's cooked.

Appetizers

Serbian Lamb Sausage Kabobs

1 pound lean ground lamb
1 pound lean ground beef
1 small yellow onion, finely
   chopped (page 68)
2 cloves garlic, minced (page 116)
1 tablespoon hot Hungarian
   paprika*
1 small egg, slightly beaten
   Salt and ground black pepper
    to taste
3 to 4 red, green or yellow bell
   peppers, cut into squares
   Rice pilaf for serving
   Tomato slices and green onion
    brushes for garnish

*You may use sweet paprika if you prefer a milder taste.

Step 2. Shaping meat squares into oblong sausages.

1. Combine lamb, beef, yellow onion, garlic, paprika and egg in large bowl; season with salt and black pepper.

2. Place meat mixture on cutting board; pat evenly into 8×6-inch rectangle. With sharp knife, cut meat into 48 (1-inch) squares; shape each square into small oblong sausage.

3. Place sausages on waxed paper-lined jelly-roll pan and freeze 30 to 45 minutes or until firm. *Do not freeze completely.*

4. Prepare barbecue grill for direct cooking (technique on page 109).

5. Alternately thread 3 sausages and 3 bell pepper pieces onto each metal skewer.

6. Grill over medium-hot coals 5 to 7 minutes. Turn kabobs, taking care not to knock sausages off. Continue grilling 5 to 7 minutes longer until meat is done. Serve with rice pilaf.

7. For green onion brushes, trim root and most of green top from green onions. Using sharp scissors, make parallel cuts, about 1½ inches long, along length of each onion at the root end or both ends. Fan out the cuts to form a brush. If desired, place brushes in bowl of ice water for several hours to open and curl. Garnish, if desired.

Makes 16 kabobs

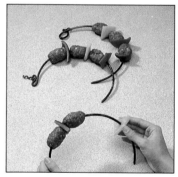

Step 5. Threading sausages and pepper pieces onto skewers.

Step 7. Cutting green onions into brushes.

Steamed Pork and Shrimp Dumplings (Siu Mai)

1 package (5 ounces) frozen cooked tiny shrimp, thawed and rinsed
1 pound lean ground pork
½ cup finely chopped water chestnuts
2 green onions with tops, finely chopped
1 tablespoon soy sauce
1 tablespoon dry sherry
2 teaspoons cornstarch
1 teaspoon minced fresh ginger (page 130)
½ teaspoon sesame oil
¼ teaspoon sugar
1 egg, separated
1 tablespoon water
36 wonton wrappers*
36 fresh green peas (5 or 6 pods)
  Additional soy sauce (optional)
  Chili oil (optional)
  Fresh tarragon sprig for garnish

*Most markets carry square wrappers. In some markets, 3-inch round wrappers are available; omit step 3 if using round wrappers.

1. Drain shrimp on paper towels. Set aside 36 shrimp. Place remaining shrimp in large bowl. Add pork, water chestnuts, green onions, 1 tablespoon soy sauce, sherry, cornstarch, ginger, sesame oil and sugar; mix well.

2. Stir egg white into pork mixture until well blended; set aside. Place egg yolk in cup. Whisk water into egg yolk; set aside.

3. To trim square wrappers into circles, stack 12 wrappers on top of each other, keeping remaining wrappers covered with plastic wrap to prevent drying. Cut into 3-inch circles with tip of paring knife using round cookie cutter as guide. Repeat procedure two more times, keeping trimmed wrappers covered with plastic wrap.

4. To fill wontons, work with about 4 trimmed wrappers at a time, keeping remaining wrappers covered with plastic wrap. Lightly brush each wrapper with egg yolk mixture.

continued on page 16

Step 2. Stirring egg white into pork mixture.

Step 3. Trimming square wonton wrappers into circles.

Step 4. Brushing trimmed wrappers with egg yolk mixture.

***Steamed Pork and Shrimp Dumplings,
continued***

5. Spoon 1½ tablespoons pork mixture onto center of each wrapper. Bring edge of wrapper up around filling in small pleats, leaving top of filling exposed. Press wrapper around filling, in middle, to form pinched "waist." Place on tray and cover with plastic wrap. Repeat with remaining wrappers and filling.

6. To steam dumplings, place 12-inch bamboo steamer in wok. Add water to ½ inch below steamer. (Water should not touch steamer.) Remove steamer. Cover wok; bring water to a boil over high heat.

7. Oil inside of bamboo steamer (bottom only). Arrange ½ of dumplings about ½ inch apart in steamer. Brush tops lightly with egg yolk mixture; place 1 pea and 1 reserved shrimp on top of each dumpling, pressing to secure in place.

8. Place steamer in wok over boiling water; reduce heat to medium. Cover and steam dumplings about 12 minutes or until pork is firm to the touch. Remove wok from heat. Transfer dumplings to serving plate with slotted spoon or spatula.

9. Repeat steps 7 and 8 with remaining dumplings. Serve immediately with soy sauce and chili oil for dipping. Garnish, if desired.   *Makes 3 dozen dumplings*

Step 5. Pressing wrappers around filling.

Step 7. Placing shrimp on top of dumplings.

Step 8. Placing steamer in wok over boiling water.

Sesame-Sour Cream Meatballs

1 medium onion
¼ cup sesame seeds, divided
1 slice fresh bread
1½ pounds ground beef
¼ cup milk
1 egg
½ teaspoon salt
⅛ teaspoon black pepper
⅛ teaspoon ground ginger
4 tablespoons vegetable oil,
    divided
4 tablespoons butter or
    margarine, divided
1 cup beef broth, divided
  Sesame-Sour Cream Sauce
    (page 18)
  Fresh Italian parsley sprigs for
    garnish

1. To chop onion in food processor, peel and quarter onion; place in bowl. Pulse 4 to 7 times until onion is finely chopped. Scrape bowl once during chopping. Chop enough onion to measure ⅔ cup. Drain onions, if needed. Set aside. (See page 68 for chopping technique with knife.)

2. To toast sesame seeds, spread seeds in large, dry skillet. Shake skillet over medium-low heat until seeds begin to pop and turn golden, about 3 minutes. Set aside 2 tablespoons toasted sesame seeds for Sesame-Sour Cream Sauce.

3. Cut bread slice into quarters. Process bread quarters in food processor or blender until fine crumbs form. Crumbs should measure ½ cup.

4. Combine ground beef, onion, bread crumbs, milk, egg, salt, pepper and ginger in large bowl.

continued on page 18

Step 1. Chopping onion in food processor.

Step 2. Shaking skillet until sesame seeds begin to pop and turn golden.

Step 3. Processing bread until fine crumbs form.

Sesame-Sour Cream Meatballs,
continued

5. Place meat mixture on cutting board; pat evenly into 8×6-inch rectangle. With sharp knife, cut meat into 48 (1-inch) squares; shape each square into 1-inch meatball.

6. Heat 2 tablespoons oil and 2 tablespoons butter in large skillet over medium heat. Cook half the meatballs until brown on all sides, 8 to 9 minutes. Add ½ cup broth. Bring to a boil over medium-high heat. Reduce heat to low. Simmer, covered, 5 to 10 minutes. Set cooked meatballs aside. Repeat with remaining meatballs, using remaining 2 tablespoons oil, 2 tablespoons butter and ½ cup broth.

7. Meanwhile, prepare Sesame-Sour Cream Sauce. Place hot meatballs in serving bowl; top with sauce. Sprinkle with remaining 2 tablespoons toasted sesame seeds. Garnish, if desired.

Makes 4 dozen meatballs

Sesame-Sour Cream Sauce

2 tablespoons butter or margarine
2 tablespoons all-purpose flour
½ teaspoon ground ginger
¼ teaspoon salt
½ cup beef broth
1 tablespoon soy sauce
2 tablespoons toasted sesame seeds
¾ cup sour cream

1. Melt butter in small saucepan over low heat. Blend in flour, ginger and salt. Cook and stir until bubbly, about 1 minute. Add beef broth. Cook until thickened, stirring constantly, for an additional minute. Add soy sauce and sesame seeds.

2. Remove from heat; pour into small bowl. Add sour cream, stirring until smooth.   *Makes 1½ cups*

Step 5. Shaping meat squares into 1-inch meatballs.

Step 6. Cooking half the meatballs until brown on all sides.

Sesame-Sour Cream Sauce: Step 1. Cooking and stirring butter mixture until bubbly.

Cheese & Chorizo Burritos

Onion-Chili Relish (recipe follows)
24 corn tortillas (4-inch diameter)
  ***or* 6 flour tortillas (8-inch**
  diameter), cut into quarters
8 ounces queso Chihuahua or
  Monterey Jack cheese
4 to 6 ounces chorizo
  Chilies for garnish

1. Prepare Onion-Chili Relish.

2. Preheat oven to 400°F. Wrap tortillas in foil.

3. Cut cheese into very thin slices. Divide slices evenly among 4 to 6 small, ovenproof plates. (Or, place slices in 1 large, shallow casserole.)

4. Remove and discard casing from chorizo. Heat medium skillet over high heat until hot. Reduce heat to medium. Crumble chorizo into skillet. Brown 6 to 8 minutes; stir to separate meat. Remove with slotted spoon; drain on paper towels. Keep warm.

5. Bake cheese 3 minutes. Place tortillas in oven; continue baking 4 minutes more or until cheese is melted.

6. Place tortillas in serving bowl; sprinkle chorizo evenly over cheese. To serve, spoon cheese mixture onto tortillas and top with relish; fold tortilla around filling. Garnish, if desired.   *Makes 4 to 6 servings*

Onion-Chili Relish

1 medium white onion
1 or 2 fresh jalapeño chilies
3 tablespoons fresh lime juice
¼ teaspoon salt

1. Cut onion and chilies lengthwise into halves. Remove and discard seeds from chilies. Cut onion and chili halves lengthwise into very thin slices; separate into slivers.

2. Combine all ingredients in bowl; mix well. Let stand, covered, at room temperature 2 hours to blend flavors.   *Makes about 1 cup*

Step 3. Cutting cheese into very thin slices.

Step 4. Removing casing from chorizo.

Onion-Chili Relish: Step 1. Cutting onion.

Dipper's Nuggets Chicken

2 whole chicken breasts, split, skinned and boned (pages 6-8)
Vegetable oil
1 egg
⅓ cup water
⅓ cup all-purpose flour
2 teaspoons sesame seeds
1½ teaspoons salt
Sweet and sour sauce, cocktail sauce and tartar sauce for dipping
Red onion rings for garnish

1. Cut chicken into 1-inch pieces on cutting board; set aside.

2. Heat 3 inches of oil in large, heavy saucepan over medium-high heat until oil registers 375°F on deep-fry thermometer. Adjust heat to maintain temperature.

3. Meanwhile, beat egg and water in large bowl until blended. Add flour, sesame seeds and salt, mixing into smooth batter.

4. Dip chicken pieces into batter, a few at a time, shaking off excess.

5. Fry chicken, a few pieces at a time, in hot oil about 4 minutes or until chicken is golden brown and no longer pink in center. With slotted spoon, remove chicken to paper towels to drain.

6. Serve with sauces. Garnish, if desired.

Makes 8 servings

Step 1. Cutting chicken into 1-inch pieces.

Step 3. Mixing batter.

Step 4. Dipping chicken pieces into batter.

Chicken Pizza

1 package (8 ounces) refrigerated
   crescent rolls
2 whole chicken breasts, split,
   skinned and boned
   (pages 6-8)
1 large green bell pepper
1 large onion
¼ cup vegetable oil
½ pound sliced mushrooms
½ cup pitted ripe olives, sliced
1 can (10½ ounces) pizza sauce
   with cheese
1 teaspoon garlic salt
1 teaspoon dried oregano leaves,
   crushed
¼ cup grated Parmesan cheese
2 cups (8 ounces) shredded
   mozzarella cheese

1. Preheat oven to 425°F.

2. Separate dough into eight triangles. Press triangles into greased 12-inch pizza pan, covering bottom of pan completely. Seal seams; set aside.

3. Cut chicken into 1-inch pieces on cutting board; set aside.

4. To prepare bell pepper, with paring knife, make circular cut around top of pepper. Pull stem from pepper to remove stem, seeds and membranes. Rinse out pepper under running water to remove any excess seeds; drain well.

5. Thinly slice pepper crosswise into rings on cutting board; remove any excess membrane.

6. Chop onion (technique on page 68).

7. Heat oil in large skillet over medium-high heat. Add chicken, pepper, onion, mushrooms and olives. Cook and stir 5 minutes or until chicken is no longer pink in center.

8. Spread pizza sauce over dough. Spoon chicken mixture over top. Sprinkle with garlic salt, oregano and Parmesan. Top with mozzarella cheese.

9. Bake 20 minutes or until crust is golden brown. Cut into wedges to serve. Garnish as desired. *Makes 8 servings*

Step 2. Pressing dough triangles into pan.

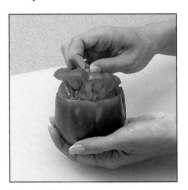

Step 4. Removing stem, seeds and membranes from pepper.

Step 5. Slicing pepper into rings.

Garlicky Gilroy Chicken Wings

2 pounds chicken wings (about 15 wings)
3 heads fresh garlic*
   Boiling water
1 cup plus 1 tablespoon olive oil, divided
10 to 15 drops hot pepper sauce
1 cup grated Parmesan cheese
1 cup Italian-style bread crumbs
1 teaspoon black pepper
   Carrot and celery slices for garnish

*The whole garlic bulb is called a head.

1. Preheat oven to 375°F.

2. Locate first and second joints in chicken wings. Cut through both joints for each wing using sharp knife on cutting board; remove and discard tips. Rinse wing sections; pat dry with paper towels.

3. To peel whole heads of garlic, drop garlic heads into enough boiling water in small saucepan to cover for 5 to 10 seconds. Immediately remove garlic with slotted spoon. Plunge garlic into cold water; drain. Peel away skins.

4. Place garlic, 1 cup oil and hot pepper sauce in food processor; cover and process until smooth.

5. Pour garlic mixture into small bowl. Combine cheese, bread crumbs and black pepper in shallow dish. Dip wing sections, one at a time, into garlic mixture, then roll in crumb mixture, coating evenly and shaking off excess.

6. Brush 13×9-inch nonstick baking pan with remaining 1 tablespoon oil; arrange wing sections in single layer in pan. Drizzle remaining garlic mixture over wing sections; sprinkle with remaining crumb mixture.

7. Bake 45 to 60 minutes or until chicken is brown and crisp. Garnish, if desired.

Makes about 6 servings

Step 2. Cutting chicken wings into sections.

Step 3. Removing blanched garlic from boiling water.

Step 5. Coating chicken wing sections.

Chicken Satay with Peanut Sauce

½ cup lime juice
⅓ cup reduced sodium soy sauce
¼ cup packed brown sugar
 4 cloves garlic, minced (page 116)
¼ teaspoon ground red pepper
 3 boneless skinless chicken breast
   halves (about 1¼ pounds)
18 bamboo skewers (10 to 12
   inches long)
¼ cup chunky or creamy peanut
   butter
¼ cup thick unsweetened coconut
   milk*
¼ cup finely chopped onion
 1 teaspoon paprika
 1 tablespoon finely chopped
   cilantro

*Coconut milk separates in the can, with thick cream (consistency may be soft like yogurt or firm like shortening) floating to the top over thin, watery milk. Spoon thick cream from top after opening can. If less than ¼ cup, make up difference with remaining coconut milk.

1. Stir lime juice, soy sauce, brown sugar, garlic and red pepper in medium bowl until sugar dissolves. Reserve ⅓ cup marinade.

2. Slice chicken lengthwise into ⅓-inch-thick strips. Add to marinade in bowl and stir to coat evenly.

3. Cover and set aside at room temperature 30 minutes or cover and refrigerate up to 12 hours.

4. Prepare barbecue grill for direct cooking (technique on page 109). Cover skewers with cold water. Soak 20 minutes to prevent them from burning; drain.

5. Place peanut butter in medium bowl. Stir in ⅓ cup reserved marinade, 1 tablespoon at a time, until smooth. Stir in coconut milk, onion and paprika. Transfer sauce to small serving bowl; set aside.

6. Drain chicken; discard marinade. Weave 1 or 2 slices chicken onto each skewer.

7. Grill skewers over hot coals or broil 2 to 3 minutes per side or until chicken is no longer pink in center. Transfer to serving platter.

8. Sprinkle sauce with cilantro; serve with skewers. Garnish as desired.

Makes 6 servings

Step 2. Slicing chicken lengthwise.

Step 6. Weaving chicken slice onto skewer.

Shrimp Butter

½ pound medium shrimp
1 cup water
½ teaspoon onion powder
½ teaspoon garlic salt
1 package (8 ounces) cream
   cheese, softened
4 tablespoons butter, softened
2 tablespoons mayonnaise
2 tablespoons cocktail sauce
1 tablespoon lemon juice
1 tablespoon chopped fresh
   parsley (page 38)
   Assorted crackers or raw
     vegetables
   Green onion, star fruit,
     kiwifruit and radish slices
     for garnish

1. To peel shrimp, remove the legs by gently pulling them off the shell. Loosen shell with fingers, then slide off; reserve shells.

2. To devein shrimp, cut a shallow slit along back of shrimp with paring knife. Lift out vein. (You may find this easier to do under cold running water.) If desired, this step may be omitted.

3. Place shrimp shells, water, onion powder and garlic salt in medium saucepan. Bring to a simmer over medium heat; simmer 5 minutes. Remove shells from water with slotted spoon; add shrimp. Simmer 1 minute or until shrimp turn pink and opaque. Remove shrimp with slotted spoon and place on cutting board; let cool. Continue cooking shrimp liquid to reduce until it just barely covers bottom of pan.

4. Blend cream cheese, butter, mayonnaise, cocktail sauce and lemon juice in large bowl until smooth. Stir in 1 tablespoon reduced cooking liquid. Discard remaining liquid.

5. Finely chop shrimp. Fold shrimp and parsley into cheese mixture with rubber spatula by gently cutting down to bottom of bowl, scraping up side of bowl, then folding over top of mixture. Repeat until shrimp and parsley are evenly incorporated.

6. Pack Shrimp Butter into decorative serving crock or plastic mold lined with plastic wrap. Cover and refrigerate overnight. Serve Shrimp Butter in decorative crock or invert mold onto serving platter and remove plastic wrap. Serve with assorted crackers. Garnish, if desired.

Makes 2½ to 3 cups

Step 1. Removing shells from shrimp.

Step 2. Deveining shrimp.

Step 5. Folding in shrimp and parsley.

Shrimp Tapas in Sherry Sauce

½ **pound large shrimp (about 16 shrimp)**
2 ounces crimini or button mushrooms
1 slice thick-cut bacon, cut into ¼-inch strips (optional)
2 tablespoons olive oil
2 cloves garlic, thinly sliced (page 48)
2 tablespoons medium dry sherry
1 tablespoon fresh lemon juice
¼ **teaspoon crushed red pepper**
 Fresh parsley for garnish
 Lemon wedge for garnish

1. To peel shrimp, remove the legs by gently pulling them off the shell. Loosen shell from body with fingers, then slide off, leaving last tail segment attached.

2. To devein shrimp, cut shallow slit along back of shrimp with paring knife. Lift out and discard vein. (You may find this easier to do under cold running water.) Rinse shrimp and pat dry with paper towels.

3. To prepare mushrooms, wipe mushrooms clean with damp paper towel. Cut thin slice from base of each mushroom stem with paring knife; discard. Slice mushrooms into quarters.

4. Cook bacon in large skillet over medium heat until brown and crispy. Remove from skillet with slotted spoon and drain on paper towels. Set aside.

5. Add oil to bacon drippings in skillet. Add mushrooms; cook and stir 2 minutes.

6. Add shrimp and garlic; cook and stir 3 minutes or until shrimp turn pink and opaque. Stir in sherry, lemon juice and crushed red pepper.

7. Remove shrimp to serving bowl with slotted spoon. Cook sauce 1 minute or until reduced and thickened. Pour over shrimp. Sprinkle with reserved bacon. Garnish, if desired.

Makes 4 appetizer servings

Step 1. Peeling shrimp, leaving last tail segment attached.

Step 2. Deveining shrimp with paring knife.

Step 6. Cooking shrimp until they turn pink and opaque.

Ruffled Tuna Kabobs

1 tuna steak, 1 inch thick
   (about ¾ pound)
1 clove garlic
⅓ cup low sodium soy sauce
3 tablespoons red wine vinegar
1 tablespoon vegetable oil
1 tablespoon packed dark brown
   sugar
1 tablespoon ground coriander
1 teaspoon ground ginger
⅛ teaspoon ground red pepper
12 (8-inch) bamboo skewers

1. Rinse tuna and pat dry with paper towels.

2. For ease in slicing, wrap fish in plastic wrap; freeze about 1 hour or until firm but not frozen.

3. Slice fish across the grain into 12 (¼-inch-thick) slices.

4. To mince garlic, trim ends of garlic clove. Slightly crush clove under flat side of chef's knife blade; peel away skin. Chop garlic with chef's knife until garlic is in uniform fine pieces.

5. To make marinade, combine soy sauce, vinegar, oil, sugar, coriander, ginger, pepper and garlic in casserole. Place fish slices in marinade, stirring to coat; cover. Marinate in refrigerator 1 to 6 hours, turning slices once or twice.

6. Cover skewers with cold water; soak 20 minutes to prevent them from burning.

7. Remove skewers from water. Weave 1 fish slice, accordion style, onto each skewer.

8. Brush fish with marinade; discard remaining marinade.*

9. Preheat broiler. Place skewers crosswise on broiler pan rack. Broil 4 inches below heat source 1 to 2 minutes or until fish is opaque and flakes easily when tested with fork. Serve immediately. *Makes 12 kabobs*

*To use marinade as a dipping sauce for kabobs, place marinade in small saucepan and bring to a full boil.

Step 3. Slicing fish into ¼-inch-thick slices.

Step 5. Stirring fish to coat.

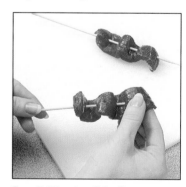
Step 7. Weaving fish slice onto skewer.

Oysters Romano

1 dozen oysters
   Salt
2 slices uncooked bacon, cut into
   1-inch pieces
½ cup Italian-seasoned dry bread
   crumbs
2 tablespoons butter or
   margarine, melted
½ teaspoon garlic salt
6 tablespoons grated Romano,
   Parmesan or provolone
   cheese
   Fresh chives for garnish

1. Scrub oysters thoroughly with stiff brush under cold running water. Soak oysters in mixture of ⅓ cup salt to 1 gallon water 20 minutes. Drain water; repeat 2 more times.

2. Place oysters on tray and refrigerate 1 hour to help them relax.

3. To shuck oysters, take pointed oyster knife in 1 hand and thick towel or glove in the other. With towel, grip shell in palm of hand. Keeping oyster level with knife, insert tip of knife between shells next to hinge; twist to pry shell until you hear a snap. (Use knife as leverage; do not force.)

4. Twist to open shell, keeping oyster level at all times to save liquor.* Cut the muscle from the shell and discard top shell.

5. Cut the muscle from the lower shell, being careful not to spill liquor; do not remove oyster from shell.

6. Preheat oven to 375°F. Place shells with oysters on baking sheet. Top each oyster with 1 piece bacon. Bake 10 minutes or until bacon is crisp.

7. Meanwhile, combine bread crumbs, butter and garlic salt in small bowl. Spoon mixture over oysters; top with cheese. Bake 5 to 10 minutes or until cheese melts. Serve immediately. Garnish, if desired.

Makes 4 appetizer servings

*Liquor is the term used to describe the natural juices of an oyster.

Step 3. Inserting tip of knife between shells next to hinge.

Step 4. Twisting to open shell.

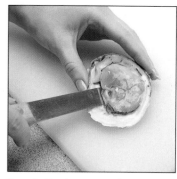

Step 5. Cutting oyster from shell.

Devilish Crab Puffs

Swiss Puffs (page 40)
2 cups crabmeat
Fresh parsley
¼ cup mayonnaise
2 tablespoons minced onion
2 teaspoons white wine
1 teaspoon Worcestershire sauce
1 teaspoon dry mustard
1 teaspoon lemon juice
¼ teaspoon ground white pepper

1. Prepare Swiss Puffs; set aside.

2. To remove cartilage and shell from crabmeat, gently squeeze a teaspoonful at a time between fingers. Feel carefully for small bits. The shell may be white or orange and cartilage milky white and thin. Discard cartilage and shell. Flake crabmeat with fork; set aside.

3. To chop parsley, place parsley in 1-cup measure. Snip enough parsley with kitchen scissors to measure ¼ cup.

4. To make filling, place crabmeat in medium bowl. Add parsley, mayonnaise, onion, wine, Worcestershire, mustard, lemon juice and pepper. Stir gently to blend.

5. Preheat oven to 375°F. Fill Swiss Puffs with crab filling.

6. Place filled appetizers on ungreased baking sheet; bake 10 minutes or until heated through. *Makes about 40 appetizers*

continued on page 40

Step 2. Removing cartilage and shell from crabmeat.

Step 3. Chopping parsley with scissors.

Step 5. Filling Swiss Puffs with crab filling.

Devilish Crab Puffs, continued

Swiss Puffs

½ cup milk
½ cup water
¼ cup butter or margarine
¼ teaspoon salt
   Pinch ground nutmeg
   Pinch ground white pepper
1 cup all-purpose flour
4 eggs, at room temperature
1 cup shredded Swiss cheese, divided

1. Preheat oven to 400°F.

2. Heat milk, water, butter, salt, nutmeg and pepper in 3-quart saucepan over medium-high heat until mixture boils. Remove pan from heat; add flour, mixing until smooth. Cook over medium-low heat, stirring constantly, until mixture leaves side of pan clean and forms a ball. Remove pan from heat.

3. Add eggs, 1 at a time, beating with wooden spoon until smooth and shiny after each addition. Continue beating until mixture loses its gloss. Stir in ¾ cup cheese.

4. Drop rounded teaspoonfuls of cheese batter 1 inch apart onto 2 large greased baking sheets. Sprinkle with remaining ¼ cup cheese.

5. Bake 30 to 35 minutes or until puffs are golden brown. Cool completely on wire racks.

6. Before filling, cut tops off puffs; scoop out and discard moist dough from centers.   *Makes about 4 dozen*

Swiss Puffs: Step 2. Stirring until mixture forms a ball.

Swiss Puffs: Step 4. Dropping by rounded teaspoonfuls onto baking sheets.

Swiss Puffs: Step 6. Scooping out moist dough from center of Swiss Puffs.

Vietnamese Vegetarian Spring Rolls

12 dried Oriental mushrooms
  (1 ounce)
1 large carrot, peeled
  (3½ ounces)
2 teaspoons sugar, divided
  Hoisin Peanut Dipping Sauce
  (page 42)
1½ cups fresh bean sprouts
  (4 ounces)
3 cups plus 2 tablespoons
  vegetable oil, divided
1 medium yellow onion, peeled,
  cut in half and sliced
1 clove garlic, minced (page 116)
1 tablespoon soy sauce
1 teaspoon sesame oil
14 egg-roll wrappers or egg-roll
  skins (7 inches in diameter)
1 egg, beaten
1 bunch fresh mint sprigs or basil
  leaves (optional)
14 large lettuce leaves (optional)

1. Place mushrooms in bowl; cover with hot water. Let stand 30 minutes.

2. Meanwhile, to cut carrot into thin strips, cut a lengthwise strip from carrot so it can lie flat on cutting board. Cut carrot into 2-inch lengths. Place pieces flat sides down on cutting board. Cut lengthwise into thin strips with utility knife.

3. Stack a few of the strips. Cut down into ¼-inch-wide strips.

4. Place carrot strips in small bowl. Add 1 teaspoon sugar and toss until mixed. Let stand 15 minutes, tossing occasionally.

5. Meanwhile, prepare Hoisin Peanut Dipping Sauce; set aside.

6. Pick over bean sprouts, discarding any green hulls. Place sprouts in strainer and rinse under cold running water; drain. Set aside.

7. Drain mushrooms, reserving ½ cup liquid. Squeeze out excess water. Cut stems off mushrooms with paring knife; discard. Cut caps into thin slices; set aside.

continued on page 42

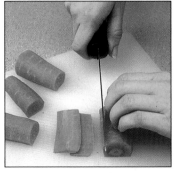

Step 2. Cutting 2-inch carrot pieces into thin strips.

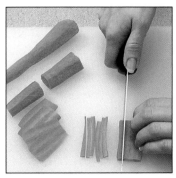

Step 3. Cutting carrots into ¼-inch-wide strips.

Step 7. Cutting mushroom caps into thin slices.

Vietnamese Vegetarian Spring Rolls,
continued

8. Heat wok over medium-high heat 1 minute or until hot. Drizzle 2 tablespoons vegetable oil into wok and heat 30 seconds. Add onion and stir-fry 1 minute. Stir in mushrooms, garlic and reserved liquid. Reduce heat to medium. Cover and cook 3 minutes or until mushrooms are tender. Uncover; add soy sauce, sesame oil and remaining 1 teaspoon sugar. Cook and stir mushroom mixture 3 to 5 minutes more until all liquid has evaporated. Transfer mushroom mixture to medium bowl; set aside to cool slightly.

9. Add carrot strips and bean sprouts to mushroom mixture; toss lightly. Place 1 wrapper on work surface like a diamond, with corner at bottom, keeping remaining wrappers covered with plastic wrap. Drain mushroom mixture; place 3 tablespoons mixture on bottom third of wrapper. Brush edges of wrapper with some beaten egg.

10. To form spring rolls, fold bottom corner of wrapper up over filling. Fold in and overlap the opposite right and left corners to form 3½-inch-wide log. Roll up filling to remaining corner and place spring roll on tray covered with plastic wrap. Repeat with remaining wrappers and filling.

11. Heat remaining 3 cups vegetable oil in wok over high heat until oil registers 375°F on deep-fry thermometer. Fry 4 rolls 2 to 3 minutes until golden brown, turning once with tongs. Repeat with remaining rolls, reheating oil between batches. Drain on paper towels. Arrange on serving plate with bowl of Hoisin Peanut Dipping Sauce. Garnish as desired. To serve, wrap mint and lettuce around rolls, if desired, then dip into sauce. *Makes 14 rolls*

Hoisin Peanut Dipping Sauce

2 tablespoons creamy peanut butter
2 tablespoons water
1 tablespoon soy sauce
⅓ cup hoisin sauce
½ teaspoon sesame oil
1 clove garlic, minced (page 116)
   Dash hot pepper sauce

Combine peanut butter, water and soy sauce in small bowl until smooth. Stir in remaining ingredients. Pour into serving bowl. *Makes about ½ cup*

Step 9. Brushing edges of wrappers with beaten egg.

Step 10. Rolling up wrappers over filling.

Stuffed Mushrooms

24 fresh medium mushrooms
   (about 1 pound)
 6 ounces boneless lean pork
 ¼ cup whole water chestnuts
   (¼ of 8-ounce can)
 3 green onions with tops
 ½ small red or green bell pepper
 1 small stalk celery
 1 teaspoon cornstarch
 1 teaspoon minced fresh ginger
 2 teaspoons dry sherry
 1 teaspoon soy sauce
 ½ teaspoon hoisin sauce
 1 egg white, lightly beaten
   Vegetable oil for frying
   Batter (recipe follows)
 ½ cup all-purpose flour
   Fresh thyme leaves for garnish

1. Clean mushrooms by wiping with damp paper towel.

2. Remove stems from mushrooms; set caps aside. Chop stems finely; transfer to large bowl.

3. Finely chop pork, water chestnuts, onions, bell pepper and celery. Add to chopped mushroom stems. Add cornstarch, ginger, sherry, soy sauce, hoisin sauce and egg white; mix well.

4. Spoon pork mixture into mushroom caps, mounding slightly in center.

5. Heat oil in wok or large skillet over high heat to 375°F. Meanwhile, prepare Batter.

6. Dip mushrooms into flour, then into batter, coating completely.

7. Add six to eight mushrooms to hot oil; cook until golden brown on all sides, about 5 minutes. Drain on paper towels. Repeat with remaining mushrooms. Garnish, if desired.

Makes 2 dozen

Batter

 ½ cup cornstarch
 ½ cup all-purpose flour
 1½ teaspoons baking powder
 ¾ teaspoon salt
 ⅓ cup milk
 ⅓ cup water

Combine cornstarch, flour, baking powder and salt in medium bowl. Add milk and water; beat with wire whisk until well blended.

Step 1. Cleaning mushrooms.

Step 4. Stuffing mushroom caps.

Step 6. Coating stuffed mushrooms with flour and batter.

Baked Garlic Bundles

3 large heads garlic,* separated into cloves
½ of 16-ounce package frozen phyllo dough, thawed to room temperature
¾ cup butter, melted
½ cup finely chopped walnuts
1 cup Italian-style bread crumbs

*The whole garlic bulb is called a head.

1. To peel whole heads of garlic, drop garlic heads into enough boiling water in small saucepan to cover for 5 to 10 seconds. Immediately remove garlic with slotted spoon. Plunge garlic into cold water; drain. Peel away skins.** Set garlic aside.

2. Preheat oven to 350°F. Remove phyllo from package; unroll and place on large sheet of waxed paper. Use scissors to cut phyllo crosswise into 2-inch-wide strips.

3. Cover phyllo with large sheet of plastic wrap and damp, clean kitchen towel. (Phyllo dries out quickly if not covered.)

4. Lay 1 strip of phyllo at a time on a flat surface and brush immediately with melted butter. Place 1 clove of garlic at one end. Sprinkle about 1 teaspoon walnuts along length of strip.

5. Roll up garlic clove and walnuts in strip, tucking in side edges as you roll.

6. Brush bundle with more butter. Roll in bread crumbs.

7. Repeat with remaining phyllo strips, garlic cloves, walnuts, butter and bread crumbs until all but the smallest garlic cloves are used. (Reserve small cloves for another use.) Place bundles on rack in shallow roasting pan. Bake 20 minutes. *Makes 24 to 27 appetizers*

**To peel garlic cloves in microwave, place the desired number of cloves in small custard cup. Microwave at HIGH (100% power) until slightly softened, 5 to 10 seconds for 1 clove or 45 to 55 seconds for a whole head. Slip the cloves out of their skins.

Step 2. Cutting phyllo crosswise into 2-inch-wide strips.

Step 4. Sprinkling walnuts along length of phyllo strip.

Step 5. Rolling up the length of the phyllo strip.

Marinated Roasted Pepper Tapas

1 large red bell pepper
1 large yellow bell pepper
1 clove garlic
3 tablespoons olive oil
1 tablespoon sherry wine vinegar
   or white wine vinegar
1 tablespoon capers, drained and
   rinsed
1 teaspoon sugar
½ teaspoon cumin seeds
1 loaf French bread
   Fresh basil leaves for garnish

1. Cover broiler pan with foil. Preheat broiler. Place peppers on foil. Broil 4 inches from heat source 15 to 20 minutes or until blackened on all sides, turning peppers every 5 minutes with tongs.

2. To steam peppers and loosen skin, place peppers in paper bag for 30 minutes.

3. To slice garlic, trim ends of clove. Slightly crush clove under flat side of knife blade; peel away skin. Cut garlic crosswise into thin slices.

4. Place garlic, oil, vinegar, capers, sugar and cumin seeds in small bowl. Whisk until combined.

5. To peel peppers, cut around core; twist and remove. Cut peppers into halves. Peel off skin with paring knife; rinse under cold water to remove seeds. Cut each half into 1-inch diamond or square-shaped pieces. Place in resealable plastic food storage bag.

6. Pour oil mixture over peppers. Cover and refrigerate at least 2 hours or overnight, turning occasionally. Bring to room temperature before serving.

7. Slice bread into rounds; toast, if desired. Arrange pepper mixture on top of rounds. Garnish, if desired.

Makes 4 to 6 appetizer servings

Step 1. Broiling peppers until blackened on all sides.

Step 3. Cutting garlic crosswise into thin slices.

Step 5. Peeling off pepper skin with paring knife.

Mushrooms Rockefeller

**18 large fresh button mushrooms
(about 1 pound)**
2 slices bacon
¼ cup chopped onion (page 68)
**1 package (10 ounces) frozen
chopped spinach, thawed and
squeezed dry**
1 tablespoon lemon juice
1 teaspoon grated lemon peel
**½ jar (2 ounces) chopped
pimiento, drained**
**Lemon slices and lemon balm
for garnish**

1. Lightly oil 13×9-inch baking dish; set aside. Preheat oven to 375°F. To prepare mushrooms, brush dirt from mushrooms; clean by wiping with damp paper towel.

2. Pull entire stem out of mushroom cap; set aside. Repeat with remaining mushrooms. Place caps in single layer in prepared baking dish.

3. Cut thin slice from base of each stem with paring knife; discard. Chop stems.

4. Cook bacon in medium skillet over medium heat until crisp. Remove bacon with tongs to paper towel; set aside.

5. Add mushroom stems and onion to hot drippings in skillet. Cook and stir until onion is soft. Add spinach, lemon juice, lemon peel and pimiento; blend well. Stuff mushroom caps with spinach mixture using spoon.

6. Crumble bacon and sprinkle on top of mushrooms. Bake 15 minutes or until heated through. Garnish, if desired. Serve immediately. *Makes 18 appetizers*

Step 1. Wiping mushroom caps with damp paper towel.

Step 2. Pulling stems out of mushrooms.

Step 5. Stuffing mushroom caps with spinach mixture.

Classic Guacamole

4 tablespoons finely chopped
    white onion, divided
1½ tablespoons coarsely chopped
    cilantro, divided
1 or 2 fresh serrano or jalapeño
    chilies, seeded, finely
    chopped
¼ teaspoon chopped garlic
    (optional)
2 large, soft-ripe avocados
1 medium, very ripe tomato
    Boiling water
1 to 2 teaspoons fresh lime juice
¼ teaspoon salt
    Corn tortilla chips
    Chilies and cilantro sprig for
    garnish

1. Combine 2 tablespoons onion, 1 tablespoon cilantro, chilies and garlic in large mortar. Grind with pestle until almost smooth. (Mixture can be processed in blender, if necessary, but it will become more watery than desired.)

2. Cut avocados lengthwise into halves; remove and discard pits. Scoop avocado flesh out of shells; place in bowl. Add chili mixture. Mash roughly with wooden spoon, bean masher or potato masher, leaving avocado slightly chunky.

3. To loosen skin from tomato, place tomato in small saucepan of boiling water 30 to 45 seconds. Rinse immediately under cold running water. Peel tomato; cut crosswise in half. Gently squeeze each half to remove seeds. Chop tomato.

4. Add tomato, lime juice, salt and remaining 2 tablespoons onion and ½ tablespoon cilantro to avocado mixture; mix well. Serve immediately or cover and refrigerate up to 4 hours. Serve with corn tortilla chips. Garnish, if desired. *Makes about 2 cups*

Step 2. Scooping avocado flesh out of shells.

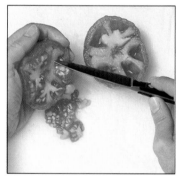
Step 3. Gently squeezing tomato half to remove seeds.

Step 4. Adding tomato to avocado mixture.

Mediterranean Frittata

¼ cup olive oil
5 small yellow onions, thinly
   sliced
1 can (14½ ounces) whole peeled
   tomatoes, drained and
   chopped
¼ pound prosciutto or cooked
   ham, chopped
¼ cup grated Parmesan cheese
2 tablespoons chopped fresh
   parsley
½ teaspoon dried marjoram
   leaves, crushed
¼ teaspoon dried basil leaves,
   crushed
¼ teaspoon salt
   Generous dash freshly ground
   black pepper
6 eggs
2 tablespoons butter or
   margarine
   Italian parsley leaves for
   garnish

1. Heat oil in medium skillet over medium-high heat until hot. Cook and stir onions in hot oil 6 to 8 minutes until soft and golden. Add tomatoes. Cook and stir over medium heat 5 minutes. Remove tomatoes and onions to large bowl with slotted spoon; discard drippings. Cool tomato-onion mixture to room temperature.

2. Stir prosciutto, cheese, parsley, marjoram, basil, salt and pepper into cooled tomato-onion mixture. Whisk eggs in small bowl; stir into prosciutto mixture.

3. Preheat broiler. Heat butter in large broilerproof skillet over medium heat until melted and bubbly; reduce heat to low.

4. Add egg mixture to skillet, spreading evenly. Cook over low heat 8 to 10 minutes until all but top ¼ inch of egg mixture is set; shake pan gently to test. *Do not stir.*

5. Broil egg mixture about 4 inches from heat 1 to 2 minutes until top of egg mixture is set. (Do not brown or frittata will be dry.) Frittata can be served hot, at room temperature or cold. To serve, cut into wedges. Garnish, if desired.   *Makes 6 to 8 appetizer servings*

Step 1. Stirring tomatoes into onion mixture.

Step 2. Stirring eggs into prosciutto mixture.

Step 4. Spreading egg mixture evenly into skillet.

Vegetable Omelets

Korean Dipping Sauce
¼ cup rice wine vinegar
2 tablespoons soy sauce
4 teaspoons sugar

Vegetable Omelets
1 large carrot, peeled
2 tablespoons plus 1 teaspoon
vegetable oil, divided
8 ounces ground pork
1 clove garlic, minced (page 116)
8 eggs
½ teaspoon salt
¼ teaspoon ground black pepper
1 cup bean sprouts
½ cup chives, cut into 1½-inch
lengths
4 (8½ ounce) pineapple cans, tops
and bottoms removed

1. To prepare Korean Dipping Sauce, combine all ingredients in small bowl. Stir until sugar is dissolved; set aside.

2. To cut carrot into thin strips, cut lengthwise strip from carrot so it can lie flat on cutting board. Cut carrot into 2-inch lengths. Place pieces flat side down on cutting board. Cut lengthwise into thin strips with utility knife.

3. Stack several strips. Cut stack lengthwise into ¼-inch-wide strips.

4. Heat 1 tablespoon oil in skillet over medium-high heat. Stir-fry carrots 2 minutes. Set aside.

5. Stir-fry ground pork and garlic about 2 minutes or until pork is well browned. Set aside.

6. Combine eggs, salt and pepper in medium bowl; whisk until frothy. Stir in bean sprouts, chives, carrots and pork mixture.

7. Spray pineapple cans with nonstick cooking spray.

8. Heat 2 teaspoons oil in large nonstick skillet over medium-high heat. Set cans in skillet; pour ½ cup egg mixture into each can. Reduce heat to medium-low; cover and cook about 3 minutes or until eggs are set.

9. Remove rings; turn omelets with spatula and cook 1 to 2 minutes more. Repeat with remaining oil and egg mixture.

10. Cut omelets into quarters; serve with Korean Dipping Sauce. *Makes 4 servings*

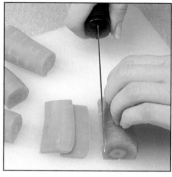

Step 2. Cutting 2-inch carrot pieces into thin strips.

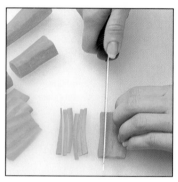

Step 3. Cutting carrots into ¼-inch-wide strips.

Step 8. Pouring egg mixture into can.

Shrimp & Chili Empadas

Empada Dough
  4 ounces cream cheese, softened
  ½ cup butter or margarine,
    softened
  ¼ cup freshly grated Parmesan
    cheese
  ½ teaspoon dried oregano leaves,
    crushed
  ¼ teaspoon ground black pepper
  1 to 1¼ cups all-purpose flour

Shrimp Filling
  8 ounces cooked, peeled shrimp
    (page 30)
  1 can (4 ounces) diced green
    chilies
  ¼ cup freshly grated Parmesan
    cheese
  2 green onions, chopped
  3 to 4 tablespoons chopped fresh
    cilantro

1. Combine cream cheese, butter, Parmesan cheese, oregano and pepper in food processor; process until smooth. Add flour; process until mixture forms dough that leaves side of bowl.

2. Form dough into 2 balls; cover with plastic wrap and refrigerate 30 minutes or until firm.

3. Place ball on lightly floured surface; flatten slightly. To knead dough, fold dough in half toward you and press dough away from you with heels of hands (technique on page 190). Give dough a quarter turn and continue folding, pushing and turning. Continue kneading 5 minutes or until smooth and elastic.

4. Roll dough to ⅛-inch thickness. Cut dough into circles using 3-inch biscuit cutter. Gather scraps into ball; cover with plastic wrap and refrigerate. Repeat kneading process with second ball. Roll out with reserved scraps to make about 36 rounds total.

5. Preheat oven to 450°F. To prepare Shrimp Filling, process filling ingredients in food processor until finely chopped.

6. To make empadas, place 1 teaspoon filling on each round. Fold in half; seal edges with fork. Place on ungreased baking sheets.

7. Bake empadas 10 minutes or until golden brown. Cool slightly on wire rack; serve warm. Garnish as desired.

Makes about 36 empadas

Step 1. Processing until mixture forms dough.

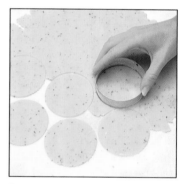
Step 4. Cutting dough into 3-inch circle.

Step 6. Sealing edge with fork.

Soups & Salads

Russian Borscht

½ head green cabbage (about
    1 pound)
1½ pounds fresh beets
  3 tablespoons vegetable oil
  1 pound beef chuck steak,
    trimmed and cut into ½-inch
    cubes
1½ cups chopped onions (page 68)
  3 cloves garlic, minced (page 116)
  5 carrots, peeled and cut into
    1-inch pieces
  1 parsnip, peeled and cut into
    1-inch pieces (page 160)
  2 quarts beef broth
  1 can (28 ounces) Italian plum
    tomatoes, undrained and
    chopped
¼ cup fresh lemon juice
  1 tablespoon sugar
  1 teaspoon ground black pepper
    Salt to taste
    Sour cream and fresh parsley
    for garnish
    Additional lemon juice and
    sugar (optional)

1. Discard any wilted or bruised outer leaves of cabbage. Cut cabbage into 4 wedges with chef's knife. Carefully cut core away. Slice cabbage wedges crosswise to form shreds.

2. Cut tops off beets; peel with vegetable peeler. Shred beets by hand* with large section of metal grater or use food processor with regular shredding disk.

3. Heat oil in 10-quart stockpot over medium-high heat until hot. Add beef; cook and stir until browned.

4. Add onions and garlic; cook and stir 3 minutes or until onions are tender.

5. Add cabbage, beets, carrots, parsnip, broth, tomatoes, lemon juice, sugar and pepper to stockpot; mix well. Bring to a boil over high heat. Reduce heat to low; cover and simmer 2 hours.

6. Season to taste with salt. Ladle borscht into soup bowls. Garnish, if desired. Serve with additional lemon juice and sugar, if desired.

Makes 12 servings

*Beet juice will stain your hands and cutting board. If shredding beets by hand, you may want to wear rubber gloves and shred the beets over a glass plate.

Step 1. Slicing cabbage wedge crosswise.

Step 2. Shredding beet with metal grater.

Step 3. Cooking and stirring beef until browned.

Classic Meatball Soup

2 pounds beef bones
3 ribs celery
2 carrots
1 medium onion, cut in half
1 bay leaf
6 cups cold water
1 egg
4 tablespoons chopped fresh parsley, divided
1 teaspoon salt, divided
½ teaspoon dried marjoram leaves, crushed
¼ teaspoon ground black pepper, divided
½ cup soft fresh bread crumbs
¼ cup grated Parmesan cheese
1 pound ground beef
1 can (14½ ounces) whole peeled tomatoes, undrained
½ cup uncooked rotini or small macaroni

1. To make stock, rinse bones. Combine bones, celery, carrots, onion and bay leaf in 6-quart stockpot. Add water. Bring to a boil; reduce heat to low. Cover partially and simmer 1 hour, skimming foam occasionally.

2. Preheat oven to 400°F. Spray 13×9-inch baking pan with nonstick cooking spray. Combine egg, 3 tablespoons parsley, ½ teaspoon salt, marjoram and ⅛ teaspoon pepper in medium bowl; whisk lightly. Stir in bread crumbs and cheese. Add beef; mix well. Place meat mixture on cutting board; pat evenly into 1-inch-thick square. With sharp knife, cut meat into 1-inch squares; shape each square into a ball. Place meatballs in prepared pan; bake 20 to 25 minutes until brown on all sides and cooked through, turning occasionally. Drain on paper towels.

3. Strain stock through sieve into medium bowl. Slice celery and carrots; reserve. Discard bones, onion and bay leaf. To degrease stock, let stand 5 minutes to allow fat to rise. Holding paper towel, quickly pull across surface only, allowing towel to absorb fat. Discard. Repeat with clean paper towels as many times as needed to remove all fat.

4. Return stock to stockpot. Drain tomatoes, reserving juice. Chop tomatoes; add to stock with juice. Bring to a boil; boil 5 minutes. Stir in rotini, remaining ½ teaspoon salt and ⅛ teaspoon pepper. Cook 6 minutes, stirring occasionally. Add reserved vegetables and meatballs. Reduce heat to medium; cook 10 minutes until hot. Stir in remaining 1 tablespoon parsley. Season to taste.

Makes 4 to 6 servings

Step 2. Cutting meat into 1-inch squares.

Step 3. Degreasing stock.

Cajun-Style Chicken Soup

1½ pounds chicken thighs
4 cups chicken broth
1 can (8 ounces) tomato sauce
2 ribs celery, sliced
1 medium onion, chopped
   (page 68)
2 garlic cloves, minced
   (page 116)
2 bay leaves
1 to 1½ teaspoons salt
½ teaspoon ground cumin
¼ teaspoon paprika
¼ teaspoon ground black pepper
¼ teaspoon ground red pepper
   Dash ground white pepper
8 ounces fresh or frozen okra
1 large green bell pepper,
   chopped (page 75)
⅓ cup uncooked rice
   Hot pepper sauce (optional)
   Fresh oregano for garnish

1. Place chicken, broth, tomato sauce, celery, onion, garlic, bay leaves, salt, cumin, paprika, black pepper, red pepper and white pepper in 5-quart Dutch oven. Bring to a boil over high heat. Reduce heat to medium-low; simmer, uncovered, 1 hour or until chicken is tender, skimming foam that rises to the surface.

2. Meanwhile, wash okra; cut into ½-inch slices. Loosely cover and refrigerate.

3. Remove chicken from soup and let cool slightly. Remove fat from soup by using large spoon and skimming off as much fat as possible. (Or, refrigerate soup several hours and remove fat that rises to the surface. *Refrigerate chicken if chilling soup to remove fat.*)

4. Remove chicken meat from bones; discard skin and bones. Cut chicken into bite-sized pieces.

5. Add chicken, bell pepper and rice to soup. Bring to a boil over high heat. Reduce heat to medium-low; simmer, uncovered, about 12 minutes or until rice is tender. Add okra; simmer an additional 8 minutes or until okra is tender. Discard bay leaves. Ladle soup into bowls; serve with hot pepper sauce. Garnish, if desired. *Makes 6 servings*

Step 1. Skimming foam that rises to the surface.

Step 2. Slicing okra.

Step 4. Removing chicken meat from bones.

Shaker Chicken and Noodle Soup

13 cups chicken broth, divided
¼ cup dry vermouth
¼ cup butter or margarine
1 cup heavy cream
1 package (12 ounces) egg
    noodles
1 cup thinly sliced celery
1½ cups water
¾ cup all-purpose flour
2 cups diced cooked chicken*
    Salt and pepper to taste
¼ cup finely chopped parsley
    (optional) (page 38)
    Parsley and carrot curls for
    garnish

*To poach and dice boneless skinless chicken breast halves, see page 96, steps 2 and 3.

1. Combine 1 cup broth, vermouth and butter in small saucepan. Bring to a boil over high heat. Continue to boil 15 to 20 minutes or until liquid is reduced to ¼ cup and has a syrupy consistency. Stir in cream. Set aside.

2. Bring remaining broth to a boil in Dutch oven. Add noodles and celery; cook until noodles are just tender.

3. Combine water and flour in medium bowl until smooth. Stir into broth mixture. Boil 2 minutes, stirring constantly.

4. Stir in reserved cream mixture; add chicken. Season with salt and pepper. Heat just to serving temperature. *Do not boil.* Sprinkle with parsley. Garnish, if desired.

Makes 15 servings

Note: This soup freezes well.

Step 2. Adding celery to boiling broth.

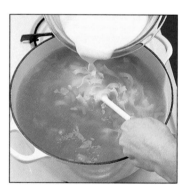

Step 3. Stirring flour mixture into broth.

Spicy
Shrimp Gumbo

1 large onion
  Fresh parsley
½ cup vegetable oil
½ cup all-purpose flour
½ cup chopped celery
½ cup sliced green onions
6 cloves garlic, minced
4 cups chicken broth or water*
1 package (10 ounces) frozen
  sliced okra, thawed
  (optional)
1 teaspoon salt
½ teaspoon ground red pepper
2 pounds medium shrimp, peeled
  and deveined (page 30)
3 cups hot cooked rice
  Fresh parsley sprigs for garnish

*Traditional gumbo's thickness is similar
to that of stew. If you prefer it thinner,
add 1 to 2 cups additional broth.

1. To chop onion, peel skin. Cut onion in half through root with utility knife. Place cut side down on cutting board. Cut onion into thin slices perpendicular to root end, holding onion with fingers to keep its shape, then turn onion and cut crosswise to root end. Repeat with remaining onion half. Set aside.

2. To chop parsley, place parsley in 1-cup measure. Snip enough parsley with kitchen scissors to measure ½ cup. Set aside.

3. For roux, blend oil and flour in large heavy stockpot. Cook over medium-high heat 10 to 15 minutes or until roux is dark brown, stirring often.

4. Add chopped onion, chopped parsley, celery, green onions and garlic to roux. Cook over medium-high heat 5 to 10 minutes or until vegetables are tender. Add broth, okra, salt and red pepper. Cover; simmer 15 minutes.

5. Add shrimp; simmer 3 to 5 minutes or until shrimp turn pink and opaque.

6. Place about ⅓ cup rice in each wide-rimmed soup bowl; top with gumbo. Garnish, if desired. *Makes 8 servings*

Step 1. Chopping onion.

Step 2. Chopping parsley with scissors.

Step 3. Cooking until roux is dark brown.

Oyster Corn Stew

40 medium oysters*
   Salt
1 cup milk
1 can (15 ounces) cream-style
   corn
¼ teaspoon salt
¼ teaspoon celery seeds
   Dash ground white pepper
4 tablespoons butter or
   margarine
1 rib celery, chopped
1 cup cream or half-and-half
   Celery leaves and lemon zest
   for garnish

*If fresh oysters in shells are not available,
substitute 1 pint shucked oysters,
including liquor. Liquor is the term used
to describe the natural juices of an oyster.

1. Scrub oysters thoroughly with stiff brush under cold running water. Soak oysters in mixture of ⅓ cup salt to 1 gallon water 20 minutes. Drain water; repeat 2 more times.

2. Place on tray and refrigerate 1 hour to help oysters relax. To shuck oysters, take pointed oyster knife in 1 hand and thick towel or glove in the other. With towel, grip shell in palm of hand. Keeping oyster level with knife, insert tip of knife between the shells next to hinge; twist to pry shell until you hear a snap. (Use knife as leverage; do not force.)

3. Twist to open shell, keeping oyster level at all times to save liquor. Cut the muscle from shell and discard top shell. Tip shell over strainer in bowl to catch oysters; discard bottom shell. Refrigerate oysters. Strain oyster liquor from bowl through triple thickness of dampened cheesecloth into small bowl; set aside oyster liquor.

4. Place milk, corn, ¼ teaspoon salt, celery seeds and pepper in large saucepan. Bring to a simmer over medium heat; set aside.

5. Melt butter in medium skillet over medium-high heat. Add celery and cook 8 to 10 minutes or until tender. Add reserved oyster liquor; cook until heated through. Add oysters; heat about 10 minutes, just until oysters begin to curl around edges.

6. Add oyster mixture and cream to milk mixture. Cook over medium-high heat until just heated through. *Do not boil.*

7. Serve in wide-rimmed soup bowls. Garnish, if desired.   *Makes 6 servings*

Step 2. Inserting tip of knife between shells next to hinge.

Step 3. Straining oyster liquor through cheesecloth.

Step 5. Cooking until oyster edges begin to curl.

Shellfish Cioppino

12 cherrystone clams*
  Salt
4 tablespoons olive oil
2 cups chopped onions (page 68)
2 red bell peppers, seeded and
  chopped
1 green bell pepper, seeded and
  chopped (page 75)
8 cloves garlic, minced
2 cups Fish Stock (page 74)
2 cups vermouth or white wine
2 cans (16 ounces each)
  tomatoes, drained and
  coarsely chopped
1 tablespoon dried basil leaves,
  crushed
1 teaspoon dried thyme leaves,
  crushed
1 bay leaf
¼ teaspoon crushed red pepper
¾ pound large shrimp, peeled
  and deveined (page 30)
½ pound sea scallops
8 crab claws or claw-shaped
  surimi
  Fresh bay leaves for garnish

*If fresh clams in shells are not available,
substitute ½ pint shucked clams. Steam in
vegetable steamer until firm. Omit steps 1
and 2.

1. To prepare clams, discard any clams that remain open when tapped with fingers. To clean clams, scrub with stiff brush under cold running water. Soak clams in mixture of ⅓ cup salt to 1 gallon water 20 minutes. Drain water; repeat 2 more times.

2. To steam clams, place 1 cup water in large stockpot. Bring to a boil over high heat. Add clams. Cover stockpot; reduce heat to medium. Steam 5 to 7 minutes or until clams open. Remove from stockpot with tongs; set aside. Discard any clams that remain unopened.

3. Heat oil in stockpot over medium-high heat. Add onions, bell peppers and garlic. Cover; reduce heat to low. Cook 20 to 25 minutes or until tender, stirring occasionally.

continued on page 74

Step 1. Scrubbing clam.

Step 2. Removing clams with tongs.

Step 3. Adding onions, bell peppers and garlic.

Shellfish Cioppino, continued

4. Add Fish Stock, vermouth, tomatoes, basil, thyme, bay leaf and crushed red pepper. Partly cover; simmer 30 minutes.

5. Add clams, shrimp, scallops and crab claws to tomato mixture. Cover; remove from heat. Let stand until shrimp turn pink and scallops turn opaque.

6. Remove bay leaf; discard. Ladle into large pasta or soup bowls. Garnish, if desired.   *Makes 4 generous servings*

Fish Stock

1¾ **pounds fish skeletons and heads from lean fish, such as red snapper, cod, halibut or flounder**
2 **medium onions**
3 **ribs celery, cut into 2-inch pieces**
10 **cups cold water**
2 **slices lemon**
¾ **teaspoon dried thyme leaves, crushed**
8 **black peppercorns**
3 **fresh parsley sprigs**
1 **bay leaf**
1 **clove garlic**

1. Rinse fish; cut out gills and discard.

2. Trim tops and roots from onions, leaving most of the dried outer skin intact; cut into wedges.

3. Combine fish skeletons and heads, onions and celery in stockpot or Dutch oven. Add water, lemon, thyme, peppercorns, parsley, bay leaf and garlic. Bring to a boil over high heat. Reduce heat to medium-low; simmer, uncovered, 30 minutes, skimming foam that rises to the surface.

4. Remove stock from heat and cool slightly. Strain stock through large sieve or colander lined with several layers of dampened cheesecloth, removing and discarding all bones, vegetables and seasonings.

5. Use stock immediately or refrigerate in tightly covered container up to 2 days. Stock can be frozen in freezer containers for several months.
Makes about 10 cups stock

Step 5. Checking scallops for doneness.

Fish Stock: Step 4. Straining stock.

Budget Fish Stew

1 green bell pepper
2 medium onions
1 jalapeño chili*
2 tablespoons peanut oil or
    vegetable oil
1 small eggplant, cut into ½-inch
    cubes
2 cloves garlic, minced
1 teaspoon salt
¼ teaspoon ground white pepper
¼ teaspoon ground red pepper
2 cups chicken broth
1 pound sweet potatoes, peeled
    and cut into 1-inch cubes
½ pound small fresh okra,
    stemmed (optional)
½ cup peanut butter
1 cup hot water
½ pound fish fillets, such as
    monkfish, hake or cusk
½ pound fish fillets, such as
    bluefish or shark
    Coarsely chopped peanuts for
    garnish

*Chili peppers can sting and irritate the skin; wear rubber gloves when handling chili peppers and do not touch eyes. Wash hands after handling chili peppers.

1. Rinse bell pepper under cold running water. To seed, stand on end on cutting board. Cut off sides in 3 to 4 lengthwise slices with utility knife. (Cut close to, but not through, stem.) Discard stem and seeds. Scrape out any remaining seeds. Rinse inside of pepper under cold running water, then coarsely chop. Set aside.

2. To chop onions, peel skin. Cut each onion in half through root with utility knife. Place cut side down on cutting board. Cut onion into thin slices perpendicular to root end, holding onion with fingers to keep its shape, then turn onion and cut crosswise to root end. Repeat with remaining onion halves; set aside.

3. Cut jalapeño chili in half lengthwise. Remove seeds, membranes and stem with small paring knife; discard. Finely chop pepper.

continued on page 76

Step 1. Cutting off side of bell pepper.

Step 2. Chopping onion.

Step 3. Removing seeds and membranes from jalapeño chili.

Budget Fish Stew, continued

4. Heat oil in large stockpot over medium heat until hot; add bell pepper. Cook bell pepper 3 to 4 minutes or until its color intensifies and pepper softens slightly; remove with slotted spoon and set aside.

5. Add onions and jalapeño chili to same stockpot and cook 6 to 8 minutes or until onions are translucent.

6. Add eggplant, garlic, salt, white pepper and red pepper. Cook 5 to 6 minutes or until eggplant softens slightly, stirring occasionally.

7. Add broth and sweet potatoes. Bring to a boil; reduce heat and simmer until potatoes are fork-tender.

8. Wash okra; cut into ¾-inch slices. Add to stew.

9. Combine peanut butter with water in small bowl. Stir into stew. Heat until stew begins to thicken.

10. Rinse fish and pat dry with paper towels. Cut fish into 1-inch cubes; stir into stew.

11. Add bell pepper. Cover and simmer 5 minutes or until fish is opaque and flakes easily when tested with fork. Garnish, if desired.

Makes 8 servings

Step 8. Cutting okra into ¾-inch slices.

Step 9. Stirring peanut butter mixture into stew.

Step 10. Cutting fish into 1-inch cubes.

Classic French Onion Soup

3 large yellow onions (about
    2 pounds)
3 tablespoons peanut oil
1 cup dry white wine
3 cans (about 14 ounces each)
    beef or chicken broth
½ teaspoon salt
¼ teaspoon ground white pepper
1 bouquet garni*
1 loaf French bread
4 ounces grated Gruyère
    cheese**
    Fresh thyme for garnish

*To prepare bouquet garni, tie together 3 sprigs parsley, 2 sprigs thyme and ½ bay leaf with cotton string or enclose herbs in square of cheesecloth secured with string.

**Gruyère is a Swiss cheese that is aged for 10 to 12 months. Any Swiss cheese may be substituted.

1. To prepare onions, peel skin from onions. Cut into halves through root with utility knife. Place onion halves, cut side down, on cutting board. Cut onion vertically into thin slices.

2. Heat oil in Dutch oven over medium-high heat until hot. Add onions; cook and stir 15 minutes or until lightly browned. Reduce heat to medium; cook, stirring occasionally, 30 to 45 minutes until onions are deep golden brown.

3. Add wine; cook over high heat 3 to 5 minutes or until liquid is reduced by half.

4. Add broth, salt, pepper and bouquet garni; bring to a boil. Reduce heat to low. Simmer 15 to 20 minutes; remove bouquet garni and discard.

5. Cut French bread into 1-inch-thick slices; toast under broiler about 3 minutes on each side.

6. Ladle soup into four broilerproof bowls; top with bread and cheese.

7. Broil 4 inches from heat 2 to 3 minutes or until cheese is bubbly and browned. Serve hot. Garnish, if desired. *Makes 4 servings*

Step 1. Cutting onion vertically into thin slices.

Step 2. Cooking and stirring onions until deep golden brown.

Step 6. Topping soup with bread and cheese.

Potato-Cheese Soup

1 small onion
2 cups water
2 cups red potatoes, peeled and
    cut into cubes
3 tablespoons butter or
    margarine
3 tablespoons all-purpose flour
    Creole seasoning to taste
    Ground red pepper to taste
    Ground black pepper to taste
3 cups milk
1 cup (4 ounces) shredded
    Cheddar cheese
1½ cups cubed cooked ham
    Chopped fresh parsley for
    garnish

1. To chop onion in food processor, peel and quarter onion; place in processor bowl. Pulse 4 to 7 times until onion is finely chopped. Scrape bowl once during chopping. Drain onion, if needed. Set aside. (See page 68 for chopping technique with knife.)

2. Bring water to a boil in large saucepan over medium-high heat. Add potatoes and cook until tender when pierced with fork, 13 to 15 minutes.

3. Meanwhile, melt butter in large skillet over medium heat. Add onion; cook and stir 4 to 5 minutes until onion is tender but not brown. Add flour. Season with Creole seasoning, red pepper and black pepper; cook and stir 3 to 4 minutes. Set aside.

4. Drain potatoes, reserving 1 cup liquid. (Add water to make 1 cup, if necessary.)

5. Gradually add onion mixture, milk and reserved liquid to potatoes in large saucepan; stir well.

6. Add cheese and ham. Bring to a boil over medium heat. Reduce heat to low. Simmer 30 minutes, stirring frequently. Garnish, if desired. *Makes 12 servings*

Step 1. Chopping onion in food processor.

Step 2. Testing tenderness of potatoes.

Step 4. Draining potatoes and reserving 1 cup liquid.

Butternut Bisque

1 medium butternut squash
(about 1½ pounds)
1 teaspoon margarine or butter
1 large onion, coarsely chopped
(page 68)
2 cans (about 14 ounces each)
reduced-sodium or regular
chicken broth, divided
½ teaspoon ground nutmeg or
freshly grated nutmeg*
⅛ teaspoon ground white pepper
Plain nonfat yogurt and chives
for garnish

*Whole nutmeg may be finely grated using
a nutmeg grater or mill.

1. Remove skin from squash with vegetable peeler. Cut squash lengthwise in half with chef's knife; discard seeds. Cut flesh into ½-inch pieces; set aside.

2. Melt margarine in large saucepan over medium heat until foamy. Add onion. Cook and stir 3 minutes.

3. Add 1 can broth and squash. Bring to a boil over high heat. Reduce heat to low. Cover and simmer 20 minutes until squash is very tender.

4. Process squash mixture, in 2 batches, in food processor until smooth.

5. Return soup to saucepan; add remaining can of broth, nutmeg and pepper. Simmer, uncovered, 5 minutes, stirring occasionally.

6. At this point, the soup may be covered and refrigerated up to 2 days before serving. Reheat in large saucepan over medium heat until hot, stirring occasionally.

7. Ladle into soup bowls. Place yogurt in pastry bag fitted with round decorating tip. Pipe onto soup in decorative design. Garnish with chives, if desired.   *Makes 6 servings*

Cream of Butternut Soup: Add ½ cup heavy cream or half-and-half with broth in step 5. Proceed as directed.

*Grating whole nutmeg with nutmeg grater.

Step 1. Peeling butternut squash.

Step 4. Processing squash mixture until smooth.

Winter Pear and Stilton Salad

⅓ cup extra-virgin olive oil

1½ tablespoons sherry wine vinegar
   or white wine vinegar

1 tablespoon Dijon-style mustard

4 teaspoons honey

¼ teaspoon salt

3 ounces assorted gourmet mixed
   salad greens, such as
   oakleaf, frisee, watercress,
   radicchio, arugula or
   escarole

1½ ounces Boston or Bibb lettuce
   leaves

2 ripe Bosc, Bartlett or Anjou
   pears
   Lemon juice

6 ounces Stilton or Gorgonzola
   cheese
   Freshly ground black pepper

1. Place oil, vinegar, mustard, honey and salt in small bowl. Whisk together until combined. Cover and refrigerate up to 2 days.

2. Wash greens in several changes of cold water. Drain well and if necessary pat with paper towels to remove excess moisture. Or, spin in salad spinner to remove moisture.

Step 2. Washing greens.

3. Discard any wilted or bruised leaves. Cut or tear off stems if they are woody.

4. Tear enough assorted gourmet mixed greens into bite-sized pieces to measure 5 packed cups. Tear enough Boston lettuce into bite-sized pieces to measure 2 packed cups.

5. Cut pears into quarters with utility knife. Remove stems and core. Cut each quarter into ½-inch pieces. To help prevent discoloration, brush pear pieces with lemon juice, if desired.

Step 4. Packing lettuce into measuring cup.

6. Crumble enough cheese with fingers to measure 1½ cups.

7. Combine all salad greens in large bowl. Add pears, cheese and dressing. Toss lightly to coat; sprinkle with pepper.

Makes 6 to 8 servings

Step 6. Crumbling cheese.

Marinated Vegetable Salad

3½ tablespoons white wine vinegar
 2 tablespoons minced fresh basil
    or ½ teaspoon dried basil
    leaves, crushed
½ teaspoon salt
⅛ teaspoon ground black pepper
    Dash sugar
 6 tablespoons olive oil
 2 ripe medium tomatoes
⅓ cup pitted green olives
⅓ cup Italian- or Greek-style ripe
    olives
 1 head leaf or red leaf lettuce
 1 small head curly endive
 2 heads Belgian endive

1. For dressing, place vinegar, basil, salt, pepper and sugar in food processor or blender. With motor running, add oil in slow, steady stream until oil is thoroughly blended.

2. Cut tomatoes into wedges. Combine tomatoes and green and ripe olives in medium bowl. Add dressing; toss lightly. Cover and let stand at room temperature 30 minutes to blend flavors, stirring occasionally.

3. Rinse leaf lettuce and curly endive; drain well. Refrigerate greens until ready to assemble salad. Core Belgian endive and separate leaves; rinse and drain well.

4. To serve, layer leaf lettuce, curly endive and Belgian endive leaves in large, shallow serving bowl.

5. Remove tomatoes and olives with slotted spoon and place on top of greens. Spoon remaining dressing over salad. Serve immediately or cover and refrigerate up to 30 minutes. *Makes 6 servings*

Step 1. Adding oil through feed tube while processing.

Step 3. Coring Belgian endive.

Step 4. Layering leaves in serving bowl.

Grilled Tri-Colored Pepper Salad

1 each large red, yellow and
    green bell pepper, cut into
    halves or quarters
⅓ cup extra-virgin olive oil
3 tablespoons balsamic vinegar
2 cloves garlic, minced
    (page 116)
¼ teaspoon salt
¼ teaspoon ground black pepper
    Fresh basil leaves
⅓ cup crumbled goat cheese
    (about 1½ ounces)

1. Prepare barbecue grill for direct cooking (technique on page 109).

2. Place bell peppers, skin side down, on grid. Grill bell peppers, on covered grill, over hot coals 10 to 12 minutes or until skin is charred.

3. To steam bell peppers and loosen skin, place charred bell peppers in paper bag. Close bag; set aside to cool 10 to 15 minutes.

4. To peel bell peppers, remove skin with paring knife; discard skin.

5. Place bell peppers in shallow glass serving dish. Combine oil, vinegar, garlic, salt and black pepper in small bowl; whisk until well combined. Pour over bell peppers. Let stand 30 minutes at room temperature. (Or, cover and refrigerate up to 24 hours. Bring bell peppers to room temperature before serving.)

6. Layer basil leaves with largest leaf on bottom, then roll up jelly-roll style. Slice basil roll into very thin slices; separate into strips. Slice enough leaves to measure ¼ cup.

7. Sprinkle bell peppers with cheese and basil just before serving. *Makes 4 to 6 servings*

Step 2. Grilling bell peppers until skin is charred.

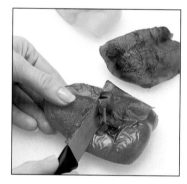

Step 4. Peeling bell peppers by removing skin with paring knife.

Step 6. Slicing basil roll into very thin slices.

Tomato, Mozzarella & Basil Salad

2 tablespoons red wine vinegar
1 clove garlic, minced
½ teaspoon salt
¼ teaspoon dry mustard
   Generous dash freshly ground
     black pepper
⅓ cup olive or vegetable oil
4 Italian plum tomatoes
6 ounces mozzarella cheese
8 to 10 fresh basil leaves

1. For dressing, combine vinegar, garlic, salt, mustard and pepper in small bowl. Add oil in slow, steady stream, whisking until oil is thoroughly blended.

2. Slice tomatoes and cheese into ¼-inch-thick slices. Trim cheese slices to size of tomato slices.

3. Place tomato and cheese slices in large, shallow bowl or glass baking dish. Pour dressing over slices. Marinate, covered, in refrigerator for at least 30 minutes or up to 3 hours, turning slices occasionally.

4. Layer basil leaves with largest leaf on bottom, then roll up jelly-roll fashion. Slice basil roll into ¼-inch-thick slices; separate into strips.

5. Arrange tomato and cheese slices alternately on serving plate or 4 individual salad plates. Sprinkle with basil strips; drizzle with remaining dressing.   *Makes 4 servings*

Step 2. Trimming cheese slices to size of tomato slices.

Step 3. Pouring dressing over cheese and tomato slices for marinating.

Step 4. Slicing basil into strips.

Avocados with Tomato Relish

1 tablespoon cider vinegar
1 tablespoon fresh orange juice
1 teaspoon grated orange peel
¼ teaspoon salt
   Dash ground black pepper
3 tablespoons olive oil
3 fresh plum tomatoes (about
   ½ pound), seeded and diced
¼ cup coarsely chopped cilantro
2 tablespoons finely chopped
   mild red onion
1 fresh jalapeño chili, seeded,
   finely chopped (page 75)
2 large, firm, ripe avocados
2 cups shredded iceberg lettuce
   Cilantro sprig, orange peel and
   tomato slice for garnish

1. Mix vinegar, orange juice, orange peel, salt and pepper in medium bowl. Gradually add oil, whisking continuously, until dressing is thoroughly blended.

2. Add tomatoes, chopped cilantro, onion and chili to dressing; toss lightly to mix. Let stand, covered, at room temperature up to 2 hours to blend flavors.

3. Just before serving, cut avocados lengthwise into halves; remove and discard pits. Pare avocados and cut lengthwise into ½-inch-thick slices.

4. Arrange avocados over lettuce-lined plates; top with tomato relish. Garnish, if desired.

Makes 4 servings

Step 1. Whisking oil into orange juice mixture.

Step 2. Adding ingredients to oil mixture to make tomato relish.

Step 3. Cutting avocados into slices.

Montmorency Cherry Chicken Salad

2 cups tart red Montmorency
    cherries*
1½ whole chicken breasts, skinned,
    split, boned (pages 6-8) and
    cooked (page 96)
3 nectarines or peaches
2 tablespoons plus 1 teaspoon
    lemon juice, divided
1½ cups sliced celery
2 tablespoons sliced green onion
1 cup mayonnaise
¼ cup sour cream
2 tablespoons honey
¼ to ½ teaspoon curry powder
⅛ teaspoon ground ginger
    Salt to taste
½ cup slivered almonds
    Boston or Bibb lettuce leaves

*If fresh Montmorency cherries are
unavailable, substitute any fresh sour
cherries. You may substitute equal
amounts of frozen pitted cherries if fresh
are unavailable; thaw and drain cherries
well and omit step 1.

1. To pit cherries, slice an "X" into ends of cherries with paring knife; squeeze out cherry pits with thumb and forefinger. Set cherries aside.

2. Dice cooked chicken on cutting board.

3. To prepare one nectarine, insert knife blade into stem end; slice in half lengthwise to the pit, turning nectarine while slicing. Remove knife blade; twist halves to pull apart. Remove pit from nectarine; discard. Cut nectarine halves into ½-inch-thick slices on cutting board; place in large bowl and set aside. Prepare remaining two nectarines in same manner; brush with 2 tablespoons lemon juice and reserve for garnish.

4. Combine cherries, chicken, celery and green onion in large bowl with nectarine slices. Set aside. Combine mayonnaise, sour cream, honey, 1 teaspoon lemon juice, curry, ginger and salt in small bowl; mix well. Pour mayonnaise mixture over chicken mixture; toss to coat. Cover; refrigerate.

5. To toast almonds, spread on baking sheet. Bake in preheated 350°F oven 8 to 10 minutes or until golden brown; stir frequently. Remove almonds from baking sheet and cool; set aside.

6. Stir all but 1 tablespoon almonds into salad just before serving; arrange salad on lettuce-lined plates. Arrange remaining nectarine slices around salad. Sprinkle salad with remaining 1 tablespoon almonds.

Makes 6 servings

Step 1. Squeezing pit from cherry.

Step 3. Removing pits from nectarines.

Step 5. Checking toasted almonds.

Chicken Salad Deluxe

1¼ cups prepared buttermilk salad
    dressing
½ cup mayonnaise
3 tablespoons half-and-half
1¾ teaspoons Beau Monde
    seasoning*
1 teaspoon salt
½ teaspoon ground black pepper
1½ pounds boneless skinless
    chicken breast halves
1 small onion, cut into slices
1 rib celery, chopped
1 carrot, coarsely chopped
10 ounces medium shell macaroni
3 cups diced celery
2½ cups seedless green grapes, cut
    lengthwise into halves
1 package (12 ounces) slivered
    almonds (reserve ½ cup for
    garnish)
2 cans (2¼ ounces each) sliced
    water chestnuts, drained
1 medium onion, chopped
    (page 68)
    Lettuce leaves (optional)
    Parsley and sliced star fruit for
    garnish
    Cantaloupe slices

*Beau Monde is a spice blend that can be
found in the spice aisle at your grocery
store.

1. Combine salad dressing, mayonnaise, half-and-half, seasoning, salt and pepper in small bowl until well blended. Cover; refrigerate overnight to blend flavors.

2. Place chicken, onion slices, chopped celery and carrot in Dutch oven. Add enough cold water to cover. Cover and bring to a boil over medium heat. Reduce heat to low. Simmer 5 to 7 minutes until chicken is no longer pink in center.

3. Drain chicken, discarding vegetables and liquid. Refrigerate chicken until it is cool enough to handle. Cut chicken into ½-inch pieces. Set aside.

4. Cook shells according to package directions. Drain well, then cover and refrigerate until chilled.

5. Combine chicken, shells, diced celery, grapes, almonds, water chestnuts and chopped onion in large bowl. Pour dressing over salad; toss gently to coat. Serve on lettuce-lined plates. Garnish, if desired. Serve with cantaloupe slices. *Makes 20 servings*

Step 2. Adding water to Dutch oven to cover chicken mixture.

Step 3. Cutting chicken into ½-inch pieces.

Warm Salmon Salad

Chive Vinaigrette
 ⅓ **cup vegetable oil**
 ¼ **cup red wine vinegar**
 2 **tablespoons finely chopped fresh chives**
 2 **tablespoons finely chopped fresh parsley (page 38)**
 ⅛ **teaspoon salt**
 ⅛ **teaspoon ground white pepper**

 2 **cups water**
 ¼ **cup chopped onion (page 68)**
 2 **tablespoons red wine vinegar**
 ¼ **teaspoon ground black pepper**
1¼ **pounds small red potatoes**
 1 **pound salmon steaks**
 6 **cups torn washed mixed salad greens**
 2 **medium tomatoes, cut into wedges**
16 **kalamata olives, sliced***

*Kalamata olives are imported from Greece and can be found at gourmet food specialty shops.

1. To prepare Chive Vinaigrette, combine oil, vinegar, chives, parsley, salt and pepper in jar with tight-fitting lid; shake well to blend. Refrigerate until ready to use.

2. Combine water, onion, vinegar and pepper in large saucepan; bring to a boil over medium-high heat.

3. Add potatoes. Cover; simmer 10 minutes or until fork-tender. Transfer potatoes to cutting board using slotted spoon; cool slightly. Reserve water.

4. Cut potatoes into thick slices with utility knife; place in medium bowl. Toss potatoes with ⅓ cup dressing; set aside.

5. Rinse salmon and pat dry with paper towels. To poach fish, add fish to reserved water and bring water just below a simmer over medium-high heat. (Water will move but not bubble. *Do not boil.* This will cause fish to break apart.) Adjust heat, if necessary. Poach fish 4 to 5 minutes or until opaque and flakes easily when tested with fork.

6. Carefully remove fish from saucepan using slotted spatula; place on cutting board. Let stand 5 minutes.

7. Remove skin and bones from fish; cut into 1-inch cubes.

8. Place salad greens on 4 plates. Arrange fish, potatoes, tomatoes and olives on top. Drizzle with remaining dressing.   *Makes 4 servings*

Step 4. Cutting potatoes into thick slices.

Step 5. Poaching fish.

Step 7. Removing skin and bones from fish.

Pineapple Crab Salad

¼ cup coarsely chopped walnuts
2 pineapples
12 ounces backfin crabmeat
½ cup drained cooked chick-peas
½ cup chopped fresh parsley
    (page 38)
¾ cup vegetable oil
2 tablespoons cider vinegar
¼ small onion
½ teaspoon salt
2 teaspoons poppy seeds
    Lettuce leaves
2 medium apples, cored and cut
    into ¼-inch-thick slices, for
    garnish
1 green onion, chopped, for
    garnish
    Red onion for garnish

1. Preheat oven to 300°F. To toast walnuts, spread in single layer on baking sheet. Bake 10 to 15 minutes or until golden brown. Set aside.

2. To make pineapple boats, cut pineapples in half lengthwise through crowns.

3. Remove fruit from shells with curved knife, leaving shells intact.

4. Remove core from each pineapple half; discard. Coarsely chop pineapple. Place pineapple with juice in glass bowl; reserve. Refrigerate pineapple shells.

5. Remove cartilage and shell from crabmeat (technique on page 38).

6. Place crabmeat in medium bowl; add 1 cup reserved chopped pineapple, chick-peas, parsley and walnuts. Gently stir to combine. Cover and refrigerate until ready to assemble salad.

7. To prepare dressing, place ⅓ cup reserved pineapple juice, ¼ cup reserved chopped pineapple, oil, vinegar, onion and salt in food processor or blender; process to combine. Add poppy seeds; process using an on/off pulsing action until mixture is blended. Set aside.

8. To assemble salad, line pineapple shells with lettuce leaves. Spoon crab mixture into shells.

9. Toss apples with 2 tablespoons reserved pineapple juice. Garnish pineapple boats with apple slices, green onion and red onion. Serve salad with pineapple-poppy seed dressing.

Makes 4 servings

Step 2. Cutting pineapple in half lengthwise.

Step 3. Removing fruit from shell.

Step 4. Removing core from pineapple half.

Butterflied Shrimp and Vermicelli Salad

¼ small yellow onion
3 tablespoons tarragon vinegar
   or white wine vinegar
2 tablespoons sugar
½ teaspoon salt
½ teaspoon dry mustard
¼ cup extra virgin olive oil
¼ cup vegetable oil
1 teaspoon celery seeds
2 oranges or 1 cup mandarin
   orange slices
1 pound medium shrimp, peeled
   and deveined (page 30)
8 ounces uncooked vermicelli
   pasta, broken into 2-inch
   lengths
1 cup finely chopped celery
1 cup seedless grapes, cut into
   halves
1 jar (4 ounces) sliced pimientos,
   drained
3 tablespoons mayonnaise
1 head Bibb lettuce
5 green onions, sliced for garnish

1. To prepare dressing, place onion and vinegar in food processor; process using an on/off pulsing action until onion is finely chopped. Add sugar, salt and mustard; process until mixture is blended.

2. With motor running, slowly pour olive oil and vegetable oil through feed tube; process until smooth. Add celery seeds; process until mixture is blended. Set aside.

3. To section orange, cut off slice from top and bottom with utility knife; set orange flat on cutting board. Starting at top and working toward bottom, slice peel and pith off orange in wide strips, following curve of orange. Repeat until all peel and pith are removed. Repeat with remaining orange.

4. Make "V-shaped" slices into center of orange just inside membrane to remove orange segments. Discard orange membrane. Repeat with remaining orange.

5. Prepare cooking water for pasta according to package directions. When water comes to a boil, add half the shrimp; simmer 1 minute or until shrimp turn pink and opaque. Remove shrimp with slotted spoon; place in large bowl. Repeat with remaining shrimp. Reserve 5 shrimp for garnish.

6. Add pasta to cooking water. Cook according to package directions. Rinse under cold water; drain. Add pasta, celery, grapes and pimientos to shrimp. Toss with mayonnaise and dressing. Gently toss with orange segments. Chill several hours or overnight. Serve on lettuce-lined plates. Garnish with reserved shrimp and onions.

Makes 5 servings

Step 2. Processing until blended.

Step 3. Slicing peel and pith off orange.

Step 4. Making "V-shaped" slices.

Scallop and Yellow Rice Salad

2 jalapeño or serrano chilies, seeded*
1 clove garlic, peeled
⅓ cup plus 2 tablespoons vegetable oil, divided
½ cup chopped onion (page 68)
2 cups water
½ teaspoon ground turmeric
½ teaspoon ground cumin
½ teaspoon salt
1 cup uncooked long-grain white rice
1 pound bay scallops or quartered sea scallops
1 can (15 ounces) black beans, rinsed and drained
1 cup chopped tomatoes
¼ cup chopped fresh cilantro or parsley
3 tablespoons lime juice
Lime wedges and zest for garnish

*Chili peppers can sting and irritate the skin; wear rubber gloves when handling chili peppers and do not touch eyes. Wash hands after handling chili peppers.

1. Combine jalapeños and garlic in food processor or blender; process until finely minced.

2. Heat 2 tablespoons oil in large saucepan over medium heat until hot. Add onion and jalapeño mixture. Cook and stir 3 to 4 minutes or until onion is softened. Add water, turmeric, cumin and salt. Bring mixture to a boil over high heat; add rice. Cover; reduce heat to low. Simmer 15 to 20 minutes or until most of liquid is absorbed.

3. Stir in scallops; cover. Simmer 2 to 3 minutes or until scallops turn opaque and are cooked through.

4. Transfer rice mixture to large bowl; set bowl in ice water to chill rice and prevent scallops from overcooking.

5. Toss mixture every few minutes. When mixture is lukewarm, stir in beans, tomatoes and cilantro.

6. Combine remaining ⅓ cup oil and lime juice in 1-cup glass measure. Pour over salad and toss. Serve immediately or refrigerate and serve chilled. Garnish just before serving.

Makes 5 servings

Step 1. Processing until finely minced.

Step 3. Cooking until opaque.

Step 4. Setting bowl in ice water.

Meats

Shredded Orange Beef

1 small beef flank steak or filet
    mignon tail (about 1 pound)
1 egg white
2 tablespoons soy sauce, divided
3 teaspoons cornstarch, divided
1½ teaspoons sesame oil
4 medium carrots, peeled
4 green onions with tops
1 large navel orange
2 to 3 fresh red or green jalapeño
    chilies*
1 tablespoon sugar
1 tablespoon dry sherry
1 tablespoon distilled white
    vinegar
2 cups vegetable oil
2 cloves garlic, minced (page 116)
3 to 4 cups shredded lettuce
    (optional)
    Orange-Peel Rose for garnish
    (page 108)

*Chilies can sting and irritate the skin;
wear rubber gloves when handling chilies
and do not touch eyes. Wash hands after
handling chilies.

1. Trim fat from beef; discard. Cut beef
lengthwise into 2 strips with chef's knife. Cut
across the grain into ¼-inch-thick slices,
holding knife on a sharp diagonal to form
2-inch-long strips (technique on page 112).

2. To prepare marinade, whisk together egg
white, 1 tablespoon soy sauce, 1 teaspoon
cornstarch and sesame oil in medium bowl.
Add beef and toss to coat. Let beef marinate
while preparing vegetables.**

3. Cut carrots into julienned strips (technique
on page 41); set aside.

4. Cut off roots from green onions with
paring knife; discard. Cut onions into 3-inch
pieces. Cut lengthwise into fine slivers; set
aside.

5. Remove 2×¾-inch strips of peel from
orange with vegetable peeler. (Remove colored
portion of skin only; the white pith has a
bitter taste.) Cut orange peel lengthwise into
⅛-inch-thick strips with paring knife; set
aside.

6. Rinse chilies; pat dry with paper towel. Cut
chilies lengthwise into halves with utility
knife. Scrape out and discard stems, seeds and
veins. Diagonally cut chili halves into slices;
set aside.

**Cover and marinate overnight in refrigerator for
added flavor.

continued on page 108

Step 4. Cutting green onion
pieces into fine slivers.

Step 5. Cutting orange peel into
⅛-inch-thick strips.

Step 6. Scraping seeds from
chilies.

7. Combine sugar, sherry, vinegar, remaining 1 tablespoon soy sauce and 2 teaspoons cornstarch in small bowl; mix well. Set aside.

8. Heat vegetable oil in wok over medium-high heat until oil registers 375°F on deep-fry thermometer. Add carrots and fry about 3 minutes or until tender. Remove carrots with slotted spoon and place in large strainer set over medium bowl. Reheat oil and fry orange peel about 15 seconds or until fragrant. Remove to paper towels; drain.

9. To double-fry beef,*** add beef to wok and fry about 1 minute or just until meat turns light in color. Remove beef to colander or strainer placed over large bowl. Reheat oil to 375°F. Place ⅓ of drained beef in oil and fry about 3 minutes or until browned. Transfer beef to strainer with carrots. Repeat with remaining beef in two batches, reheating oil to maintain temperature.

10. Pour off all oil from wok. Reheat wok over medium-high heat. Add onions, garlic and chilies; stir-fry about 30 seconds or until fragrant. Stir cornstarch mixture and add to wok. Cook and stir until sauce boils and thickens. Add beef, carrots and orange peel; stir-fry until thoroughly heated. Serve spooned over lettuce on serving platter. Garnish, if desired.

Makes 4 main-dish servings or 6 servings for multi-course meal

***This technique helps keep the meat moist inside and crispy on the outside. The first frying "seals" in the juices while the second frying cooks the meat until crisp.

Orange-Peel Rose

1 orange
2 or 3 fresh mint leaves

1. Peel orange, starting at top, with vegetable peeler, cutting continuous narrow strip of peel in spiral fashion around entire orange and pressing firmly with peeler.

2. Wrap strip around itself to form coil. Continue wrapping peel tightly, tapering bottom as much as possible.

3. Insert one or two toothpicks horizontally into base to secure. Tuck mint leaves under base of rose.

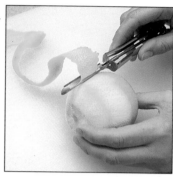
Orange-Peel Rose: Step 1.
Cutting strip of peel from orange.

Orange-Peel Rose: Step 2.
Wrapping peel into tight coil.

Orange-Peel Rose: Step 3.
Inserting toothpick into base.

Fajitas with Avocado Salsa

1 to 2 fresh or drained, bottled jalapeño chilies*
1 beef flank steak (1¼ to 1½ pounds)
¼ cup tequila or nonalcoholic beer
3 tablespoons fresh lime juice (page 370)
2 large cloves garlic, minced (page 116)
1 large red bell pepper
1 large green bell pepper
Avocado Salsa (page 110)
8 flour tortillas (6- to 7-inch diameter)
4 slices red onion, cut ¼ inch thick (page 143)

*Jalapeño chilies can sting and irritate the skin; wear rubber gloves when handling chilies and do not touch eyes. Wash hands after handling chilies.

1. Slit jalapeños open lengthwise using scissors or knife. Under cold running water, carefully pull out and discard the seeds and veins. Rinse jalapeños well and drain; pat dry with paper towels. Mince enough jalapeños to measure 1 tablespoon.

2. Place steak in large resealable plastic food storage bag. Combine tequila, lime juice, jalapeños and garlic in small bowl; pour over steak. Seal bag tightly, turning to coat. Marinate in refrigerator 1 to 4 hours, turning once.

3. Rinse bell peppers under cold running water. To seed peppers, stand on end on cutting board. Cut off sides into 4 lengthwise slices with utility knife. (Cut close to, but not through, stem.) Discard stem and seeds. Scrape out any remaining seeds. Rinse inside of peppers under cold running water. Set aside.

4. Prepare barbecue grill for direct cooking.

5. Meanwhile, prepare Avocado Salsa.

6. Wrap tortillas in heavy-duty foil using Drugstore Wrap technique (technique on page 260).

continued on page 110

Step 1. Removing seeds and veins from jalapeño chili.

Step 3. Cutting sides off bell pepper.

Step 4. Briquets arranged in grill for direct cooking.

Fajitas with Avocado Salsa, continued

7. Drain steak; discard marinade. Place steak, bell peppers and onion slices on grid. Grill, on covered grill, over medium-hot coals 14 to 18 minutes for medium or until desired doneness is reached, turning steak, bell peppers and onion slices halfway through grilling time. Place tortilla packet on grid during last 5 to 7 minutes of grilling; turn halfway through grilling time to heat through.

8. Transfer steak to carving board. Carve steak across the grain into thin slices. Slice bell peppers into thin strips. Separate onion slices into rings. Divide among tortillas; roll up and top with Avocado Salsa. *Makes 4 servings*

Avocado Salsa

1 large ripe avocado
1 large tomato, seeded and diced (page 52)
3 tablespoons chopped cilantro
1 tablespoon vegetable oil
1 tablespoon fresh lime juice (page 370)
2 teaspoons minced fresh or drained, bottled jalapeño chilies (page 136)
1 clove garlic, minced (page 116)
½ teaspoon salt

1. To prepare avocado, place avocado on cutting board. Insert utility knife into stem end of avocado; slice in half lengthwise to the pit, turning avocado while slicing. Remove knife blade; twist both halves to pull apart. Press knife blade into pit; twist knife to pull pit from avocado.

2. Scoop avocado flesh out of shells with large spoon; place on cutting board. Coarsely chop avocado flesh into ½-inch cubes. Transfer to medium bowl.

3. Gently stir in tomato, cilantro, oil, lime juice, jalapeños, garlic and salt until well combined. Let stand at room temperature while grilling steak. Cover; refrigerate if preparing in advance. Bring to room temperature before serving. *Makes about 1½ cups*

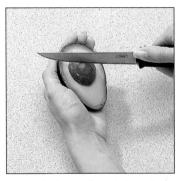

Avocado Salsa: Step 1. Pressing knife blade into pit of avocado.

Avocado Salsa: Step 2. Scooping avocado flesh out of shells.

Cantonese Tomato Beef

1 small beef flank steak or filet
   mignon tail (about 1 pound)
2 tablespoons soy sauce
2 tablespoons sesame oil, divided
1 tablespoon plus 1 teaspoon
   cornstarch, divided
1 pound fresh Chinese-style thin
   wheat noodles or 12 ounces
   dry spaghetti
3 small onions (about 7 ounces),
   peeled
5 large ripe tomatoes (about 2
   pounds), cored
1 cup beef broth
2 tablespoons brown sugar
1 tablespoon cider vinegar
2 tablespoons vegetable oil,
   divided
1 tablespoon minced fresh ginger
   (page 130)
1 green onion with tops,
   diagonally cut into thin slices
   (page 116)
  Edible flowers, such as
   nasturtiums, for garnish

1. Trim fat from beef; discard. Cut beef lengthwise into 2 strips with chef's knife. Cut across the grain into ¼-inch-thick slices, holding knife on a sharp diagonal to form 2-inch-long strips.

2. Combine soy sauce, 1 tablespoon sesame oil and 1 teaspoon cornstarch in large bowl. Add beef slices; toss to coat. Set aside to marinate.

3. Cook noodles according to package directions just until tender. Cut each onion and tomato into 8 wedges. Combine broth, sugar, remaining 1 tablespoon cornstarch and vinegar in small bowl; mix well. Set aside.

4. Drain cooked noodles in colander and return to stockpot. Add remaining 1 tablespoon sesame oil; toss. Keep warm.

5. Heat wok over high heat 1 minute or until hot. Drizzle 1 tablespoon vegetable oil into wok and heat 30 seconds. Add ginger and stir-fry about 30 seconds or until fragrant. Add beef mixture and stir-fry 5 minutes or until lightly browned. Remove beef and ginger to bowl and set aside. Reduce heat to medium.

6. Add remaining 1 tablespoon vegetable oil to wok. Add onion wedges; cook and stir about 2 minutes or until wilted. Stir in ½ of tomato wedges. Stir broth mixture and add to wok. Cook and stir until liquid boils and thickens.

7. Return beef and any juices to wok. Add remaining tomato wedges; cook and stir until heated through. Place cooked noodles in shallow serving bowl. Spoon tomato-beef mixture over noodles. Sprinkle with green onion. Garnish, if desired. Serve immediately.

Makes 4 servings

Step 1. Cutting beef across the grain into ¼-inch-thick slices.

Step 6. Stirring broth mixture into stir-fried onions and tomatoes.

Hickory Beef Kabobs

**2 ears fresh corn,* shucked and
   cleaned (page 256)**
**1 pound boneless beef top sirloin
   or tenderloin steak, cut into
   1¼-inch pieces**
**1 green or red bell pepper, cut
   into 1-inch squares**
**1 small red onion, cut into ½-inch
   wedges**
½ cup beer or nonalcoholic beer
½ cup chili sauce
1 teaspoon dry mustard
2 cloves garlic, minced (page 116)
1½ cups hickory chips
4 metal skewers (12 inches long)
3 cups hot cooked white rice
¼ cup chopped fresh parsley
   **Fresh parsley sprigs and plum
   tomatoes for garnish**

*Four small ears frozen corn, thawed, can
be substituted for fresh corn.

1. Place corn on cutting board. Cut crosswise
with chef's knife into 1-inch pieces.

2. Place beef, bell pepper, onion and corn in
large resealable plastic food storage bag.
Combine beer, chili sauce, mustard and garlic
in small bowl; pour over beef and vegetables.
Seal bag tightly, turning to coat. Marinate in
refrigerator at least 1 hour or up to 8 hours,
turning occasionally.

3. Prepare barbecue grill for direct cooking.

4. Meanwhile, cover hickory chips with cold
water; soak 20 minutes.

5. Drain beef and vegetables; reserve
marinade. Alternately thread beef and
vegetables onto skewers. Brush with reserved
marinade.

6. Drain hickory chips; sprinkle over coals.
Place kabobs on grid. Grill kabobs, on
covered grill, over medium-hot coals 5
minutes. Brush with reserved marinade; turn
and brush again. Discard remaining
marinade. Continue to grill, covered, 5 to 7
minutes for medium or until desired doneness
is reached.

7. Combine rice and chopped parsley; serve
kabobs over rice mixture. Garnish, if desired.

Makes 4 servings

Step 1. Cutting corn crosswise
into 1-inch pieces.

Step 3. Briquets arranged in grill
for direct cooking.

Step 5. Alternately threading
beef and vegetables onto
skewers.

Korean Broiled Beef (Bulgogi)

Sesame Salt
  ½ cup sesame seeds
  ¼ teaspoon salt

1½ pounds sirloin steak
  3 green onions
  2 cloves garlic
  ¼ cup soy sauce
  2 tablespoons rice wine, beef
      broth or water
  1 tablespoon sesame oil
  1 tablespoon sugar
  ¼ teaspoon ground black pepper
    Leaf lettuce
    Cooked rice, roasted garlic,
      kimchi or Korean hot bean
      paste (optional)
    Carrot ribbon and additional
      green onion slices for garnish

1. To prepare Sesame Salt, toast sesame seeds (technique on page 120); cool. Crush toasted sesame seeds together with salt with mortar and pestle *or* process in clean coffee or spice mill. Refrigerate in covered glass jar until used. Unused portion may be saved for future Korean recipes.

2. Trim fat from beef; discard. Slice beef on the diagonal across the grain into ⅛-inch-thick strips 3 inches long.

3. Cut off roots from green onions. Cut onions diagonally into thin slices.

4. Trim ends of garlic cloves. Slightly crush cloves under flat side of knife blade; peel away skin. Chop with chef's knife until garlic is in uniform fine pieces.

5. To prepare marinade, combine soy sauce, rice wine, 2 tablespoons Sesame Salt, sesame oil, sugar and pepper in large bowl. Add green onions, garlic and beef; toss to coat. Cover and refrigerate at least 30 minutes.

6. Preheat broiler. Spray broiler rack with nonstick cooking spray. Place strips of beef on broiler rack. Broil about 4 inches from heat source for 2 minutes; turn beef and broil 1 minute for medium or until desired doneness.

7. Line platter with leaf lettuce; arrange beef on top. Serve as is or use lettuce leaves to wrap beef with choice of accompaniments and eat burrito-style. Garnish, if desired.

Makes 4 servings

Step 2. Slicing beef across the grain.

Step 3. Cutting onions diagonally into thin slices.

Step 6. Broiling beef until desired doneness.

Peppered Beef Rib Roast

4½ teaspoons black peppercorns
2 cloves garlic
1 boneless beef rib roast (2½ to 3 pounds), well trimmed
¼ cup Dijon-style mustard
¾ cup sour cream
2 tablespoons prepared horseradish
1 tablespoon balsamic vinegar
½ teaspoon sugar

1. Prepare barbecue grill with rectangular metal or foil drip pan. Bank briquets on either side of drip pan for indirect cooking.

2. Meanwhile, to crack peppercorns, place peppercorns in heavy, small resealable plastic food storage bag. Squeeze out excess air; seal bag tightly. Pound peppercorns using flat side of meat mallet or rolling pin until cracked. Set aside.

3. To mince garlic, trim off ends of garlic cloves. Slightly crush cloves under flat side of chef's knife blade; peel away skin. Chop garlic with chef's knife until garlic is in uniform fine pieces.

4. Pat roast dry with paper towels. Combine mustard and garlic in small bowl; spread with spatula over top and sides of roast. Sprinkle pepper over mustard mixture.

5. Insert meat thermometer into center of thickest part of roast. Place roast, pepper-side up, on grid directly over drip pan. Grill roast, on covered grill, over medium coals 1 hour to 1 hour 10 minutes or until thermometer registers 150°F for medium-rare or until desired doneness is reached, adding 4 to 9 briquets to both sides of the fire after 45 minutes to maintain medium coals.

6. Meanwhile, combine sour cream, horseradish, vinegar and sugar in small bowl; mix well. Cover; refrigerate until serving.

7. Transfer roast to carving board; tent with foil. Let stand 5 to 10 minutes before carving. Serve with horseradish sauce.

Makes 6 to 8 servings

Step 2. Pounding peppercorns with meat mallet until cracked.

Step 3. Crushing garlic clove to remove peel.

Step 4. Spreading mustard mixture over top and sides of roast.

Korean Beef Short Ribs

1 tablespoon sesame seeds
6 to 8 green onions
2½ pounds flanken-style beef short
    ribs, cut ⅜ to ½ inch thick*
¼ cup soy sauce
¼ cup water
1 tablespoon sugar
2 teaspoons sesame oil
2 teaspoons minced fresh ginger
    (page 130)
2 cloves garlic, minced (page 116)
½ teaspoon ground black pepper

*Flanken-style ribs may be ordered from your meat retailer. They are cross-cut short ribs sawed through the bones, ⅜ to ½ inch thick.

1. To toast sesame seeds, spread seeds in large, dry skillet. Shake skillet over medium-low heat until seeds begin to pop and turn golden, about 3 minutes. Set aside.

2. Rinse green onions under cold running water; pat dry with paper towels. Cut off root ends; discard. Finely chop enough green onions with tops to measure ¼ cup.

3. Place ribs in large resealable plastic food storage bag. Combine soy sauce, water, green onions, sugar, oil, ginger, garlic and pepper in small bowl; pour over ribs. Seal bag tightly, turning to coat. Marinate in refrigerator at least 4 hours or up to 24 hours, turning occasionally.

4. Prepare barbecue grill for direct cooking (technique on page 109).

5. Drain ribs; reserve marinade. Place ribs on grid. Grill ribs, on covered grill, over medium-hot coals 5 minutes. Brush tops lightly with reserved marinade; turn and brush again. Discard remaining marinade. Continue to grill, covered, 5 to 6 minutes for medium or until desired doneness is reached. Sprinkle with sesame seeds. *Makes 4 to 6 servings*

Step 1. Shaking skillet until sesame seeds begin to pop and turn golden.

Step 2. Finely chopping green onions.

Step 3. Pouring marinade over ribs.

Mexicali Burgers

Guacamole
1 ripe avocado, pitted (page 110)
1 tablespoon purchased salsa or picante sauce
1 teaspoon fresh lime or lemon juice (page 370)
¼ teaspoon garlic salt

Burgers
⅓ cup crushed tortilla chips
1 pound ground chuck
⅓ cup purchased salsa or picante sauce
3 tablespoons finely chopped cilantro
2 tablespoons finely chopped onion
1 teaspoon ground cumin
4 slices Monterey Jack or Cheddar cheese
4 Kaiser rolls or hamburger buns, split
Lettuce leaves (optional)
Sliced tomatoes (optional)

1. Prepare barbecue grill with rectangular metal or foil drip pan. Bank briquets on either side of drip pan for indirect cooking.

2. Meanwhile, to prepare Guacamole, scoop avocado flesh out of shells with large spoon; place in medium bowl. Mash roughly with fork or wooden spoon, leaving avocado slightly chunky.

3. Stir in salsa, lime juice and garlic salt. Cover; let stand at room temperature while grilling burgers. Refrigerate if preparing in advance. Bring to room temperature before serving.

4. Place tortilla chips in large resealable plastic food storage bag; seal. Finely crush chips with rolling pin or mallet to measure ⅓ cup.

5. Combine ground chuck, salsa, tortilla chips, cilantro, onion and cumin in medium bowl. Mix lightly but thoroughly. Shape mixture into four ½-inch-thick burgers, 4 inches in diameter.

6. Place burgers on grid directly over drip pan. Grill burgers, on covered grill, over medium coals 8 to 10 minutes for medium or until desired doneness is reached, turning halfway through grilling time.

7. Place 1 slice cheese on each burger to melt during last 1 to 2 minutes of grilling. If desired, place rolls, cut-sides down, on grid to toast lightly during last 1 to 2 minutes of grilling. To serve, place burgers between rolls; top burgers with Guacamole. Serve with lettuce and tomatoes. *Makes 4 servings*

Step 2. Mashing avocado until slightly chunky.

Step 4. Crushing tortilla chips.

Step 5. Shaping beef mixture into burgers.

String Pie

8 ounces spaghetti
1 medium onion
1 pound ground beef
¼ cup chopped green bell pepper
1 jar (about 14 ounces) spaghetti
    sauce
⅓ cup grated Parmesan cheese
2 eggs, beaten
2 teaspoons butter, melted
1 cup cottage cheese
½ cup (2 ounces) shredded
    mozzarella cheese

1. Cook pasta according to package directions. Drain in colander.

2. To chop onion, peel skin. Cut onion in half through the root with a utility knife. Place cut side down on cutting board. Holding knife horizontally, make cuts parallel to the board, almost to root end. Next, cut onion vertically into thin slices, holding onion with fingers to keep its shape, then turn onion and cut crosswise to root end. (The closer the cuts are, the finer the onion is chopped.) Repeat with remaining onion half.

3. Preheat oven to 350°F.

4. Cook beef, onion and green pepper in large skillet over medium-high heat until meat is brown, stirring to separate meat; drain drippings. Stir in spaghetti sauce; mix well.

5. Combine spaghetti, Parmesan cheese, eggs and butter in large bowl; mix well. Place in bottom of 13×9-inch baking pan. Spread cottage cheese over top. Pour sauce mixture over cottage cheese. Sprinkle mozzarella over top of casserole.

6. Bake 20 minutes or until hot and cheese has melted. *Makes 6 to 8 servings*

Step 2. Chopping onion.

Step 4. Stirring ground beef to separate meat.

Step 5. Spreading cottage cheese over spaghetti sauce.

Lasagna Supreme

8 ounces lasagna noodles
½ pound ground beef
½ pound mild Italian sausage,
    casings removed
1 medium onion, chopped
    (page 68)
2 cloves garlic, minced
1 can (14½ ounces) whole peeled
    tomatoes, undrained and
    cut up
1 can (6 ounces) tomato paste
2 teaspoons dried basil leaves,
    crushed
1 teaspoon dried marjoram,
    crushed
1 can (4 ounces) sliced
    mushrooms, drained
2 eggs
1 pound cream-style cottage
    cheese
¾ cup Parmesan cheese, divided
2 tablespoons parsley flakes
½ teaspoon salt
½ teaspoon ground black pepper
2 cups (8 ounces) shredded
    Cheddar cheese
3 cups (12 ounces) shredded
    mozzarella cheese
    Mixed salad (optional)

1. Cook lasagna noodles according to package directions. Drain in colander.

2. Cook meats, onion and garlic in large skillet over medium-high heat until meat is brown, stirring to separate meat. Drain drippings.

3. Add tomatoes with juice, tomato paste, basil and marjoram. Reduce heat to low. Cover; simmer 15 minutes, stirring often. Stir in mushrooms; set aside.

4. Preheat oven to 375°F.

5. Beat eggs in large bowl; add cottage cheese, ½ cup Parmesan cheese, parsley, salt and pepper. Mix well.

6. Place half the noodles in bottom of 13×9-inch baking pan. Spread half the cottage cheese mixture over noodles, then half the meat mixture and half the Cheddar cheese and mozzarella cheese.

7. Repeat layers. Sprinkle with remaining ¼ cup Parmesan cheese.

8. Bake lasagna 40 to 45 minutes or until bubbly. Let stand 10 minutes before cutting. Serve with mixed salad.

Makes 8 to 10 servings

Note: Lasagna may be assembled, covered and refrigerated up to 2 days in advance. Bake, uncovered, in preheated 375°F oven 60 minutes or until bubbly.

Step 3. Stirring mushrooms into skillet.

Step 6. Layering lasagna.

Swedish Meatballs

3 slices fresh bread
1 cup heavy cream
  Fresh parsley sprigs
2 tablespoons butter or
  margarine, divided
1 small onion, chopped
1 pound ground beef
½ pound ground pork
1½ teaspoons salt
¼ teaspoon ground black pepper
¼ teaspoon ground allspice
1 cup beef broth
1 cup sour cream
1 tablespoon all-purpose flour
  Red pepper curls for garnish

1. Cut bread slices into quarters. Process bread in food processor or blender until fine crumbs form. Measure 1½ cups crumbs. Combine bread crumbs and cream in small bowl; mix well. Let stand 10 minutes.

2. To chop parsley, place parsley in 1-cup measuring cup. Snip enough parsley with kitchen scissors to measure 3 tablespoons.

3. Melt 1 tablespoon butter in large skillet over medium heat. Add onion. Cook and stir 5 minutes or until onion is tender.

4. Combine beef, pork, bread crumb mixture, onion, 2 tablespoons parsley, salt, pepper and allspice in large bowl; mix well. Cover; refrigerate 1 hour.

5. Place meat mixture on cutting board; pat evenly into 1-inch-thick square. Cut into 36 squares and shape each square into a ball.

6. Melt remaining 1 tablespoon butter in same large skillet over medium heat. Add meatballs. Cook 10 minutes or until browned on all sides and no longer pink in center. Remove meatballs from skillet; drain on paper towels.

7. Drain and discard drippings. Add broth to skillet to deglaze. Heat over medium-high heat, stirring and scraping up any browned bits. Reduce heat to low.

8. Combine sour cream and flour; mix well. Stir mixture into skillet. Cook 5 minutes, stirring constantly. *Do not boil.* Add meatballs. Cook 5 minutes more. Sprinkle with remaining 1 tablespoon parsley. Garnish, if desired.   *Makes 5 to 6 servings*

Step 1. Pouring cream over bread crumbs.

Step 2. Chopping parsley with kitchen scissors.

Step 5. Shaping meat mixture into balls.

Malaysian Curried Beef

1 piece fresh ginger (about 1 inch
   square)
2 large baking potatoes (1 pound)
2 tablespoons vegetable oil
2 large yellow onions, chopped
   (page 68)
2 cloves garlic, minced (page 116)
2 tablespoons curry powder
1 teaspoon salt
1 cup beef broth
2 ripe tomatoes (12 ounces)
1 pound ground chuck
   Hot cooked rice
   Purple kale and watercress
     sprigs for garnish

1. To mince ginger, peel with vegetable peeler and chop with paring knife until ginger is in uniform fine pieces; set aside.

2. Peel potatoes and cut into 1-inch chunks with utility knife; set aside.

3. Heat wok over medium-high heat 1 minute or until hot. Drizzle oil into wok and heat 30 seconds. Add onions and stir-fry 2 minutes. Add ginger, garlic, curry and salt. Cook and stir about 1 minute or until fragrant. Add potatoes; cook and stir 2 to 3 minutes.

4. Add broth to potato mixture. Cover and bring to a boil. Reduce heat to low; simmer about 20 minutes or until potatoes are fork-tender.

5. Meanwhile, to loosen skin from tomatoes, place in large saucepan of boiling water for 30 seconds. Drain in colander and rinse immediately in cold water. Gently peel skin from tomatoes.

6. Cut tomatoes in half lengthwise. Remove stems and seeds; discard. Cut tomatoes into 1-inch chunks; set aside.

7. Stir ground chuck into potato mixture. Cook and stir about 5 minutes or until beef is browned and no longer pink; spoon off fat, if necessary.

8. Add tomato chunks and stir gently until thoroughly heated. Spoon beef mixture into serving dish. Top center with rice. Garnish, if desired. *Makes 4 servings*

Step 1. Mincing ginger.

Step 5. Peeling skin from tomato.

Step 6. Scraping seeds from tomato.

Classic Veal Florentine

6 ounces fresh spinach
6 tablespoons butter or
    margarine, divided
2 cloves garlic, minced
1 can (14½ ounces) whole peeled
    tomatoes, undrained
¼ cup dry white wine
¼ cup water
1 tablespoon tomato paste
½ teaspoon sugar
¾ teaspoon salt, divided
¼ teaspoon ground black pepper,
    divided
¼ cup all-purpose flour
4 veal cutlets, cut ⅜ inch thick
    (about 4 ounces each)
1 tablespoon olive oil
4 ounces mozzarella cheese,
    shredded
  Hot cooked angel hair pasta
    (optional)
  Flat-leaf parsley for garnish

1. To steam spinach, rinse spinach thoroughly in large bowl of water; drain, but do not squeeze dry. Trim and discard stems. Stack leaves; cut crosswise into coarse shreds. Place spinach in large saucepan over medium heat. Cover and steam 4 minutes or until tender, stirring occasionally. Add 2 tablespoons butter; cook and stir until butter is absorbed. Remove from pan; set aside.

2. Heat 2 tablespoons butter in medium saucepan over medium heat until melted and bubbly. Add garlic; cook and stir 30 seconds. Press tomatoes and juice through sieve into garlic mixture; discard seeds. Add wine, water, tomato paste, sugar, ½ teaspoon salt and ⅛ teaspoon pepper to tomato mixture. Bring to a boil; reduce heat to low. Simmer, uncovered, 10 minutes, stirring occasionally. Remove from heat; set aside.

3. Mix flour, remaining ¼ teaspoon salt and ⅛ teaspoon pepper in small plastic bag. Pound veal with meat mallet to ¼-inch thickness (technique on page 134). Pat dry with paper towels. Shake veal, 1 cutlet at a time, in seasoned flour to coat evenly.

4. Heat oil and remaining 2 tablespoons butter in large skillet over medium heat until bubbly. Add veal to skillet; cook 2 to 3 minutes per side until light brown. Remove from heat. Spoon off excess fat. Top veal with spinach, then cheese. Pour tomato mixture into skillet, lifting edges of veal to let sauce flow under. Cook over low heat until bubbly. Cover and simmer 8 minutes or until heated through. Serve with pasta. Garnish, if desired.

Makes 4 servings

Step 4. Topping veal with spinach and cheese.

Step 4. Adding tomato sauce to veal.

Veal Scallopine

4 veal cutlets, cut ⅜ inch thick
    (about 4 ounces each)
¼ cup butter or margarine
½ pound fresh mushrooms, thinly
    sliced
2 tablespoons olive oil
1 small onion, finely chopped
¼ cup dry sherry
2 teaspoons all-purpose flour
½ cup beef broth
¼ teaspoon salt
⅛ teaspoon ground black pepper
2 tablespoons heavy or whipping
    cream
    Hot cooked pasta (optional)
    Fresh bay leaf and marjoram
      sprigs for garnish

1. Place each veal cutlet between sheets of waxed paper on cutting board. Pound veal with meat mallet to ¼-inch thickness. Pat dry with paper towels; set aside.

2. Heat butter in large skillet over medium heat until melted and bubbly. Cook and stir mushrooms in hot butter 3 to 4 minutes until light brown. Remove mushrooms with slotted spoon to small bowl; set aside.

3. Add oil to butter remaining in skillet; heat over medium heat. Add veal; cook 2 to 3 minutes per side until light brown. Remove veal with slotted spatula to plate; set aside.

4. Add onion to same skillet; cook and stir 2 to 3 minutes until soft. Stir sherry into onion mixture. Bring to a boil over medium-high heat; boil 15 seconds. Stir in flour; cook and stir 30 seconds. Remove from heat; stir in broth. Bring to a boil over medium heat, stirring constantly. Stir in mushrooms, salt and pepper. Add veal to sauce mixture; reduce heat to low. Cover and simmer 8 minutes or until veal is tender. Remove from heat.

5. Push veal to one side of skillet. Stir cream into sauce mixture; mix well. Cook over low heat until heated through. Serve immediately with pasta. Garnish, if desired.

Makes 4 servings

Step 1. Pounding veal.

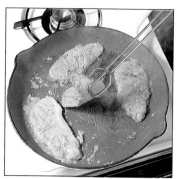

Step 3. Cooking veal.

Step 5. Stirring cream into sauce mixture.

Jerked Pork

2 jalapeño chilies*
4 green onions, coarsely chopped
2 tablespoons brown sugar
1 tablespoon dried thyme leaves, crushed
½ teaspoon ground cinnamon
½ teaspoon ground nutmeg
½ teaspoon ground allspice
½ teaspoon ground cloves
½ teaspoon ground black pepper
6 pork chops (5 to 6 ounces each)
Fresh thyme sprigs for garnish

*Chilies can sting and irritate the skin; wear rubber gloves when handling chilies and do not touch eyes. Wash hands after handling chilies.

1. Rinse chilies; pat dry with paper towels. Cut chilies lengthwise into halves with utility knife. Scrape out and discard stems, seeds and veins. Cut halves crosswise into thirds.

2. Combine onions, chilies, sugar, thyme, cinnamon, nutmeg, allspice, cloves and pepper in food processor; process until onions and chilies are finely chopped.

3. Trim fat from pork; discard. Rub both sides of pork with spice mixture.

4. Preheat broiler. Place pork on broiler pan. Broil 2 to 3 inches from heat source for 5 to 6 minutes per side or until pork is barely pink in center. Garnish, if desired.

Makes 6 servings

Step 1. Scraping out stems, seeds and veins.

Step 2. Processing spice mixture until onions and chilies are finely chopped.

Step 3. Rubbing both sides of pork with spice mixture.

Wok-Roasted Pork Loin

2 pounds boneless pork loin
2 tablespoons vegetable oil,
    divided
1½ pounds small red potatoes,
    unpeeled and scrubbed
½ cup ketchup
2 tablespoons hoisin sauce
1 tablespoon soy sauce
1 teaspoon sugar
1 clove garlic, minced (page 116)
1 medium onion, peeled and
    sliced
3 large zucchini (1½ pounds),
    scrubbed and cut diagonally
    into ¼-inch-thick slices
¼ teaspoon salt
¼ teaspoon ground black pepper

1. Trim excess fat layer from pork with large chef's knife; discard. To butterfly pork loin, or split loin in half, make horizontal cut, starting from one long edge through center of pork to within 1 inch of opposite long edge. (Be careful not to cut all the way through.)

2. Open pork and press uncut edge to flatten as much as possible.

3. Heat wok over medium-high heat 1 minute or until hot. Add 1 tablespoon oil and heat 30 seconds. Add pork, cut side down, and cook about 5 minutes or until browned. Turn pork over and cook about 5 minutes or until other side is browned. Remove pork to plate.

4. Cut potatoes in half. Add to bottom of wok. Place pork, cut side down, over potatoes. Cover; reduce heat to low. Simmer 20 minutes, stirring if necessary to loosen potatoes.

5. To prepare glaze, combine ketchup, hoisin sauce, soy sauce, sugar and garlic in small saucepan. Heat over low heat; keep warm.

6. Spoon ½ of glaze over pork. Cover and cook about 15 minutes more or until pork and potatoes are fork-tender. Remove pork and potatoes. Cover; keep warm.

7. Rinse wok and heat over medium-high heat until dry. Add remaining 1 tablespoon oil and heat 30 seconds. Add onion; cook and stir about 1 minute or until wilted. Add zucchini and stir-fry until crisp-tender. Sprinkle with salt and black pepper. Transfer zucchini, onion and potatoes to serving platter. Cut pork crosswise into thin slices; add to platter. Top with remaining glaze. Serve immediately.

Makes 8 servings

Step 1. Cutting loin in half to butterfly.

Step 2. Opening loin and pressing to flatten.

Mu Shu Pork

4 teaspoons cornstarch, divided
8 teaspoons soy sauce, divided
5 teaspoons dry sherry, divided
8 ounces boneless lean pork, cut
    into matchstick pieces
3 dried mushrooms
2 dried wood ears
    Water
½ teaspoon sugar
1 teaspoon sesame oil
2 tablespoons plus 1 teaspoon
    vegetable oil, divided
2 eggs, lightly beaten
1 teaspoon minced fresh ginger
    (page 116)
½ cup sliced bamboo shoots
    (½ of 8-ounce can), cut into
    matchstick pieces
1 small carrot, shredded
½ cup chicken broth
2 cups bean sprouts (about
    4 ounces)
2 green onions with tops, cut into
    1½-inch slivers (page 106)
¾ cup hoisin sauce
16 Mandarin Pancakes (recipe
    follows on page 142)

1. For marinade, combine 1 teaspoon cornstarch, 2 teaspoons soy sauce and 2 teaspoons sherry in large bowl. Add meat; stir to coat. Let stand 30 minutes.

2. Meanwhile, place dried mushrooms and wood ears in small bowl; add enough water to cover. Let stand 30 minutes; drain. Squeeze out excess water. Cut off and discard mushroom stems; cut caps into thin slices.

3. Pinch out hard nobs from centers of wood ears; discard.

4. Cut wood ears into thin strips.

5. Combine remaining 3 teaspoons cornstarch, 6 teaspoons soy sauce and 3 teaspoons sherry in small bowl. Add additional 1 tablespoon water, sugar and sesame oil; mix well.

6. Heat ½ teaspoon vegetable oil in small nonstick skillet over medium-high heat. Add ½ of eggs, tilting skillet to cover bottom.

7. Cook egg just until set. Loosen edges and turn omelet over; cook 5 seconds.

8. Remove omelet from skillet; set aside to cool. Repeat with another ½ teaspoon vegetable oil and remaining egg.

9. Cut omelets in half. Stack halves; cut crosswise into thin strips.

10. Heat remaining 2 tablespoons vegetable oil in wok or large skillet over high heat. Stir in ginger. Add meat; stir-fry until meat is no longer pink in center, about 2 minutes. Add mushrooms, wood ears, bamboo shoots, carrot and chicken broth; stir-fry 2 minutes.

Step 3. Removing nobs from wood ears.

Step 6. Tilting skillet to cover bottom with eggs.

Step 7. Loosening omelet from skillet.

continued on page 142

***Mu Shu Pork,* continued**

11. Add bean sprouts and onions; stir-fry 1 minute.

12. Stir cornstarch mixture; add to wok. Cook, stirring constantly, until sauce bubbles and thickens. Stir in omelet strips.

13. To serve, spread about 2 teaspoons hoisin sauce onto each pancake. Spoon about 3 tablespoons pork mixture down center. Fold over bottom; roll up.

Makes 8 servings

Mandarin Pancakes

2 cups all-purpose flour
¾ cup boiling water
2 tablespoons sesame oil

1. Place flour in bowl; make well in center. Pour in boiling water.

2. Stir flour mixture with wooden spoon until dough looks like lumpy meal.

3. Press dough into ball. On lightly floured surface, knead dough until smooth and satiny, about 5 minutes (technique on page 190). Cover with clean towel and let rest 30 minutes.

4. Roll dough into log, 10 inches long. Cut into 1-inch pieces; cover with plastic wrap.

5. Cut each piece of dough in half, keeping remaining dough pieces covered with plastic wrap. Shape each half into ball. Place on lightly floured surface; flatten slightly. With lightly floured rolling pin, roll each dough piece into 3-inch circle; brush with small amount of sesame oil. Stack two dough circles together, oil-side in.

6. Roll each pair of dough circles into 6- to 7-inch circle; cover and set aside. Repeat with remaining dough circles.

7. Heat nonstick skillet over medium-low heat. Cook pancakes, one pair at a time, turning every 30 seconds, until cakes are flecked with brown and feel dry, 2 to 3 minutes. (Be careful not to overcook pancakes or they will become brittle.)

8. Remove pancakes from pan. Separate each pancake into two pancakes while still hot. Stack pancakes on plate; keep covered while cooking remaining pancakes. Fold pancakes into quarters and arrange in serving basket. Serve immediately.

Makes about 20 pancakes

Note: Pancakes may be prepared ahead and refrigerated or frozen in resealable plastic food storage bags. To reheat, wrap pancakes in clean towel (thaw completely, if using frozen). Steam over simmering water 5 minutes.

Mandarin Pancakes: Step 2. Stirring flour mixture to form dough.

Mandarin Pancakes: Step 6. Rolling out dough circles.

Mandarin Pancakes: Step 7. Cooking pancakes.

Barbecued Pork Tenderloin Sandwiches

1 clove garlic
1 large red onion
½ cup ketchup
⅓ cup packed brown sugar
2 tablespoons bourbon or whiskey
    (optional)
1 tablespoon Worcestershire
    sauce
½ teaspoon dry mustard
¼ teaspoon ground red pepper
2 whole pork tenderloins (about
    ¾ pound each), well trimmed
6 hoagie rolls or Kaiser rolls,
    split

1. Prepare barbecue grill for direct cooking (technique on page 109).

2. To mince garlic, trim off ends of garlic clove. Slightly crush clove under flat side of chef's knife blade; peel away skin. Chop garlic with chef's knife until garlic is in uniform fine pieces. Set aside.

3. Meanwhile, to slice onion, slice off stem and root end; discard. Peel away skin. Cut onion crosswise into six ¼-inch-thick slices. Set aside.

4. Combine ketchup, sugar, bourbon, Worcestershire sauce, mustard, ground red pepper and garlic in small, heavy saucepan with ovenproof handle; mix well. (If not ovenproof, wrap heavy-duty foil around handle.)

continued on page 144

Step 1. Briquets arranged in grill for direct cooking.

Step 2. Crushing garlic clove to remove peel.

Step 3. Cutting onion crosswise into ¼-inch-thick slices.

Barbecued Pork Tenderloin Sandwiches, continued

5. Set saucepan on one side of grid.* Place tenderloins on center of grid. Grill tenderloins, on uncovered grill, over medium-hot coals 8 minutes. Simmer sauce 5 minutes or until thickened, stirring occasionally.

6. Turn tenderloins with tongs; continue to grill, uncovered, 5 minutes. Add onion slices to grid. Set aside half of sauce; reserve. Brush tenderloins and onions with a portion of remaining sauce.

7. Continue to grill, uncovered, 7 to 10 minutes or until pork is juicy and barely pink in center, brushing with remaining sauce and turning onions and tenderloins halfway through grilling time. (If desired, insert instant-read thermometer** into center of thickest part of tenderloins. Thermometer should register 160°F.)

8. Carve tenderloins crosswise into thin slices; separate onion slices into rings. Divide meat and onion rings among rolls; drizzle with reserved sauce.

Makes 6 servings

*If desired, sauce may be prepared on rangetop. Combine ketchup, sugar, bourbon, Worcestershire sauce, mustard, ground red pepper and garlic in small saucepan. Bring to a boil over medium-high heat. Reduce heat to low and simmer, uncovered, 5 minutes or until thickened, stirring occasionally.

**Do not leave instant-read thermometer in tenderloins during grilling since the thermometer is not heatproof.

Step 6. Brushing tenderloins and onions with portion of sauce.

Step 7. Inserting instant-read thermometer into thickest part of tenderloin.

Step 8. Carving tenderloins crosswise into thin slices.

Grilled Pork and Potatoes Vesuvio

1 center-cut boneless pork loin
  roast (1½ pounds), well
  trimmed
½ cup dry white wine
2 tablespoons olive oil
4 cloves garlic, minced, divided
  (page 116)
1½ to 2 pounds small red potatoes
  (about 1½ inches in
  diameter), scrubbed
6 metal skewers (12 inches long)
6 lemon wedges
  Salt (optional)
  Ground black pepper (optional)
¼ cup chopped fresh Italian or
  curly leaf parsley
1 teaspoon finely grated lemon
  peel

1. Cut pork into 1-inch cubes. Place pork in large resealable plastic food storage bag. Combine wine, oil and 3 cloves minced garlic in small bowl; pour over pork.

2. Place potatoes in single layer in microwave-safe dish. Pierce each potato with tip of sharp knife. Microwave at HIGH (100% power) 6 to 7 minutes or until almost tender when pierced with fork. (Or, place potatoes in large saucepan. Cover with cold water. Bring to a boil over high heat. Simmer about 12 minutes or until almost tender when pierced with fork.) Immediately rinse with cold water; drain. Add to pork in bag. Seal bag tightly, turning to coat. Marinate in refrigerator at least 2 hours or up to 8 hours, turning occasionally.

3. Prepare barbecue grill for direct cooking (technique on page 109).

4. Meanwhile, drain pork mixture; discard marinade. Alternately thread about 3 pork cubes and 2 potatoes onto each skewer. Place 1 lemon wedge on end of each skewer. Sprinkle salt and pepper over pork and potatoes.

5. Place skewers on grid. Grill skewers, on covered grill, over medium coals 14 to 16 minutes or until pork is juicy and barely pink in center and potatoes are tender, turning halfway through grilling time.

6. Remove skewers from grill. Combine parsley, lemon peel and remaining minced garlic clove in small bowl. Sprinkle over pork and potatoes. Squeeze lemon wedges over pork and potatoes. *Makes 6 servings*

Step 4. Alternately threading pork and potatoes onto skewers.

Step 6. Sprinkling parsley mixture over pork and potatoes.

Honey-Glazed Spareribs

1 side pork spareribs (about
    2 pounds)
¼ cup plus 1 tablespoon soy
    sauce, divided
3 tablespoons hoisin sauce
3 tablespoons dry sherry, divided
1 tablespoon sugar
1 teaspoon minced fresh ginger
2 cloves garlic, minced (page 116)
¼ teaspoon Chinese five-spice
    powder
2 tablespoons honey
1 tablespoon cider vinegar
   Green Onion Curls (page 12),
    slivered green onions and
    edible flowers for garnish

1. Have your butcher cut ribs down length of slab into two pieces so that each half is 2 to 3 inches wide. Cut between bones to make 6-inch pieces.

2. Trim excess fat from ribs. Place ribs in heavy resealable plastic food storage bag.

3. For marinade, combine ¼ cup soy sauce, hoisin sauce, 2 tablespoons sherry, sugar, ginger, garlic and five-spice powder in small cup or bowl; mix well. Pour over ribs.

4. Seal bag tightly; place in large bowl. Refrigerate at least 8 hours or overnight, turning bag occasionally.

5. Preheat oven to 350°F. Line large baking pan with foil. Place ribs on rack in pan, reserving marinade. Bake 30 minutes; turn ribs over. Brush with marinade; continue baking 40 minutes or until ribs are tender when pierced with fork.

6. For glaze, combine honey, vinegar, remaining 1 tablespoon soy sauce and 1 tablespoon sherry in small bowl; mix well. Brush ½ of mixture over ribs. Place under preheated broiler 4 to 6 inches from heat source; broil until glaze is hot and bubbly, 2 to 3 minutes. Turn ribs over. Brush with remaining honey glaze.

7. Broil until hot and bubbly. Cut into serving-size pieces. Garnish, if desired.

Makes about 4 servings

Step 1. Cutting ribs into 6-inch pieces.

Step 3. Pouring marinade over ribs.

Step 6. Brushing ribs with glaze.

Rosemary-Crusted Leg of Lamb

2 large cloves garlic
¼ cup Dijon-style mustard
1 boneless butterflied leg of lamb
   (sirloin half, about 2½
   pounds), well trimmed
3 tablespoons chopped fresh
   rosemary leaves *or* 1
   tablespoon dried rosemary
   leaves, crushed
Fresh rosemary sprigs
Mint jelly (optional)

1. Prepare barbecue grill for direct cooking (technique on page 109).

2. Meanwhile, to mince garlic, trim off ends of garlic cloves. Slightly crush cloves under flat side of chef's knife blade; peel away skin. Chop garlic with chef's knife until garlic is in uniform fine pieces.

3. Combine mustard and garlic in small bowl; spread half of mixture with fingers or spatula over one side of lamb. Sprinkle with half of chopped rosemary; pat into mustard mixture. Turn lamb over; repeat with remaining mustard mixture and rosemary.

4. Insert meat thermometer into center of thickest part of lamb.

5. Place lamb on grid. Grill lamb, on covered grill, over medium coals 39 to 42 minutes or until thermometer registers 130°F for medium-rare doneness. For medium doneness, grill lamb for 43 to 46 minutes or until thermometer registers 145°F. Turn lamb every 10 minutes.

6. Meanwhile, soak rosemary sprigs in water. Place rosemary sprigs directly on coals during last 10 minutes of grilling.

7. Transfer lamb to carving board; tent with foil. Let stand about 15 minutes* before carving into thin slices. Serve with mint jelly.

Makes 8 servings

*Stand time allows lamb to reach desired final temperature. Internal temperature will rise another 15 degrees in about 15 minutes after lamb is removed from grill.

Step 2. Crushing garlic clove to remove peel.

Step 3. Patting rosemary into mustard mixture.

Step 7. Carving lamb into thin slices.

Mongolian Lamb

Sesame Sauce

   1 tablespoon sesame seeds
   ¼ cup soy sauce
   1 tablespoon dry sherry
   1 tablespoon red wine vinegar
   1½ teaspoons sugar
   1 clove garlic, minced
   1 green onion with top, finely
      chopped
   ½ teaspoon sesame oil

Lamb

   1 pound boneless lean lamb* (leg
      or shoulder)
   2 small leeks
   4 green onions with tops, slivered
   2 medium carrots, shredded
   1 medium zucchini, shredded
   1 each green and red bell pepper,
      cut into matchstick pieces
   ½ small head napa cabbage,
      thinly sliced
   1 cup bean sprouts
   4 tablespoons vegetable oil,
      divided
   4 slices peeled fresh ginger
      Chili oil (optional)

*Or, substitute beef flank steak or
boneless lean pork for the lamb.

1. For Sesame Sauce, place sesame seeds in small skillet. Carefully shake or stir over medium heat until seeds begin to pop and turn golden brown, about 2 to 3 minutes; cool.

2. Crush seeds with mortar and pestle (or place between paper towels and crush with rolling pin); scrape up sesame paste with knife and transfer to small serving bowl. Add remaining sauce ingredients; mix well.

3. Slice meat across grain into 2×¼-inch strips.

4. Cut leeks into 2-inch slivers. Rinse leek slivers well under cold running water to remove sand and dirt. Pat dry with paper towels.

5. Arrange meat and all vegetables on large platter. Have Sesame Sauce, vegetable oil, ginger and chili oil near cooking area.

6. Heat wok or electric griddle to 350°F. Cook one serving at a time: For each serving, heat 1 tablespoon vegetable oil. Add one slice ginger; cook and stir 30 seconds. Discard ginger. Add ½ cup meat strips; stir-fry until lightly browned, about 1 minute. Add 2 cups assorted vegetables; stir-fry 1 minute. Drizzle with 2 tablespoons Sesame Sauce; stir-fry 30 seconds. Season with a few drops chili oil. Repeat with remaining ingredients. *Makes 4 servings*

Step 4. Cutting leek into slivers.

Step 5. Arranging cut-up ingredients on platter.

Poultry

Pesto-Stuffed Grilled Chicken

2 tablespoons pine nuts or
    walnuts
  Fresh basil leaves
2 cloves garlic, peeled
¼ teaspoon ground black pepper
5 tablespoons extra-virgin olive
    oil, divided
¼ cup grated Parmesan cheese
1 fresh or thawed frozen roasting
    chicken or capon (6 to 7
    pounds)
2 tablespoons fresh lemon juice
  Additional fresh basil leaves
    and fresh red currants for
    garnish

1. Preheat oven to 350°F. To toast pine nuts, spread in single layer on baking sheet. Bake 8 to 10 minutes or until golden brown, stirring frequently. Remove pine nuts from baking sheet; cool completely. Set aside.

2. Rinse basil leaves under cold running water. Remove stems; discard. Pat leaves dry with paper towel. Prepare enough basil leaves to measure ½ cup packed. Set aside.

3. Meanwhile, prepare barbecue grill with rectangular metal or foil drip pan. Bank briquets on either side of drip pan for indirect cooking.

4. To prepare pesto, drop garlic cloves through feed tube of food processor with motor running. Add basil, pine nuts and pepper; process until basil is minced. With processor running, add 3 tablespoons oil in slow, steady stream until smooth paste forms, scraping down side of bowl once. Add cheese; process until well blended.

continued on page 156

Step 1. Toasting pine nuts until golden brown.

Step 2. Removing stems from basil leaves.

Step 4. Processing pesto in food processor until well blended.

Pesto-Stuffed Grilled Chicken, continued

5. Remove giblets from chicken cavity; reserve for another use. Rinse chicken with cold water; pat dry with paper towels. Loosen skin over breast of chicken by pushing fingers between skin and meat, taking care not to tear skin. Do not loosen skin over wings and drumsticks.

6. Using rubber spatula or small spoon, spread pesto under breast skin; massage skin to evenly spread pesto.

7. Combine remaining 2 tablespoons oil and lemon juice in small bowl; brush over chicken skin.

8. Insert meat thermometer into center of thickest part of thigh, not touching bone.

9. Tuck wings under back; tie legs together with wet kitchen string. Place chicken, breast-side up, on grid directly over drip pan. Grill chicken, on covered grill, over medium-low coals 1 hour 10 minutes to 1 hour 30 minutes or until thermometer registers 185°F, adding 4 to 9 briquets to both sides of the fire after 45 minutes to maintain medium-low coals.

10. Transfer chicken to carving board; tent with foil. Let stand 15 minutes before carving. Garnish, if desired.

Makes 6 servings

Step 5. Loosening skin over chicken breast by pushing fingers between skin and meat.

Step 6. Spreading pesto under breast skin.

Step 8. Inserting meat thermometer into thickest part of thigh, not touching bone.

Sweet and Pungent Chicken

1 whole frying chicken* (about 3½ pounds)
⅓ cup plus 4 teaspoons cornstarch, divided
⅓ cup all-purpose flour
1 teaspoon sugar
½ teaspoon salt, divided
¼ teaspoon baking powder
⅓ cup water
1 can (20 ounces) pineapple chunks in juice, undrained
⅓ cup distilled white vinegar
3 tablespoons light brown sugar
3 tablespoons ketchup
3 to 4 cups vegetable oil
1 medium yellow onion, peeled and cut into wedges
1 small red bell pepper, stemmed, seeded (page 270) and cut into 12 chunks
1 small green bell pepper, stemmed, seeded and cut into ½-inch-wide strips
Hot cooked rice (optional)

*To save time, use 1 pound boneless skinless chicken breast halves cut into 1-inch pieces for whole frying chicken. (Omit steps 1 through 5.)

1. Remove neck and giblets from chicken and cut off wings; wrap and freeze for another use, such as soup or stock. Rinse chicken and cavity under cold running water; pat dry with paper towels. Place chicken, breast-side down, on cutting board with neck end away from you. Working from neck to tail, cut along one side of backbone, cutting as close to bone as possible with sharp utility knife. Cut down other side of backbone; remove backbone.

2. Open chicken as much as possible. Cut small slit through membrane and cartilage at the "V" of the neck end. Grasp chicken breast with both hands and gently bend both sides backward to snap breast bone. With fingers, work along both sides of breast bone to loosen triangular keel bone. Pull out bone, using knife to loosen if necessary.

3. Turn chicken breast side up. Cut lengthwise down center of chicken to split into halves.

continued on page 158

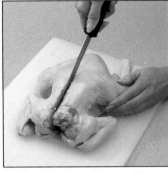

Step 1. Cutting along backbone of chicken to remove.

Step 2. Pulling out keel bone from chicken using knife to loosen.

Step 3. Cutting chicken in half.

Sweet and Pungent Chicken, *continued*

4. To cut into quarters, cut through skin, separating thighs from breast.

5. To skin chicken, grasp skin with paper towel and pull away from meat; discard skin. With tip of sharp knife, cut and scrape meat from breast, thigh and leg bones, pulling bones away from meat; wrap and freeze bones for another use, such as soup or stock. Cut chicken meat into 1-inch pieces; set aside.

6. Combine ⅓ cup cornstarch, flour, sugar, ¼ teaspoon salt and baking powder in medium bowl. Stir in water to form smooth batter. Add chicken and mix well.

7. Drain pineapple, reserving ½ cup juice; set aside pineapple. Combine juice, remaining 4 teaspoons cornstarch, ¼ teaspoon salt, vinegar, brown sugar and ketchup in small bowl; set aside.

8. Heat oil in wok over medium-high heat until oil registers 375°F on deep-fry thermometer. Add ⅓ of chicken, shaking off excess batter. Fry about 4 minutes or until golden brown and chicken is no longer pink in center, stirring to break up pieces with spoon. Remove chicken with slotted spoon to tray or plate lined with paper towels; drain. Repeat two more times with remaining chicken, reheating oil between batches.

9. Pour off oil. Return 1 tablespoon oil to wok; heat over medium heat 30 seconds. Add onion and stir-fry about 2 minutes or until onion is wilted. Add peppers and stir-fry 1 minute. Stir cornstarch mixture and add to wok. Add pineapple; cook and stir until sauce thickens and boils. Return chicken to wok; mix well. Transfer to serving platter or place wok on table over wok ring stand or trivet. Serve with rice. *Makes 4 servings*

Step 4. Cutting chicken into quarters.

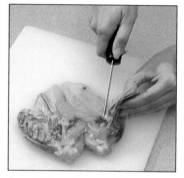

Step 5. Scraping meat from breast bone.

Step 8. Deep-frying battered chicken pieces.

Guinness Chicken

5 carrots
2 parsnips
2 large cloves garlic
2 tablespoons vegetable oil
1 medium onion, chopped
    (page 68)
1 whole frying chicken (3 to 4
    pounds), cut into serving
    pieces
1 teaspoon dried thyme leaves,
    crushed
¾ teaspoon salt
½ teaspoon ground black pepper
¾ cup Guinness Stout
½ pound fresh button mushrooms
¾ cup frozen peas
    Fresh parsley for garnish

1. To prepare carrots and parsnips, peel with vegetable peeler. Trim ends and cut into 1-inch pieces.

2. To mince garlic, trim ends of cloves. Slightly crush clove under flat side of chef's knife blade; peel away skin. Chop garlic with chef's knife until garlic is in uniform fine pieces. Set aside.

3. Heat oil in large skillet over medium heat until hot. Add garlic and onion; cook and stir 3 minutes or until tender. Remove vegetables with slotted spoon to small bowl.

4. Arrange chicken in single layer in skillet. Cook over medium-high heat 5 minutes per side or until lightly browned.

5. Add onion, garlic, carrots, parsnips, thyme, salt and pepper to skillet. Pour stout over chicken and vegetables. Bring to a boil over high heat. Reduce heat to low. Cover and simmer 35 minutes.

6. Wipe mushrooms with damp paper towel. Cut thin piece from stem; discard. Add mushrooms and peas to skillet. Cover; cook 10 minutes.

7. Uncover skillet; increase heat to medium. Cook 10 minutes or until sauce is slightly reduced and chicken is no longer pink in center. Garnish, if desired.

Makes 4 servings

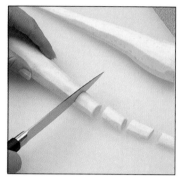

Step 1. Cutting parsnips into 1-inch pieces.

Step 2. Crushing garlic clove under flat side of chef's knife blade.

Step 6. Wiping mushrooms with damp paper towel.

Barbecued Chicken with Chili-Orange Glaze

1 or 2 dried de árbol chilies*
½ cup fresh orange juice
2 tablespoons tequila
2 cloves garlic, minced
1½ teaspoons shredded orange peel
¼ teaspoon salt
¼ cup vegetable oil
**1 broiler-fryer chicken (about
    3 pounds), cut into quarters**
**Orange slices and cilantro
    sprigs for garnish**

*For milder flavor, seed some or all of the chilies.

1. Crush chilies into coarse flakes in mortar with pestle.

2. Combine chilies, orange juice, tequila, garlic, orange peel and salt in small bowl. Gradually add oil, whisking continuously, until marinade is thoroughly blended.

3. Arrange chicken in single layer in shallow glass baking dish. Pour marinade over chicken; turn pieces to coat. Marinate, covered, in refrigerator 2 to 3 hours, turning chicken over and basting with marinade several times.

4. Prepare coals for direct grilling or preheat broiler. Drain chicken, reserving marinade. Bring marinade to a boil in small saucepan over high heat.

5. Grill or broil chicken 6 to 8 inches from heat 15 minutes, brushing frequently with marinade. Turn chicken over. Grill or broil 15 minutes more or until chicken is tender and juices run clear, brushing frequently with marinade. Garnish, if desired.

Makes 4 servings

Step 2. Whisking oil into orange juice mixture.

Step 3. Basting chicken with marinade.

Step 5. Brushing grilled chicken with marinade.

Roast Chicken & Kiwi with Raspberry Glaze

**2 (3½- to 4-pound) frying
    chickens, cut into halves
    (page 157)**
1 teaspoon salt
¼ teaspoon ground black pepper
**½ cup butter, melted
    Raspberry Glaze (recipe
    follows)**
2 kiwifruit

1. Preheat oven to 400°F. Sprinkle chicken halves with salt and pepper.

2. Place chicken halves, skin sides up, in single layer in large shallow baking pan. Brush chicken with butter.

3. Roast chicken, basting frequently with butter, 45 minutes or until chicken is tender.

4. Meanwhile, prepare Raspberry Glaze.

5. To prepare kiwifruit, remove peel from kiwifruit with vegetable peeler or paring knife.

6. Cut kiwifruit into thin slices; set aside.

7. When chicken is done, spoon off drippings from baking pan.

8. Spoon Raspberry Glaze over chicken; top with kiwifruit slices.

9. Bake chicken 3 minutes or until kiwifruit and chicken are well glazed, spooning glaze frequently from bottom of pan over chicken and kiwifruit.   *Makes 4 servings*

Raspberry Glaze

1 cup seedless raspberry preserves
**½ cup white port wine
    Grated peel of 1 lemon (page 332)**

Combine preserves, wine and lemon peel in small saucepan; cook over low heat 5 minutes or until thickened slightly.

Makes about 1 cup

Step 5. Peeling kiwifruit.

Step 6. Slicing peeled kiwifruit.

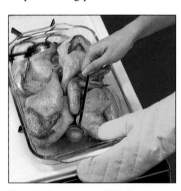
Step 7. Spooning off drippings.

Chicken Cacciatore

1 broiler-fryer chicken (3 to
   3½ pounds), cut into 8 pieces
1 tablespoon olive oil
4 ounces fresh mushrooms, finely
   chopped
1 medium onion, chopped
1 clove garlic, minced
½ cup dry white wine
4½ teaspoons white wine vinegar
½ cup chicken broth
1 teaspoon dried basil leaves,
   crushed
½ teaspoon dried marjoram
   leaves, crushed
½ teaspoon salt
⅛ teaspoon ground black pepper
1 can (14½ ounces) whole peeled
   tomatoes, undrained
8 Italian- or Greek-style ripe
   olives
1 tablespoon chopped fresh
   parsley
   Hot cooked pasta
   Fresh marjoram leaves for
   garnish

1. Rinse chicken; drain and pat dry with paper towels. Heat oil in large skillet over medium heat until hot. Add chicken pieces in single layer, without crowding. Cook 8 minutes per side or until chicken is brown; remove chicken with slotted spatula to Dutch oven. Repeat with remaining chicken pieces; set aside.

2. Add mushrooms and onion to drippings remaining in skillet. Cook and stir over medium heat 5 minutes or until onion is soft. Add garlic; cook and stir 30 seconds. Add wine and vinegar; cook over medium-high heat 5 minutes or until liquid is almost evaporated. Stir in broth, basil, marjoram, salt and pepper. Remove from heat.

3. Press tomatoes and juice through sieve into onion mixture; discard seeds. Bring to a boil over medium-high heat; boil, uncovered, 2 minutes.

4. Pour tomato-onion mixture over chicken. Bring to a boil; reduce heat to low. Cover and simmer 25 minutes or until chicken is tender and juices run clear when pierced with fork. Remove chicken with slotted spatula to heated serving dish; keep warm.

5. Bring tomato-onion mixture to a boil over medium-high heat; boil, uncovered, 5 minutes. Cut olives in half; remove and discard pits.

6. Add olives and parsley to sauce; cook 1 minute more. Pour sauce over chicken and pasta. Garnish, if desired.

Makes 4 to 6 servings

Step 1. Cooking chicken pieces.

Step 4. Piercing chicken with fork to test for doneness.

Step 5. Pitting olives.

Jamaican Rum Chicken

½ cup dark rum

2 tablespoons lime juice or lemon juice

2 tablespoons soy sauce

2 tablespoons brown sugar

4 large cloves garlic, minced (page 116)

1 to 2 jalapeño chilies, seeded and minced (page 75)

1 tablespoon minced fresh ginger (page 130)

1 teaspoon dried thyme leaves, crushed

½ teaspoon ground black pepper

6 boneless skinless chicken breast halves

1. To prepare marinade, combine rum, lime juice, soy sauce, sugar, garlic, chilies, ginger, thyme and black pepper in 2-quart glass measuring cup.

2. Rinse chicken and pat dry with paper towels. Place chicken in resealable plastic food storage bag. Pour marinade over chicken. Press air out of bag and seal tightly. Turn bag over to completely coat chicken with marinade. Refrigerate 4 hours or overnight, turning bag once or twice.

3. Prepare barbecue grill for direct grilling by spreading hot coals in single layer that extends 1 to 2 inches beyond area of food.

4. Drain chicken; reserve marinade. Place chicken on grid. Grill chicken, on uncovered grill, over medium-hot coals 6 minutes per side or until chicken is no longer pink in center.

5. Meanwhile, bring remaining marinade to a boil in small saucepan over medium-high heat. Boil 5 minutes or until marinade is reduced by about half.

6. To serve, drizzle marinade over chicken. Garnish as desired. *Makes 6 servings*

Step 2. Pouring marinade over chicken.

Step 4. Grilling chicken until no longer pink in center.

Step 5. Boiling remaining marinade until reduced by half.

Chicken Avocado Melt

2 tablespoons cornstarch
1 teaspoon ground cumin
1 teaspoon garlic salt
1 egg
1 tablespoon water
⅓ cup yellow cornmeal
2 whole chicken breasts, skinned,
    boned and split (pages 6-8)
3 tablespoons vegetable oil
1 firm ripe avocado
1½ cups (6 ounces) shredded
    Monterey Jack cheese
½ cup sour cream
¼ cup sliced green onion tops
¼ cup chopped red bell pepper
    Steamed crinkle-cut carrots
4 green onion brushes for garnish
    (page 12)

1. Preheat oven to 325°F. Combine cornstarch, cumin and garlic salt in shallow dish; set aside. Beat egg with water in shallow dish; set aside. Place cornmeal in shallow dish; set aside.

2. Flatten chicken breasts to ¼-inch thickness (technique on page 6).

3. Coat chicken in cornstarch mixture, shaking off excess. Dip chicken into egg mixture, then roll in cornmeal, shaking off excess.

4. Heat oil in large skillet over medium-high heat. Add chicken to skillet in single layer; cook 4 minutes, turning once.

5. Remove chicken to shallow baking dish; set aside.

6. Remove pit from avocado (technique on page 110); cut avocado halves lengthwise in half on cutting board. From stem end, carefully peel skin away from each avocado quarter.

7. Cut avocado quarters lengthwise into slices; set aside.

8. Arrange avocado slices over chicken in dish; sprinkle with cheese.

9. Bake chicken 15 minutes or until chicken is tender and cheese is melted. Transfer chicken to serving platter. Top each serving with a dollop of sour cream; sprinkle with sliced green onion tops and red pepper. Serve with carrots. Garnish, if desired.

Makes 4 servings

Step 3. Coating chicken in cornstarch mixture.

Step 6. Peeling skin from avocado quarters.

Step 7. Cutting avocado into slices.

Swimming Rama

1 fresh red chili pepper* *or* ¼ cup
    diced red bell pepper
1¾ to 2 pounds fresh spinach or
    2 packages (10 ounces each)
    washed and stemmed fresh
    spinach
3 boneless skinless chicken breast
    halves (about 1¼ pounds)
    Peanut Sauce (page 174)
    Marigold petals for garnish

*Chili peppers can sting and irritate the skin; wear rubber gloves when handling peppers and do not touch eyes. Wash hands after handling.

1. Rinse chili pepper; pat dry with paper towel. Cut lengthwise into halves with utility knife. Scrape out and discard stems, seeds and veins. Finely chop pepper; set aside.

2. Separate spinach into leaves. Swish in cold water. Repeat several times with fresh water to remove sand and grit. Pat dry with paper towels.

3. To remove stems from spinach leaves, fold each leaf in half, then pull stem toward top of leaf. Discard stems.

4. Set steamer basket in Dutch oven or large skillet; add water to within ¼ inch of bottom of basket.

5. Bring water to a boil over high heat. Layer about ¼ of spinach in basket; cover and steam 15 seconds. Quickly turn leaves over with tongs. Cover and steam 15 seconds or until leaves are bright green and barely wilted. (Some leaves will wilt but most should just turn bright green.)

6. Transfer spinach to colander with tongs. Repeat with remaining spinach. Lay spinach on serving platter or individual plates.

continued on page 174

Step 3. Removing stems from spinach leaves.

Step 4. Adding water to within ¼ inch of bottom of basket.

Step 5. Covering and steaming spinach until bright green.

Swimming Rama, continued

7. Bring 6 cups water to a boil in large saucepan over high heat. Meanwhile, trim fat from chicken breasts and discard. Cut chicken crosswise into ½-inch-wide strips with utility knife.

8. Add chicken to boiling water; remove saucepan from heat. Let stand, covered, 5 minutes or until chicken is no longer pink in center.

9. Prepare Peanut Sauce.

10. Drain chicken; stir into hot Peanut Sauce and pour mixture over spinach. Sprinkle with reserved chili pepper. Garnish, if desired.

Makes 4 servings

Peanut Sauce

1 to 2 limes
2 teaspoons vegetable oil
½ cup finely chopped onion
3 cloves garlic, minced (page 116)
½ cup chunky or creamy peanut butter
3 tablespoons packed brown sugar
2 tablespoons fish sauce
1 teaspoon paprika
¼ teaspoon ground red pepper
1 cup unsweetened coconut milk *or*
    1 cup milk plus 1 teaspoon
      coconut extract
1 tablespoon water
1 tablespoon cornstarch

1. To juice limes, cut in half on cutting board. With tip of knife, remove any visible seeds. Using citrus reamer or squeezing tightly with hand, squeeze juice into bowl. Remove any remaining seeds and measure 2 tablespoonfuls; set aside.

2. Heat oil in medium saucepan over medium-high heat until hot. Add onion and garlic; cook and stir 2 to 3 minutes or until tender.

3. Reduce heat to medium. Add peanut butter, brown sugar, fish sauce, paprika and ground red pepper; stir until smooth. Slowly stir in coconut milk until well blended. (At this point, sauce may be cooled, covered and refrigerated up to 2 days in advance.)

4. Stir sauce constantly over medium heat until bubbling gently. Reduce heat to medium-low. Combine water and cornstarch in small cup; stir into sauce. Cook and stir 1 to 2 minutes or until sauce is thickened. Stir in 2 tablespoons lime juice. *Makes about 2 cups*

Step 7. Cutting chicken crosswise into ½-inch-wide strips.

Peanut Sauce: Step 1. Squeezing juice from lime with reamer.

Cranberry Smothered Chicken

3 cloves garlic
½ cup all-purpose flour
   Salt and ground white pepper
      to taste
3 whole chicken breasts, skinned
      and split (pages 6-8)
¼ cup vegetable oil
½ cup chicken broth
2 medium green bell peppers
3 medium onions
2 tablespoons butter or
      margarine
10 large mushrooms, sliced
½ cup raspberry or balsamic
      vinegar
1 can (16 ounces) whole berry
      cranberry sauce
1 cup orange juice
1 tablespoon cornstarch
1 tablespoon Worcestershire
      sauce
   Water
   Hot cooked rice and steamed
      fresh asparagus
   Orange slices and parsley
      sprigs for garnish

1. To prepare garlic, trim ends of garlic cloves. Slightly crush garlic under flat side of chef's knife blade; peel away skins. Arrange garlic together in small pile; chop until minced.

2. Combine flour, salt and white pepper in large resealable plastic bag.

3. Add chicken to bag; shake to coat completely with flour mixture.

4. Heat oil in large skillet over medium-high heat until hot. Add garlic; cook until soft. Add chicken; cook until chicken is browned on both sides. Drain drippings from skillet. Add chicken broth; bring to a boil over high heat. Reduce heat to low. Cover; simmer 30 minutes.

5. To prepare bell peppers, with paring knife, make circular cuts around tops of peppers. Pull stems from peppers to remove stems, seeds and membranes. Rinse out peppers under running water to remove any excess seeds; drain well. Slice peppers lengthwise in half on cutting board; remove any excess membrane. Thinly slice each half lengthwise into thin strips.

continued on page 176

Step 1. Crushing garlic.

Step 3. Coating chicken with flour mixture.

Step 5. Slicing pepper into thin strips.

Cranberry Smothered Chicken,
continued

6. To prepare onions, peel skins from onions; cut onions in half through the roots. Place, cut sides down, on cutting board. To coarsely chop onions, hold knife horizontally. Make cuts parallel to board, almost to root ends. Next, make vertical, lengthwise cuts, then slice across cuts to root ends. (The closer the cuts are spaced, the finer the onions are chopped.)

7. Melt butter in another large skillet over medium-high heat. Cook and stir bell peppers, onions and mushrooms in hot butter until vegetables are softened. Stir in vinegar, cranberry sauce and orange juice. Reduce heat to medium. Cook and stir about 5 minutes until cranberry sauce melts and mixture is heated through.

8. Mix cornstarch and Worcestershire sauce with enough water to make a smooth paste; add to sauce and vegetables in skillet. Stir gently over low heat until thickened. Season with salt and white pepper.

9. Arrange chicken, rice and asparagus on individual serving plates. Pour sauce over chicken. Garnish, if desired.

Makes 6 servings

Step 6. Chopping onions.

Step 8. Adding cornstarch mixture to sauce and vegetables.

Cheesy Chicken Roll-Ups

1 package (8 ounces) cream cheese
3 tablespoons sliced almonds
6 lasagna noodles
¼ cup butter
1 medium onion, chopped (page 68)
4 ounces fresh mushrooms, cleaned (page 44) and sliced
3 boneless skinless chicken breast halves, cut into bite-sized pieces
¾ cup dry white wine
½ teaspoon dried tarragon leaves, crushed
½ teaspoon salt
½ teaspoon ground black pepper
½ cup heavy cream
½ cup dairy sour cream
1½ cups (6 ounces) shredded Swiss cheese, divided
1 cup (4 ounces) shredded Muenster cheese, divided
Chopped parsley (optional) (page 38)

1. Place cream cheese in opened wrapper on cutting board. Cut cream cheese lengthwise into ½-inch slices with utility knife. Then cut crosswise into ½-inch pieces; set aside. Let stand at room temperature until softened.

2. Preheat oven to 350°F. To toast almonds, spread on baking sheet. Bake 8 to 10 minutes or until golden brown, stirring frequently. Remove almonds from pan and cool; set aside. *Reduce oven temperature to 325°F.* Grease 13×9-inch baking pan; set aside.

3. Cook lasagna noodles according to package directions. Drain in colander. Rinse under warm running water; drain well. When cool enough to handle, cut noodles lengthwise into halves.

4. Melt butter in large skillet over medium-high heat. Cook and stir onion and mushrooms in hot butter until tender. Add chicken, wine, tarragon, salt and pepper; bring to a boil over high heat. Reduce heat to low. Simmer 10 minutes.

5. Curl each lasagna noodle half into a circle; arrange in prepared pan. With slotted spoon, fill center of lasagna rings with chicken mixture.

6. To remaining liquid in skillet, add cream cheese, heavy cream, sour cream, ¾ cup of Swiss cheese and ½ cup of Muenster cheese. Cook and stir over medium-low heat until cheese melts. *Do not boil.* Pour over lasagna rings. Sprinkle remaining cheeses and almonds on top.

7. Bake 35 minutes or until bubbly. Sprinkle with parsley. Garnish as desired.

Makes 6 servings

Step 1. Cutting cream cheese into ½-inch pieces.

Step 2. Toasting almonds.

Step 5. Filling noodle circle with chicken mixture.

Caramelized Lemongrass Chicken

1½ **pounds skinless chicken thighs**
   (4 to 6 thighs)
  2 **stalks lemongrass**
  2 **cloves garlic**
  3 **tablespoons fish sauce**
  ¼ **cup sugar**
  ¼ **teaspoon ground black pepper**
  1 **tablespoon vegetable oil**
  1 **tablespoon lemon juice**

1. Rinse chicken and pat dry with paper towels.

2. Remove outer leaves from lemongrass and discard. Trim off and discard upper stalks. Flatten lemongrass with meat mallet or flat side of cleaver.

3. Cut flattened lemongrass into 1-inch pieces with utility knife.

4. Cut garlic lengthwise into thin slices with paring knife. Stack several slices; cut into slivers.

5. Place chicken in large resealable plastic food storage bag; add fish sauce, sugar, garlic, pepper and lemongrass. Seal bag tightly; turn to coat. Marinate in refrigerator at least 1 hour or up to 4 hours, turning occasionally.

6. Heat oil in large skillet over medium heat until hot. Remove chicken from food storage bag; reserve marinade. Cook chicken 10 minutes or until browned, turning once.

7. Pour reserved marinade into skillet; bring to a boil. Boil 1 to 2 minutes. Reduce heat to low; cover and simmer 30 minutes or until chicken is tender and no longer pink in center, turning chicken occasionally.

8. Stir lemon juice into skillet. Turn chicken pieces over to coat. Garnish as desired.

Makes 4 servings

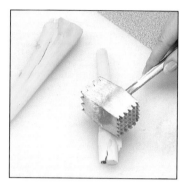

Step 2. Flattening lemongrass with meat mallet.

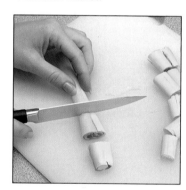

Step 3. Cutting lemongrass into 1-inch pieces.

Step 4. Cutting garlic into slivers.

Kung Pao Chicken

3½ teaspoons cornstarch, divided
5 teaspoons soy sauce, divided
5 teaspoons dry sherry, divided
¼ teaspoon salt
3 boneless skinless chicken breast halves, cut into bite-sized pieces
1 tablespoon red wine vinegar
2 tablespoons chicken broth or water
1½ teaspoons sugar
3 tablespoons vegetable oil, divided
⅓ cup salted peanuts
6 to 8 small dried hot chili peppers
1½ teaspoons minced fresh ginger (page 130)
2 green onions with tops, cut into 1½-inch pieces
Additional green onion and dried hot chili pepper for garnish

1. For marinade, combine 2 teaspoons cornstarch, 2 teaspoons soy sauce, 2 teaspoons sherry and salt in large bowl; mix well. Add chicken; stir to coat well. Let stand 30 minutes.

2. Combine remaining 1½ teaspoons cornstarch, 3 teaspoons soy sauce, 3 teaspoons sherry, vinegar, chicken broth and sugar in small bowl; mix well. Set aside.

3. Heat 1 tablespoon oil in wok or large skillet over medium heat. Add peanuts; cook and stir until lightly toasted. Remove peanuts from wok; set aside.

4. Heat remaining 2 tablespoons oil in wok over medium heat. Add chili peppers; stir-fry until peppers just begin to char, about 1 minute.

5. Increase heat to high. Add chicken mixture; stir-fry 2 minutes. Add ginger; stir-fry until chicken is no longer pink in center, about 1 minute.

6. Add peanuts and onions; stir-fry 1 minute.

7. Stir cornstarch mixture; add to wok. Cook and stir until sauce boils and thickens. Garnish, if desired.   *Makes 3 servings*

Step 3. Toasting peanuts.

Step 4. Stir-frying chili peppers.

Step 6. Stir-frying peanuts and onions with chicken mixture.

Walnut Chicken

1 tablespoon cornstarch
3 tablespoons soy sauce
1 tablespoon rice wine or dry
    sherry
2 tablespoons minced fresh
    ginger (page 130)
2 cloves garlic, minced (page 116)
½ teaspoon crushed red pepper
    flakes
1 pound boneless skinless chicken
    thighs, cut into 1-inch pieces
¾ pound fresh green beans
3 tablespoons vegetable oil
½ cup walnut halves or pieces
½ cup sliced water chestnuts
2 green onions with tops, cut into
    1-inch pieces
¼ cup water
    Hot cooked rice (optional)

1. To prepare marinade, combine cornstarch, soy sauce, rice wine, ginger, garlic and red pepper in large bowl; mix well. Add chicken and stir to combine. Let stand 30 minutes to marinate.

2. Meanwhile, snap off tip and stem ends from beans, pulling strings down to remove if present (technique on page 244). Cut beans diagonally into 2-inch lengths. Place 4 cups water in wok; bring to a boil over high heat. Add beans and cook 3 to 5 minutes until crisp-tender, stirring occasionally. Drain in colander. Rinse with cold water; set aside.

3. To toast walnuts, heat wok over high heat 1 minute or until dry and hot. Drizzle oil into wok and heat 30 seconds. Add walnuts; stir-fry with slotted spoon about 1 minute or until lightly browned. Remove walnuts to small bowl; set aside.

4. Add chicken and marinade to wok; cook and stir about 5 to 7 minutes until chicken is tender and no longer pink in center. Add water chestnuts, beans, green onions and water, stirring to loosen browned bits from bottom. Sprinkle with walnuts. Serve with rice. Garnish as desired. *Makes 4 servings*

Step 1. Adding chicken to marinade.

Step 2. Cooking beans in wok.

Step 3. Toasting walnuts.

Buffalo Chicken Drumsticks

1 clove garlic
8 large chicken drumsticks
   (about 2 pounds)
3 tablespoons hot pepper sauce
1 tablespoon vegetable oil
¼ cup mayonnaise
3 tablespoons sour cream
1½ tablespoons white wine vinegar
¼ teaspoon sugar
⅓ cup (1½ ounces) crumbled
   Roquefort or blue cheese
2 cups hickory chips
   Celery sticks

1. To mince garlic, trim off ends of garlic clove. Slightly crush clove under flat side of chef's knife blade; peel away skin. Chop garlic with chef's knife until garlic is in uniform fine pieces.

2. Place chicken in large resealable plastic food storage bag. Combine hot pepper sauce, oil and garlic in small bowl; pour over chicken. Seal bag tightly, turning to coat. Marinate in refrigerator at least 1 hour or, for hotter flavor, up to 24 hours, turning occasionally.

3. For blue cheese dressing, combine mayonnaise, sour cream, vinegar and sugar in another small bowl. Stir in cheese; cover and refrigerate until serving.

4. Prepare barbecue grill for direct cooking.

5. Meanwhile, cover hickory chips with cold water; soak 20 minutes.

6. Drain chicken; discard marinade. Drain hickory chips; sprinkle over coals.

7. Place chicken on grid. Grill chicken, on covered grill, over medium-hot coals 25 to 30 minutes or until chicken is no longer pink in center and juices run clear, turning 3 to 4 times. Serve with blue cheese dressing and celery sticks. *Makes 4 servings*

Step 2. Pouring marinade over chicken.

Step 5. Covering hickory chips with cold water to soak.

Step 6. Sprinkling hickory chips over coals.

Chicken Enchiladas

1 broiler-fryer chicken (about
    3 pounds), cut into 8 pieces
3 fresh poblano chilies, roasted,
    peeled, seeded, deveined,
    diced (page 10)
1 large tomato, peeled, seeded,
    chopped (page 52)
½ cup finely chopped white onion
1 clove garlic, minced
½ teaspoon ground cumin
¼ teaspoon salt
½ cup chicken broth
1½ cups heavy cream
12 corn tortillas (6-inch diameter)
2 cups (8 ounces) shredded
    Monterey Jack cheese
    Green onions and slivered red
    bell peppers for garnish
    Arroz Rojos (page 276)
    (optional)

1. Place chicken in single layer in 12-inch skillet. Sprinkle with chilies, tomato, white onion, garlic, cumin and salt; add broth. Bring to a boil over medium-high heat. Reduce heat. Cover; simmer 1 hour or until chicken is tender.

2. Remove chicken from skillet with tongs, shaking off vegetable pieces. Let stand until cool enough to handle.

3. Skim and discard fat from skillet. Bring remaining broth mixture to a boil over medium-high heat. Boil 4 to 8 minutes until mixture is reduced to 2 cups. Pour reduced broth mixture into 13×9-inch baking dish.

4. Remove and discard skin and bones from chicken. Using fingers, pull chicken into coarse shreds.

5. Preheat oven to 375°F. Heat cream in medium skillet over medium heat to just below boiling; remove from heat.

6. Dip 1 tortilla in cream with tongs a few seconds or until limp. Remove, draining off excess cream. Spread about 3 tablespoons chicken down center of tortilla.

7. Roll up; place on sauce in baking dish. Repeat with remaining tortillas, cream and chicken. Pour any remaining cream over enchiladas.

8. Sprinkle cheese over enchiladas. Bake 25 to 30 minutes until sauce is bubbly and cheese is melted. Garnish, if desired. Serve with Arroz Rojos. *Makes 4 to 6 servings*

Step 1. Adding broth to skillet.

Step 6. Dipping tortilla in cream.

Step 7. Forming enchilada.

Chicken Tortellini with Mushroom-Cream Sauce

2 cups plus 1 tablespoon
   all-purpose flour
½ teaspoon salt, divided
4 eggs
1 tablespoon milk
1 teaspoon olive oil
2 small boneless skinless chicken
   breast halves (about 4 ounces
   each), cooked and minced
2 ounces fresh spinach, cleaned,
   cooked (page 132), squeezed
   dry and minced
2 ounces prosciutto or cooked
   ham, minced
⅓ cup plus 2 tablespoons grated
   Parmesan cheese, divided
2 cups heavy or whipping cream
   (1 pint), divided
Dash ground black pepper
3 tablespoons butter or
   margarine
½ pound fresh mushrooms, thinly
   sliced
3 tablespoons chopped fresh
   parsley

1. Combine flour and ¼ teaspoon salt on pastry board, cutting board or countertop; make well in center. Whisk 3 eggs, milk and oil in small bowl until well blended; gradually pour into well in flour mixture while mixing with fingertips or fork to form ball of dough.

2. Place dough on lightly floured surface; flatten slightly. To knead dough, fold dough in half toward you and press dough away from you with heels of hands. Give dough a quarter turn and continue folding, pushing and turning. Continue kneading 5 minutes or until smooth and elastic, adding more flour to prevent sticking if necessary. Wrap dough in plastic wrap; set aside. Allow dough to stand at least 15 minutes.

3. Combine chicken, spinach, prosciutto and remaining egg in medium bowl; mix well. Add 2 tablespoons cheese, 1 tablespoon cream, remaining ¼ teaspoon salt and pepper to spinach mixture; mix well.

4. Unwrap dough and knead briefly (as described in step 2) on lightly floured surface; divide into 3 pieces. Using lightly floured rolling pin, roll out 1 dough piece to ¹⁄₁₆-inch thickness on lightly floured surface. (Keep remaining dough pieces wrapped in plastic wrap to prevent drying.)

Step 1. Mixing egg mixture into flour with fingertips to form dough.

Step 2. Kneading dough.

continued on page 192

Chicken Tortellini with Mushroom-Cream Sauce, continued

5. Cut out dough circles with 2-inch round cutter. Cover rolled dough with clean kitchen towel to prevent drying while working.

6. Place ½ teaspoon chicken filling in center of 1 dough circle; brush edge of circle lightly with water using tip of index finger.

7. Fold circle in half to enclose filling, making sure all air has been pushed out. Pinch outside edges together firmly to seal.

8. Brush end of half circle with water; wrap around finger, overlapping ends. Pinch to seal. Place tortellini on clean kitchen towel. Repeat with remaining dough circles, rerolling dough scraps as needed. Repeat with remaining 2 dough pieces and chicken filling.

9. Let tortellini dry on towel for 30 minutes before cooking.

10. Heat butter in 3-quart saucepan over medium heat until melted and bubbly; cook and stir mushrooms in hot butter 3 minutes. Stir in remaining cream. Bring to a boil over medium heat; immediately reduce heat to low. Simmer, uncovered, 3 minutes. Stir in remaining ⅓ cup cheese; cook and stir 1 minute. Remove from heat.

11. Cook tortellini, ⅓ at a time, in large pot of boiling salted water 2 to 3 minutes, just until al dente.

12. Drain well; add to mushroom-cream sauce. Bring mushroom-cream sauce and tortellini just to a boil over medium heat; reduce heat to low. Simmer 2 minutes. Sprinkle with parsley. Serve immediately.

Makes 6 to 8 servings

Step 6. Brushing edge of circle lightly with water.

Step 7. Pinching dough edges together firmly to seal.

Step 8. Pinching tortellini ends together to seal.

Mesquite-Grilled Turkey

2 cups mesquite chips, divided
1 fresh or thawed frozen turkey
   (10 to 12 pounds)
1 small sweet or Spanish onion,
   peeled and quartered
1 lemon, quartered
3 fresh tarragon sprigs
1 metal skewer (6 inches long)
2 tablespoons butter or
   margarine, softened
   Salt and ground black pepper
   (optional)
   Additional fresh tarragon
   sprigs
¼ cup butter or margarine,
   melted
2 tablespoons fresh lemon juice
2 tablespoons chopped fresh
   tarragon leaves *or* 2
   teaspoons dried tarragon
   leaves, crushed
2 cloves garlic, minced (page 116)

1. Prepare barbecue grill with rectangular metal or foil drip pan. Bank briquets on either side of drip pan for indirect cooking.

2. Meanwhile, cover mesquite chips with cold water; soak 20 minutes.

3. Remove giblets from turkey cavity; reserve for another use. Rinse turkey with cold running water; pat dry with paper towels. Place onion, lemon and 3 tarragon sprigs in cavity. Pull skin over neck; secure with metal skewer. Tuck wing tips under back; tie legs together with wet kitchen string.

4. Using fingers or paper towel, spread softened butter over turkey skin; sprinkle with salt and pepper to taste.

continued on page 194

Step 2. Covering mesquite chips with cold water to soak.

Step 3. Securing skin pulled over neck with metal skewer.

Step 4. Spreading softened butter over turkey skin.

Mesquite-Grilled Turkey, continued

5. Insert meat thermometer into center of thickest part of thigh, not touching bone.

6. Drain mesquite chips; sprinkle 1 cup over coals. Place turkey, breast-side up, on grid directly over drip pan. Grill turkey, on covered grill, over medium coals 11 to 14 minutes per pound, adding 4 to 9 briquets to both sides of the fire each hour to maintain medium coals and adding remaining 1 cup mesquite chips after 1 hour of grilling.

7. Meanwhile, soak additional fresh tarragon sprigs in water.

8. Combine melted butter, lemon juice, chopped tarragon and garlic in small bowl. Brush half of mixture over turkey during last 30 minutes of grilling. Place soaked tarragon sprigs directly on coals to additionally flavor the smoke. Continue to grill, covered, 20 minutes. Brush turkey with remaining mixture. Continue to grill, covered, about 10 minutes or until thermometer registers 180°F.

9. Transfer turkey to carving board; tent with foil. Let stand 15 minutes before carving. Discard onion, lemon and tarragon sprigs from cavity. Garnish as desired.

Makes 8 to 10 servings

Step 5. Inserting meat thermometer into thickest part of thigh, not touching bone.

Step 6. Adding additional briquets to fire to maintain medium coals.

Stir-Fried Turkey with Broccoli

1 lemon
1 teaspoon dried thyme leaves
½ teaspoon salt
¼ teaspoon ground white pepper
1 pound turkey cutlets
1 pound fresh broccoli
1 cup chicken broth
1 tablespoon cornstarch
3 tablespoons vegetable oil,
    divided
1 tablespoon butter
¼ pound fresh button mushrooms,
    cleaned (page 44) and sliced
1 medium red onion, peeled,
    sliced and separated into
    rings
1 can (14 ounces) pre-cut baby
    corn, drained and rinsed*
Hot cooked rice
Lemon slices for garnish

*Or, substitute 15-ounce can whole baby corn, cut into 1-inch lengths.

1. Finely grate peel of lemon into large bowl. Cut lemon crosswise in half; squeeze with citrus reamer or juicer to extract juice. Measure 2 tablespoons lemon juice. Add juice, thyme, salt and pepper to lemon peel; stir.

2. Cut turkey cutlets into 2½×1-inch strips with utility knife. Add turkey to lemon mixture; coat well. Marinate 30 minutes.

3. To prepare broccoli, trim leaves from stalks. Trim off tough ends with paring knife. Cut broccoli tops into 2-inch-long flowerets by removing each head to include a piece of stem. Peel stems with vegetable peeler, then diagonally trim stems; set aside.

4. Place 4 cups water in wok; bring to a boil over medium-high heat. Add flowerets; cook 2 minutes more or until crisp-tender. Drain in colander; rinse with cold water. Stir broth into cornstarch in cup until dissolved; set aside.

5. Heat wok over medium-high heat until dry and hot. Add 1 tablespoon oil and butter; heat until butter is melted. Add mushrooms; stir-fry 2 minutes. Add onion; stir-fry 2 minutes. Remove to large bowl.

6. Heat 1 tablespoon oil in wok. Stir-fry ½ of turkey strips in single layer 1½ minutes or until well browned. Transfer to mushroom mixture. Repeat with remaining 1 tablespoon oil and turkey.

7. Add baby corn to wok and heat 1 minute. Stir cornstarch mixture; add to wok and cook until bubbly. Add turkey, broccoli, mushrooms and onions; cook and stir until heated through. Serve over rice. Garnish, if desired. *Makes 4 to 6 servings*

Step 2. Cutting turkey cutlets into 2½×1-inch strips.

Step 3. Cutting broccoli tops into flowerets.

Crispy Duck

1 whole duck (about 5 pounds)
1 tablespoon dried rubbed sage
1 teaspoon salt
¼ teaspoon ground black pepper
3 cups vegetable oil
1 tablespoon butter or margarine
2 large Granny Smith or Rome
    Beauty apples, cored and cut
    into thin wedges
½ cup clover honey
   Fresh sage sprigs and
     crabapples for garnish

1. Remove neck and giblets from duck. Cut wing tips and second wing sections off duck; wrap and freeze for another use. Trim excess fat and excess skin from duck; discard. Rinse duck and cavity under cold running water; pat dry with paper towels.

2. Cut duck into quarters, removing backbone and breast bone. (Follow techniques for chicken on pages 157 and 158.) Place duck in 13×9-inch baking pan. Combine sage, salt and pepper in cup. Rub duck with sage mixture. Cover; refrigerate 1 hour.

3. To steam duck, place wire rack in wok. Add water to 1 inch below rack. (Water should not touch rack.) Cover wok; bring water to a boil over medium-high heat. Arrange quarters, skin sides up, on wire rack. Cover; steam 40 minutes or until fork-tender. (Add boiling water to wok to keep water at same level.)

4. Transfer cooked duck to plate. Carefully remove rack from wok; discard water. Rinse wok and dry. Heat oil in wok over medium-high heat until oil registers 375°F on deep-fry thermometer. Add ½ of duck, skin sides down, with long-handled tongs. Fry 5 to 10 minutes until crisp and golden brown, turning once. Drain duck on paper towels. Repeat with remaining duck, reheating oil.

5. Pour off oil. Melt butter in wok over medium heat. Add apples; cook and stir with slotted spoon 5 minutes or until wilted. Stir in honey and bring to a boil. Transfer apples with slotted spoon to warm serving platter. Arrange duck on apples. Drizzle honey mixture over duck. Garnish, if desired.

Makes 4 servings

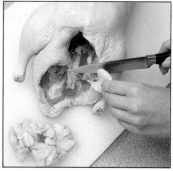
Step 1. Removing excess skin from duck.

Step 2. Rubbing duck with sage mixture.

Step 3. Arranging duck on rack in wok.

Braised Cornish Hens

2 Cornish hens, thawed if frozen
  (1½ to 1¾ pounds each)
¼ cup soy sauce
2 tablespoons dry sherry
1 teaspoon sugar
⅔ cup plus 1 tablespoon
  cornstarch, divided
¼ cup vegetable oil
1 piece fresh ginger (about 1 inch
  square), peeled and cut into 4
  slices
2 cloves garlic, minced (page 116)
1 cup chicken broth
1 large yellow onion, coarsely
  chopped (page 68)
12 ounces fresh snow peas
  (Chinese pea pods),
  destemmed (page 270)
  Yellow squash, zucchini, carrot
  and red bell pepper crescents
  for garnish

1. Remove neck and giblets from hens; wrap and freeze for another use, such as soup or stock. Rinse hens and cavities under cold running water; pat dry with paper towels. Cut each hen into quarters, removing backbone and breast bone. (Follow techniques for chicken on pages 157 and 158.)

2. To prepare marinade, combine soy sauce, sherry and sugar in large bowl; mix well. Add hen quarters; stir to coat well. Cover and refrigerate 1 hour to marinate, stirring occasionally.

3. Drain hens and reserve marinade. Place ⅔ cup cornstarch in shallow dish or pie plate. Coat hens with cornstarch. Combine remaining 1 tablespoon cornstarch with marinade; mix well and set aside.

4. Heat wok over medium-high heat about 1 minute or until hot. Drizzle oil into wok and heat 30 seconds. Add ginger and garlic; cook and stir about 1 minute or until oil is fragrant. Remove and discard ginger and garlic with slotted spoon. Add hens to oil and fry about 10 to 15 minutes until well browned on all sides, turning occasionally.

5. Add broth and onion to wok; bring to a boil. Cover and reduce heat to low; simmer hens about 20 minutes or until fork-tender, turning occasionally. Move hens up side of wok and add snow peas to bottom of wok. Cover and cook 3 to 5 minutes until peas are crisp-tender. Stir cornstarch mixture and add to wok. Cook and stir until sauce thickens and boils. Transfer to serving platter. Garnish, if desired. Serve immediately.

Makes 2 to 4 servings

Step 3. Coating hens with cornstarch.

Step 4. Browning hens on all sides.

Seafood

Tuna with Peppercorns on a Bed of Greens

4 tuna steaks (about 1½ pounds)
  Salt
2 teaspoons coarsely ground
  black pepper
1 tablespoon butter or margarine
1 large onion, thinly sliced
¼ cup dry white wine
½ pound fresh kale or spinach
1 tablespoon olive oil
½ teaspoon sugar
¼ teaspoon ground black pepper
12 thin strips carrot (page 41)
  Lemon slices and purple kale
  for garnish

1. Preheat oven to 325°F.

2. Rinse tuna and pat dry with paper towels. Lightly sprinkle fish with salt, then press coarsely ground pepper into both sides of steaks; set aside.

3. Melt butter in large skillet over medium heat. Add onion; cook and stir 5 minutes or until crisp-tender. Add wine and remove from heat. Spread onion mixture on bottom of 13×9-inch glass baking dish. Place fish on top of onion mixture.

4. Bake 15 minutes. Spoon liquid over fish and bake 15 minutes more or until fish flakes easily when tested with fork.

5. Meanwhile, rinse kale well in large bowl of cold water. Place in colander; drain.

6. Discard any discolored leaves from kale. To trim away tough stems, make "V-shaped" cut at stem end; discard tough stems. Stack leaves and cut into 1-inch strips.

7. Heat oil in medium skillet over medium-high heat. Add kale, sugar and black pepper. Cook and stir 2 to 3 minutes or until tender.

8. Place kale on plates. Top with fish and onion mixture. Top fish with carrot strips. Garnish, if desired. *Makes 4 servings*

Step 2. Pressing coarsely ground pepper into steaks.

Step 3. Placing fish on top of onion mixture.

Step 6. Making "V-shaped" cut at stem end.

Blackened Snapper with Red Onion Salsa

Cajun Seasoning Mix
2 tablespoons salt
1 tablespoon paprika
1½ teaspoons garlic powder
1 teaspoon onion powder
1 teaspoon ground red pepper
½ teaspoon ground white pepper
½ teaspoon ground black pepper
½ teaspoon dried thyme leaves, crushed
½ teaspoon dried oregano leaves, crushed

Red Onion Salsa
1 tablespoon vegetable oil
1 large red onion, chopped
1 clove garlic, minced (page 116)
½ cup Fish Stock (page 74) or chicken broth
¼ cup dry red wine or red wine vinegar
¼ teaspoon dried thyme leaves, crushed
Salt and ground black pepper to taste

4 red snapper fillets (about 6 ounces each)
2 tablespoons butter

1. To prepare Cajun Seasoning Mix, combine salt, paprika, garlic powder, onion powder, red pepper, white pepper, ½ teaspoon black pepper, ½ teaspoon thyme and oregano in small bowl; set aside.

2. To prepare Red Onion Salsa, heat oil in small saucepan over medium-high heat until hot. Add onion; cover and cook 5 minutes. Add garlic; cook 1 minute. Add Fish Stock, wine, ¼ teaspoon thyme and salt and black pepper. Cover and cook about 10 minutes. Uncover and cook until liquid reduces to ¼ cup. Set aside.

3. Rinse red snapper and pat dry with paper towels. Sprinkle with Cajun Seasoning Mix.

4. Heat large, heavy skillet over high heat until very hot. Add butter and swirl skillet to coat bottom. When butter no longer bubbles, place fish in pan.

5. Cook fish 6 to 8 minutes or until surface is very brown and fish flakes easily when tested with fork, turning halfway through cooking. Serve with Red Onion Salsa.

Makes 4 servings

Step 3. Sprinkling fish with Cajun Seasoning Mix.

Step 4. Swirling skillet to coat bottom.

Step 5. Testing with fork.

Fillets with Mole Verde

¼ cup vegetable oil, divided
¼ cup chopped white onion
1 or 2 fresh jalapeño chilies, seeded, finely chopped*
1 cup fresh tomatillos, husked and chopped, *or* 1 can (8 ounces) tomatillos, drained and chopped
2 cloves garlic, minced
¼ teaspoon ground cumin
⅓ cup plus 1 tablespoon water, divided
⅓ cup coarsely chopped cilantro
½ teaspoon salt, divided
⅓ cup all-purpose flour
⅛ teaspoon ground black pepper
1 egg
2 tablespoons butter or margarine
1½ to 2 pounds small red snapper fillets or skinless sole fillets
Cilantro sprigs and tomatillos for garnish
Carrot sticks (optional)

*Chilies can sting and irritate the skin; wear rubber gloves when handling chilies and do not touch eyes. Wash hands after handling chilies.

1. Heat 2 tablespoons oil in small skillet over medium heat until hot. Add onion and chilies. Cook and stir 4 minutes or until softened. Add tomatillos, garlic and cumin. Cook and stir 1 minute.

2. Add ⅓ cup water, chopped cilantro and ¼ teaspoon salt. Bring to a boil over high heat. Reduce heat to low. Cover and simmer 20 minutes. Pour into blender; blend until smooth. Return sauce to skillet; remove from heat and set aside.

3. Combine flour, remaining ¼ teaspoon salt and pepper on plate. Beat egg with remaining 1 tablespoon water in shallow bowl.

4. Heat butter and remaining 2 tablespoons oil in large skillet over medium-high heat until foamy. Working with as many fillets as will fit in skillet in single layer, lightly coat each fillet on both sides with flour mixture; shake off excess. Dip into egg mixture; let excess drain off. Cook 4 to 8 minutes or until light brown on outside and opaque in center, turning once. Remove to serving plate; keep warm. Repeat with remaining fillets.

5. Quickly heat sauce over medium heat until hot, stirring frequently. Pour over and around fish. Garnish, if desired. Serve with carrot sticks. *Makes 4 to 6 servings*

Step 1. Cooking tomatillos.

Step 2. Returning puréed sauce to skillet.

Step 4. Dipping fillets into egg mixture.

Soleful Roulettes

1 package (6¼ ounces) long-grain
   and wild rice mix
1 package (3 ounces) cream
   cheese, softened
2 tablespoons milk
32 medium fresh spinach leaves
4 sole fillets (about 1 pound)
   Salt and ground black pepper
½ cup water
¼ cup dry white wine

1. Cook rice mix according to package directions. Place 2 cups cooked rice in large bowl. Cover and refrigerate remaining rice and save for another use. Combine cream cheese and milk in medium bowl. Stir into rice; set aside.

2. Swish spinach leaves in cold water. Repeat several times with fresh cold water to remove sand and grit.

3. Place spinach in heatproof bowl. Pour very hot water (not boiling) over spinach to wilt leaves slightly.

4. Rinse sole and pat dry with paper towels. Place fish on work surface. Sprinkle both sides of each fillet with salt and pepper. Cover each fillet with spinach leaves.

5. Divide rice mixture evenly and spread over top of each spinach-lined fillet.

6. To roll fillets, begin with thin end of fillet, roll up and secure with wooden toothpicks.

7. Combine water and wine in large, heavy saucepan.

8. Stand fillets upright on rolled edges in saucepan; cover.

9. Simmer over low heat. *(Do not boil. This will cause fish to break apart.)* Simmer 10 minutes or until fish flakes easily when tested with fork.   *Makes 4 servings*

Step 5. Spreading with rice mixture.

Step 6. Rolling up fillets.

Step 8. Standing fillets upright.

Poached Salmon with Tarragon Cream Sauce

2 to 3 shallots
2 tablespoons butter or margarine
1 clove garlic, minced
1 cup dry white wine, divided
½ cup clam juice
½ cup heavy cream
½ teaspoon dried tarragon leaves, crushed
1 tablespoon chopped fresh parsley (page 38)
2 salmon steaks, 1 inch thick (about 8 ounces each)
Fish Stock (page 74), clam juice or water
Fresh tarragon for garnish

1. Remove papery outer skins from shallots. Cut off root ends. Finely chop enough shallots with chef's knife to measure 3 tablespoons.

2. To make Tarragon Cream Sauce, melt butter in medium saucepan over medium heat. Add shallot and garlic; reduce heat to low and cook 5 minutes or until shallot is tender.

3. Add ½ cup wine and clam juice to shallot mixture. Bring to a simmer. Simmer 10 minutes or until sauce is reduced to ½ cup. Add heavy cream and simmer 5 minutes or until sauce is reduced by half. Sauce should heavily coat the back of metal spoon. Stir in ½ teaspoon tarragon and parsley; keep warm over very low heat.

4. Rinse salmon and pat dry with paper towels. To poach fish, place in saucepan just large enough to hold it. Add remaining ½ cup wine and enough Fish Stock to barely cover fish. Bring liquid to a simmer over medium heat. *(Do not boil. This will cause fish to break apart.)* Adjust heat, if necessary, to keep liquid at a simmer. Simmer 10 minutes or until center is no longer red and fish flakes easily when tested with fork.

5. Remove fish with slotted spatula; transfer to serving plates.

6. Top fish with Tarragon Cream Sauce. Garnish, if desired. *Makes 2 servings*

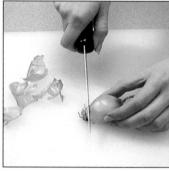
Step 1. Removing papery outer skin from shallot.

Step 3. Coating back of spoon.

Step 4. Poaching fish.

Seared Salmon Teriyaki

2 medium zucchini (12 ounces)
2 medium yellow squash
   (12 ounces)
¼ cup soy sauce
¼ cup sake
2 tablespoons sugar
1½ pounds salmon fillet with skin
   (1¼ inches thick)
2 tablespoons vegetable oil,
   divided
1 tablespoon butter
¼ teaspoon each salt and ground
   black pepper
1 tablespoon sesame seeds,
   toasted (page 120)
   Lemon slices (optional)

1. Cut tip and stem ends from zucchini and yellow squash with paring knife; discard. Cut vegetables crosswise into halves, then cut each half lengthwise into ⅛- to ¼-inch slices. Stack a few slices; cut lengthwise into ⅛- to ¼-inch strips. Repeat with remaining slices; set aside.

2. Combine soy sauce, sake and sugar in cup; stir until sugar dissolves. Set aside.

3. Rinse and dry salmon. Run fingers over cut surface of salmon; remove any bones that remain. Cut crosswise into 4 pieces.

4. Heat wok over high heat until hot. Add 1 tablespoon oil; heat 30 seconds. Add zucchini, yellow squash and butter. Cook and stir 4 to 5 minutes until lightly browned and tender. Sprinkle squash mixture with salt and pepper. Transfer to serving platter. Sprinkle with sesame seeds; cover and keep warm.

5. Add remaining 1 tablespoon oil to wok and heat until sizzling hot. Carefully place fish in wok, skin sides up. Cook about 4 minutes or until browned. Reduce heat to medium-high. Turn fish over using 2 pancake turners or flat spatulas. Cook, skin sides down, 8 to 10 minutes or until fish flakes easily when tested with fork, loosening fish on bottom occasionally to prevent sticking. Place fish over squash mixture on platter. Cover and keep warm.

6. Pour off fat from wok. Stir soy mixture and pour into wok. Boil until mixture is reduced by half and slightly thickened. Spoon sauce over fish. Serve with lemon, if desired.

Makes 4 servings

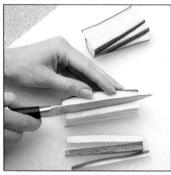
Step 1. Cutting zucchini slices into ¼-inch-thick strips.

Step 3. Cutting salmon into 4 pieces.

Step 5. Turning fish to cook both sides.

Trout with Apples and Toasted Hazelnuts

⅓ cup whole hazelnuts or walnuts
5 tablespoons butter or
   margarine, divided
1 large Red Delicious apple,
   cored and cut into 16 wedges
2 butterflied rainbow trout*
   (about 8 ounces each)
   Salt and ground black pepper
3 tablespoons all-purpose flour
1 tablespoon lemon juice
1 tablespoon snipped fresh chives
   Lemon slices and fresh chives
   for garnish

* A butterflied trout has head, gills and entrails removed and is split horizontally so that both sides of the fish are connected by an uncut strip of skin on the belly. Request this preparation from the seafood department at the supermarket or at a fish market.

1. Preheat oven to 350°F. To toast hazelnuts, spread in single layer on baking sheet. Bake 8 to 10 minutes or until skins split.

2. Wrap hazelnuts in kitchen towel; set aside for 5 minutes to cool slightly. Rub hazelnuts in towel to remove as much of the papery skins as possible.

3. Place hazelnuts in food processor. Process using on/off pulsing action until hazelnuts are coarsely chopped; set aside.

4. Melt 3 tablespoons butter in medium skillet over medium-high heat. Add apple; cook 4 to 5 minutes or until crisp-tender. Remove apple from skillet with slotted spoon; set aside.

5. Rinse trout and pat dry with paper towels. Open trout and press flat to resemble butterfly. Sprinkle fish with salt and pepper, then coat with flour.

6. Place fish in skillet. Cook 4 minutes or until golden and fish flakes easily when tested with fork, turning halfway through cooking time. Return apple to skillet. Reduce heat to low and keep warm.

7. Melt remaining 2 tablespoons butter in small saucepan over low heat. Stir in lemon juice, 1 tablespoon chives and hazelnuts.

8. Drizzle fish and apple with hazelnut mixture. Garnish, if desired.

Makes 2 servings

Step 1. Toasting hazelnuts until skins split.

Step 2. Rubbing hazelnuts in towel to remove papery skins.

Step 3. Processing until coarsely chopped.

Orange Roughy in Parchment Hearts

8 ounces fresh asparagus
   Parchment paper or foil
4 orange roughy fillets (about
   1½ pounds)
   Butter
1 yellow bell pepper, cut into
   16 thin strips
1 red bell pepper, cut into
   16 thin strips
1 medium carrot, cut into thin
   strips (page 41)
¼ cup dry white wine
3 tablespoons Dijon mustard
2 tablespoons lemon juice
1 teaspoon dried marjoram
   leaves, crushed
¼ teaspoon ground black pepper

1. Peel tough stem ends of asparagus with vegetable peeler. To steam asparagus, bring 2 inches of water in large saucepan to a boil over high heat. Place asparagus in metal steamer basket and set in saucepan. (Water should not touch bottom of basket.) Cover pan; steam 2 to 3 minutes or until asparagus turns bright green. Remove steamer basket from heat and rinse asparagus with cold water until cool. Cut asparagus diagonally into 2-inch pieces.

2. Preheat oven to 375°F. Cut parchment paper into 4 (12-inch) squares. Fold each square in half diagonally and cut into half-heart shape.

3. Rinse orange roughy and pat dry with paper towels.

4. Lightly butter inside of each heart. Place 1 fillet on 1 side of each heart.

5. Divide asparagus over fish. Place 4 strips each yellow and red bell pepper over fish, then divide carrot strips over fish.

6. Combine wine, mustard, lemon juice, marjoram and black pepper in small bowl. Divide wine mixture over fish.

7. Fold parchment hearts in half. Beginning at top of heart, fold edges together, 2 inches at a time. At tip of heart, fold paper over.

8. Place parchment hearts on large baking sheet. Bake 20 to 25 minutes or until fish flakes easily when tested with fork. To serve, place hearts on plates and cut an "X" through top layer of parchment, folding points back to display contents. *Makes 4 servings*

Step 1. Steaming asparagus.

Step 4. Placing fish on side of parchment heart.

Step 7. Folding edges of heart together.

Southern Fried Catfish with Hush Puppies

Hush Puppy Batter (recipe follows)
4 catfish fillets (about 1½ pounds)
½ cup yellow cornmeal
3 tablespoons all-purpose flour
1½ teaspoons salt
¼ teaspoon ground red pepper
Vegetable oil for frying
Fresh parsley sprigs for garnish

1. Prepare Hush Puppy Batter; set aside.

2. Rinse catfish and pat dry with paper towels.

3. Combine cornmeal, flour, salt and red pepper in shallow dish. Dip fish in cornmeal mixture.

4. Heat 1 inch of oil in heavy, deep skillet over medium heat until a fresh bread cube placed in oil browns in 45 seconds (about 365°F). Discard bread cube.

5. Fry fish, a few pieces at a time, 4 to 5 minutes or until golden brown and fish flakes easily when tested with fork. Adjust heat to maintain temperature. (Allow temperature of oil to return to 365°F between each batch.) Drain fish on paper towels.

6. Drop batter by tablespoonfuls into hot oil. Fry a few Hush Puppies at a time, 2 minutes or until golden brown. Serve with catfish. Garnish, if desired.   *Makes 4 servings*

Hush Puppy Batter

1½ cups yellow cornmeal
½ cup all-purpose flour
2 teaspoons baking powder
½ teaspoon salt
1 egg
1 cup milk
1 small onion, minced

Combine cornmeal, flour, baking powder and salt in medium bowl. Add egg, milk and onion. Stir until well combined. Allow batter to stand 5 to 10 minutes before frying.
Makes about 24 Hush Puppies

Step 3. Dipping fish in cornmeal mixture.

Step 4. Browning bread cube.

Step 5. Frying fish.

Grilled Swordfish
à l'Orange

1 orange
¾ cup orange juice
1 tablespoon lemon juice
1 tablespoon sesame oil
1 tablespoon soy sauce
4 swordfish, halibut or shark
    steaks (about 1½ pounds),
    rinsed and patted dry
1 teaspoon cornstarch
   Salt and ground black pepper
    to taste

1. To grate orange peel, rinse orange under cold running water, then dry. Grate orange peel using finest side of box-shaped grater, being careful to remove only the outermost layer of skin and not any of the bitter, white pith. Grate enough peel to measure 1 teaspoon. Set aside.

2. To section orange, cut off slice from top and bottom with utility knife; set orange flat on cutting board. Starting at top and working toward bottom, slice remaining peel and pith off orange in wide strips, following curve of orange. Repeat until all peel and pith are removed.

3. Make "V-shaped" slices into center of orange just inside membrane to remove orange segments. Set aside. Discard orange membrane.

4. Combine orange juice, lemon juice, oil and soy sauce in small bowl. Pour half the orange juice mixture into shallow glass dish. Add ½ teaspoon grated orange peel to orange juice mixture. Coat fish in mixture; cover and marinate in refrigerator for at least 1 hour.

5. Pour remaining orange juice mixture into small saucepan. Stir in cornstarch and remaining ½ teaspoon orange peel. Heat over medium-high heat, stirring constantly, 3 to 5 minutes or until sauce thickens; set aside.

6. Remove fish from marinade; discard remaining marinade. Lightly sprinkle fish with salt and pepper to taste. Grill 3 to 4 minutes per side or until fish is opaque and flakes easily when tested with fork. Top with orange sections and orange sauce. Serve immediately. *Makes 4 servings*

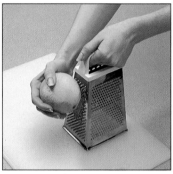
Step 1. Grating orange peel.

Step 2. Slicing peel and pith off orange.

Step 3. Making "V-shaped" slices.

Shrimp in Chili Sauce

1 pound large shrimp (about 23 shrimp)
1 tablespoon rice wine or dry sherry
4 cloves garlic, chopped (page 116)
1 teaspoon paprika
¼ teaspoon ground red pepper
1 or 2 fresh green jalapeno chilies*
2 tablespoons water
2 tablespoons ketchup
1 teaspoon cornstarch
½ teaspoon sugar
¼ teaspoon salt
2 tablespoons vegetable oil
Edible flowers, such as violets, and zucchini "leaves" for garnish

*Chilies can sting and irritate the skin; wear rubber gloves when handling chilies and do not touch eyes. Wash hands after handling chilies.

1. To peel shrimp, remove the legs by gently pulling them off the shell. Loosen shell from body with fingers then slide off, leaving last tail segment attached.

2. To devein shrimp, cut shallow slit along back of shrimp with paring knife. Lift out and discard vein. (You may find this easier to do under cold running water.) Rinse shrimp and pat dry with paper towels.

3. Combine shrimp, rice wine, garlic, paprika and red pepper in medium bowl; mix well. Cover and refrigerate 1 to 4 hours to marinate.

4. Rinse chilies; pat dry with paper towel. Cut chilies lengthwise into halves with utility knife. Scrape out and discard stems, seeds and veins. Cut halves crosswise into ⅛-inch slices.

5. Combine water, ketchup, cornstarch, sugar and salt in small bowl; mix well. Set aside.

6. Heat wok over high heat about 1 minute or until hot. Drizzle oil into wok and heat 30 seconds. Add shrimp mixture and chilies; stir-fry about 3 minutes or until shrimp turn pink and opaque.

7. Stir cornstarch mixture; add to wok. Cook and stir about 2 minutes or until sauce coats shrimp and thickens. Transfer shrimp to serving dish or individual serving plates. Garnish, if desired. Serve immediately.

Makes 4 servings

Step 1. Removing shells from shrimp.

Step 2. Deveining shrimp.

Step 4. Scraping seeds from chilies.

Shrimp Noodle Supreme

1 package (3 ounces) cream
    cheese
1½ pounds medium shrimp
1 package (8 ounces) spinach
    noodles
½ cup butter
    Salt and ground black pepper
    to taste
1 can (10¾ ounces) condensed
    cream of mushroom soup
1 cup dairy sour cream
½ cup half-and-half
½ cup mayonnaise
1 tablespoon chopped chives
1 tablespoon chopped parsley
    (page 38)
½ teaspoon Dijon-style mustard
¾ cup (3 ounces) shredded sharp
    Cheddar cheese
    Lemon slices and paprika for
    garnish

1. Place cream cheese on opened wrapper on cutting board. Cut cream cheese lengthwise into ½-inch slices with utility knife. Then cut crosswise into ½-inch pieces; set aside. Let stand at room temperature until softened.

2. To peel shrimp, remove the legs by gently pulling them off the shell. Loosen shell with fingers, then slide shell off.

3. To devein shrimp, cut a shallow slit along back of shrimp with paring knife. Lift out and discard vein. (You may find this easier to do under cold running water.) If desired, this step may be omitted.

4. Cook pasta according to package directions. Drain in colander.

5. Preheat oven to 325°F. Grease 13×9-inch glass dish.

6. Combine cream cheese and noodles in medium bowl. Spread noodle mixture in bottom of prepared dish.

7. Heat butter in large skillet over medium-high heat. Cook shrimp in hot butter about 5 minutes or until shrimp turn pink and opaque. Season to taste with salt and pepper. Place shrimp on noodles.

8. Combine soup, sour cream, half-and-half, mayonnaise, chives, parsley and mustard in another medium bowl. Spread over shrimp. Sprinkle Cheddar cheese over top of casserole.

9. Bake 25 minutes or until hot and cheese melts. Garnish, if desired.

Makes 6 servings

Step 1. Cutting cream cheese into ½-inch pieces.

Step 2. Removing shell from shrimp.

Step 3. Deveining shrimp.

Crab-Stuffed Shrimp

Sauce

- 2 tablespoons vegetable oil
- 1 small yellow onion, finely chopped
- 1 teaspoon curry powder
- 1½ tablespoons dry sherry
- 1 tablespoon satay sauce
- 2 teaspoons soy sauce
- 1 teaspoon sugar
- ¼ cup cream or milk

Shrimp

- 2 egg whites, lightly beaten
- 4 teaspoons cornstarch
- 1 tablespoon dry sherry
- 1 tablespoon soy sauce
- 2 cans (6½ ounces each) crabmeat, drained and flaked
- 8 green onions with tops, finely chopped
- 2 ribs celery, finely chopped
- 1½ pounds large shrimp, peeled and deveined (page 30), leaving tails intact
- ½ cup all-purpose flour
- 3 eggs
- 3 tablespoons milk
- 2 to 3 cups soft bread crumbs (from 8 to 10 bread slices)
- Vegetable oil for frying

1. Heat 2 tablespoons oil in small saucepan over medium heat. Add yellow onion; cook and stir until tender, about 3 minutes. Add curry powder; cook and stir 1 minute. Add 1½ tablespoons sherry, satay sauce, 2 teaspoons soy sauce and sugar; cook and stir 2 minutes. Stir in cream; bring to a boil. Simmer 2 minutes, stirring occasionally. Keep warm.

2. Blend egg whites, cornstarch, 1 tablespoon sherry and 1 tablespoon soy sauce in medium bowl. Add crabmeat, green onions and celery; mix well.

3. Cut deep slit into, but not through, back of each shrimp.

4. Flatten shrimp slightly by pounding gently with mallet or rolling pin. Stuff crab mixture into slit of each shrimp.

5. Coat each shrimp lightly with flour.

6. Beat eggs and milk with fork in shallow bowl until blended. Place each shrimp, stuffed-side up, in egg mixture; spoon egg mixture over shrimp to coat completely.

7. Coat each shrimp with bread crumbs, pressing crumbs lightly onto shrimp. Place shrimp in single layer on baking sheets or plates. Refrigerate 30 minutes.

8. Heat oil in wok or large skillet over high heat to 375°F. Add four or five shrimp at a time; cook until golden brown, about 3 minutes. Drain on paper towels. Serve with sauce.

Makes 4 servings

Step 3. Slitting back of shrimp.

Step 4. Stuffing shrimp.

Braised Shrimp with Vegetables

1 teaspoon cornstarch
½ cup chicken broth
1 teaspoon oyster sauce
½ teaspoon minced fresh ginger
   (page 130)
¼ teaspoon sugar
⅛ teaspoon ground black pepper
8 ounces fresh broccoli
1 pound large shrimp
1 tablespoon vegetable oil
2 cans (4 ounces each) whole
   button mushrooms, drained
1 can (8 ounces) sliced bamboo
   shoots, drained

1. Combine cornstarch, broth, oyster sauce, ginger, sugar and pepper in small bowl; mix well. Set aside.

2. Remove woody stems from broccoli; discard.

3. Coarsely chop head of broccoli and remaining stems; set aside.

4. Peel shells from shrimp. To devein shrimp, cut a shallow slit along back of shrimp with paring knife. Lift out and discard vein. (You may find this easier to do under cold running water.)

5. Heat oil in wok or large skillet over high heat until hot. Add shrimp; stir-fry until shrimp turn pink, about 3 minutes.

6. Add broccoli to wok; stir-fry 1 minute. Add mushrooms and bamboo shoots; stir-fry 1 minute.

7. Stir cornstarch mixture; add to wok. Cook and stir until sauce boils and thickens, about 2 minutes.

Makes 4 servings

Step 2. Removing broccoli stems.

Step 4. Deveining shrimp.

Step 5. Stir-frying shrimp.

Seafood Paella

1 pound small squid
½ pound medium shrimp
16 mussels
1 cup plus 2 teaspoons salt,
 divided
½ cup olive oil
2 green bell peppers, chopped
 (page 75)
1 medium onion, chopped
 (page 68)
8 cloves garlic, minced
2 cups uncooked short-grain or
 long-grain rice
1 teaspoon ground turmeric
1 teaspoon paprika
1 bay leaf
6 to 7 cups Fish Stock, heated,
 divided (page 74)
½ cup dry white wine
1 can (16 ounces) tomatoes,
 drained and chopped
1 pound cod, monkfish or other
 firm whitefish, rinsed, patted
 dry and cut into 1-inch pieces
½ pound scallops
1 cup fresh or frozen peas
¼ cup chopped fresh parsley
 (page 38)
1 jar (2 ounces) sliced pimientos,
 drained

1. To clean each squid, hold body of squid firmly in one hand. Grasp head firmly with other hand; pull head, twisting gently from side to side. (Head and contents of body should pull away in 1 piece.) Set aside tubular body sac. Cut tentacles off head; set aside. Discard head and contents of body.

2. Grasp tip of pointed, thin, clear cartilage protruding from body sac; pull out and discard. Rinse squid under cold running water. Peel off and discard spotted outer membrane covering body sac and fins. Pull off side fins; set aside. Rinse inside of squid thoroughly under cold running water. Repeat with remaining squid.

3. Cut body sac crosswise into ¼-inch rings; finely chop tentacles and fins. (Rings, fins and tentacles are all edible parts.) Pat pieces dry with paper towels.

4. To peel shrimp, remove the legs by gently pulling them off the shell. Loosen shell with fingers, then slide off.

5. To devein shrimp, cut shallow slit along back of shrimp with paring knife. Lift out vein. (You may find this easier to do under cold running water.) If desired, this step may be omitted.

continued on page 232

Step 1. Removing head from squid.

Step 2. Peeling outer membrane from squid.

Step 3. Cutting squid into rings.

Seafood Paella, continued

6. Discard any mussels that remain open when tapped with fingers. To clean mussels, scrub with stiff brush under cold running water. To debeard, pull threads from shells with fingers. Soak mussels in mixture of ⅓ cup salt to 1 gallon water 20 minutes. Drain water; repeat 2 more times.

7. Preheat oven to 375°F.

8. Heat oil in 14- to 15-inch paella pan or heavy 14-inch skillet over medium-high heat. Add peppers, onion and garlic. Cook and stir 5 to 8 minutes or until vegetables are tender. Stir in rice, remaining 2 teaspoons salt, turmeric, paprika and bay leaf. Reduce heat to medium. Add 5 cups Fish Stock, wine and tomatoes. Simmer 15 to 20 minutes, adding additional stock as needed until rice is almost tender, stirring frequently.

9. Stir in squid, shrimp, cod, scallops, peas and parsley.

10. Garnish top of paella with pimientos and mussels. Place paella in oven and bake 15 minutes or until seafood is opaque and liquid is absorbed. Remove bay leaf; discard. Serve immediately or cool to lukewarm.*   *Makes 8 servings*

*Lukewarm is the preferred Spanish serving temperature for paella.

Step 6. Removing beard from mussel.

Step 9. Stirring in ingredients.

Spaghetti with Seafood Marinara Sauce

8 fresh oysters
1 pound fresh medium shrimp
½ pound fresh sea scallops
6 flat anchovy fillets, canned
    in oil
2 tablespoons olive oil
⅓ cup chopped onion
1 clove garlic, minced
½ cup dry white wine
10 ounces uncooked dry spaghetti
5 large ripe fresh tomatoes,
    seeded and chopped
1 tablespoon tomato paste
¾ teaspoon dried basil, crumbled
¾ teaspoon salt
½ teaspoon dried oregano,
    crumbled
⅛ teaspoon ground black pepper
3 tablespoons chopped fresh
    parsley
    Fresh basil leaves for garnish

1. Scrub oysters thoroughly with stiff brush under cold running water. Place on tray and refrigerate 1 hour to help oysters relax.

2. To shuck oysters, take pointed oyster knife in one hand and thick towel or glove in the other. With towel, grip shell in palm of hand. Keeping oyster level with knife, insert tip of knife between the shell next to hinge; twist to pry shell until you hear a snap. (Use knife as leverage; do not force.)

3. Twist to open shell, keeping oyster level at all times to save liquor. Cut the muscle from shell and discard top shell. Tip shell over strainer in bowl to catch oysters; discard bottom shell. Refrigerate oysters.

4. Strain oyster liquor from bowl through triple thickness of dampened cheesecloth into small bowl; set aside oyster liquor.

5. Remove shells from shrimp under cold running water. To devein, cut shallow slit down back of shrimp; pull out and discard vein (techniques on page 30). If desired, this step may be omitted.

continued on page 234

Step 2. Twisting to pry open shell with oyster knife.

Step 3. Cutting muscle from shell.

Step 4. Straining oyster liquor through cheesecloth.

Spaghetti with Seafood Marinara Sauce, continued

6. Cut scallops into ¾-inch pieces. Drain and mince anchovies. Refrigerate seafood.

7. Heat oil in 3-quart saucepan over medium-high heat until hot; cook and stir onion 4 minutes or until soft. Add garlic; cook 30 seconds. Add wine; cook 4 to 5 minutes until wine has evaporated. Remove from heat; cover and set aside.

8. Cook spaghetti in large pot of boiling salted water 8 to 10 minutes just until al dente; drain well.

9. Stir oyster liquor and anchovies into onion mixture in saucepan; add tomatoes, tomato paste, basil, salt, oregano and pepper. Mix well.

10. Bring to a boil over high heat; reduce heat to medium. Cook, uncovered, 20 minutes or until sauce thickens, stirring occasionally.

11. Stir in shrimp, scallops and oysters.

12. Cover and cook 2 to 3 minutes until shrimp turn opaque and are cooked through, stirring occasionally. Stir in parsley.

13. Combine hot spaghetti with seafood sauce in large serving bowl; toss until well coated. Garnish, if desired. Serve immediately.   *Makes 4 to 5 servings*

Step 6. Mincing anchovies.

Step 10. Simmering sauce until thickened.

Step 11. Stirring shrimp, scallops and oysters into sauce.

Scallops with Vegetables

1 ounce dried mushrooms
    Water
4 teaspoons cornstarch
2½ tablespoons dry sherry
4 teaspoons soy sauce
2 teaspoons instant chicken
    bouillon granules
8 ounces fresh green beans
1 pound fresh or thawed frozen
    sea scallops
2 tablespoons vegetable oil
2 yellow onions, cut into 8 wedges
    and separated
3 ribs celery, diagonally cut into
    ½-inch pieces
2 teaspoons minced fresh ginger
    (page 130)
1 clove garlic, minced (page 116)
6 green onions with tops,
    diagonally cut into thin slices
    (page 116)
1 can (15 ounces) baby corn,
    drained

1. Place mushrooms in bowl. Add enough water to cover; let stand 30 minutes. Drain. Squeeze out as much water as possible from mushrooms. Cut off and discard stems; cut caps into thin slices.

2. Combine cornstarch and additional 1 cup water in small bowl; stir in sherry, soy sauce and bouillon granules. Set aside.

3. Trim green beans; discard ends. Diagonally cut beans into 1-inch pieces.

4. Cut scallops into quarters; set aside.

5. Heat oil in wok or large skillet over high heat until hot. Add green beans, yellow onions, celery, ginger and garlic; stir-fry 3 minutes.

6. Stir cornstarch mixture; add to wok. Cook and stir until sauce boils and thickens.

7. Add mushrooms, scallops, green onions and baby corn.

8. Cook and stir until scallops turn opaque, about 4 minutes. Garnish as desired.

Makes 4 to 6 servings

Step 3. Trimming beans.

Step 4. Quartering scallops.

Step 7. Adding corn to wok.

Steamed Maryland Crabs with Corn on the Cob

1 pint water or beer
1 pint cider vinegar or white
   vinegar
2 dozen live Maryland blue crabs
½ pound seafood seasoning
½ pound salt
4 ears fresh corn, cooked

1. Place water and vinegar in 10-gallon stockpot. Place rack in bottom of pot. Place 1 layer of crabs on rack. Mix seafood seasoning with salt and sprinkle half over crabs.

2. Repeat with remaining crabs, layering with remaining seasoning mixture.

3. Cover pot. Heat on high until liquid begins to steam. Steam about 25 minutes or until crabs turn red and meat is white. Remove crabs to large serving platter using tongs.

4. Cover table with disposable paper cloth.

5. To pick crabs, place crab on its back. With thumb or knife point, pry off "apron" flap (the "pull tab" looking shell in the center) and discard.

6. Lift off top shell and discard.

7. Break off toothed claws and set aside. With knife edge, scrape off 3 areas of lungs and debris over hard semi-transparent membrane covering edible crabmeat; discard.

8. Hold crab at each side; break apart at center. Discard legs. Remove membrane with knife, exposing large chunks of meat; remove with fingers or knife.

9. Crack claws with mallet or knife handle to expose meat.

10. Serve with corn on the cob.

Makes 4 servings

Step 5. Prying off "apron" flap.

Step 7. Scraping off lungs.

Step 8. Breaking crab apart.

Chesapeake Crab Cakes

1 pound backfin crabmeat
½ cup soft bread crumbs
1 tablespoon minced onion
1 tablespoon finely chopped green or red bell pepper
1 tablespoon chopped fresh parsley (page 38)
¼ cup mayonnaise
1 egg
2 teaspoons white wine Worcestershire sauce
2 teaspoons lemon juice
1 teaspoon prepared mustard
½ teaspoon salt
¼ teaspoon ground white pepper
Vegetable oil for frying (optional)
Tartar sauce

Serving Suggestions: Serve large crab cakes on plate or as sandwiches with round buns. Serve bite-sized cakes on plate or with toothpicks as appetizers. Accompany with tartar sauce.

1. To remove cartilage and shell from crabmeat, gently squeeze a teaspoonful at a time between fingers. Feel carefully for small bits. The shells may be white or orange and cartilage milky white and thin. Discard cartilage and shells. Flake crabmeat with fork.

2. Place crabmeat in medium bowl. Add bread crumbs, onion, bell pepper and parsley; set aside.

3. Mix remaining ingredients except oil and tartar sauce in small bowl. Stir well to combine. Pour mayonnaise mixture over crabmeat mixture. Gently mix so large lumps will not be broken. Shape mixture into 6 large (¾-inch-thick) cakes or 36 bite-sized cakes.

To Pan-Fry Crab Cakes:

Pour enough oil into large skillet to cover bottom. Heat oil over medium-high heat until hot. Fry crab cakes 10 minutes for large cakes or 6 minutes for bite-sized cakes or until cakes are lightly browned on bottom, turning halfway through cooking.

To Broil Crab Cakes:

Preheat broiler. Place crab cakes on broiler pan. Broil 4 to 6 inches below heat 10 minutes for large cakes or 6 minutes for bite-sized cakes or until cakes are lightly browned on surface, turning halfway through cooking.

Makes 6 servings

Step 1. Removing cartilage and shell from crabmeat.

Pan-Frying: Turning crab cakes.

Boiled Whole Lobster with Burned Butter Sauce

8 tablespoons butter
2 tablespoons chopped fresh
   parsley (page 38)
1 tablespoon cider vinegar
1 tablespoon capers
2 live lobsters*

*Purchase live lobsters as close to the time of cooking as possible. Store in refrigerator.

1. Fill 8-quart stockpot with enough water to cover lobsters. Cover stockpot; bring water to a boil over high heat.

2. Meanwhile, to make Burned Butter Sauce, melt butter in medium saucepan over medium heat. Cook and stir butter until it turns dark chocolate brown. Remove from heat. Add parsley, vinegar and capers. Pour into 2 individual ramekins; set aside.

3. Holding lobster by its back, submerge head first in boiling water; repeat with second lobster. Cover and continue to heat. When water returns to a boil, cook lobsters for 10 to 18 minutes, according to size:

1 pound—10 minutes
1¼ pounds—12 minutes
1½ pounds—15 minutes
2 pounds—18 minutes

4. Transfer to 2 large serving platters. Remove bands restraining claws. To remove meat from claws, first break them from the body. Pull off the "thumb" part of the claw.

5. Then, using a metal nutcracker, crack claw gently to avoid damaging the meat. Using seafood fork, gently remove claw meat.

6. Crack legs gently with nutcracker. Pick out meat.

7. To remove tail meat, place lobster tail with underside facing up. With kitchen scissors, cut through underside of shell. Pull shell apart and slide your index finger between meat and shell to loosen meat; gently pull out meat from shell.

8. Serve lobster with Burned Butter Sauce.

Makes 2 servings

Step 4. Pulling off the "thumb" part of claw.

Step 5. Removing claw meat.

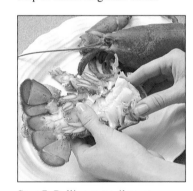
Step 7. Pulling out tail meat.

Vegetables & Side Dishes

Frenched Beans with Celery

½ teaspoon vegetable oil
2 tablespoons shelled sunflower
   seeds
¾ pound fresh green beans
2 ribs celery
   Water
2 tablespoons butter, melted
   Celery leaves and carrot slices
     for garnish

1. To toast sunflower seeds, heat oil in small skillet over medium heat. Add sunflower seeds; cook and stir 3 minutes or until lightly browned, shaking pan constantly. Remove with slotted spoon to paper towels.

2. Place beans in colander; rinse well. To prepare beans, snap off stem end from each bean, pulling off strings if present. (Young, tender beans may not have strings.)

3. Slice beans lengthwise on cutting board with chef's knife; set aside.

4. To prepare celery, trim stem ends and leaves from ribs on cutting board with chef's knife. Reserve leaves for garnish, if desired. Slice ribs thinly on the diagonal.

5. Bring 1 inch of water in medium saucepan to a boil over high heat. Add beans and celery. Cover; reduce heat to medium-low. Simmer 8 minutes or until beans are crisp-tender; drain.

6. Toss beans and celery with butter. Transfer to warm serving dish. Sprinkle with sunflower seeds. Garnish, if desired. Serve immediately.

Makes 6 servings

Step 2. Snapping off stem ends from beans.

Step 3. Slicing beans lengthwise.

Step 4. Slicing celery on the diagonal.

Green Beans and Shiitake Mushrooms

10 to 12 dried shiitake mushrooms (about 1 ounce)
2 green onions
¾ cup water, divided
3 tablespoons oyster sauce
1 tablespoon cornstarch
4 cloves garlic, minced (page 116)
⅛ teaspoon red pepper flakes
1 tablespoon vegetable oil
¾ to 1 pound fresh green beans, ends trimmed
⅓ cup fresh basil leaves or chopped cilantro
⅓ cup roasted peanuts (optional)

1. Place mushrooms in bowl; cover with hot water. Let stand 30 minutes or until caps are soft.

2. Drain mushrooms; squeeze out excess water. Remove and discard stems. Slice caps into thin strips.

3. Cut roots from green onions with paring knife; discard. Cut onions diagonally into thin slices (technique on page 116). Set aside.

4. Combine ¼ cup water, oyster sauce, cornstarch, garlic and pepper flakes in small bowl; mix well. Set aside.

5. Heat medium skillet or wok over medium-high heat. Add oil and swirl to coat surface. Add mushrooms, beans and remaining ½ cup water; cook and stir until water boils.

6. Reduce heat to medium-low; cover and cook 8 to 10 minutes or until beans are crisp-tender, stirring occasionally.

7. Break off and discard stems from basil. Rinse leaves; pat dry with paper towels. Layer some of leaves on cutting board with largest leaf on bottom, then roll up jelly-roll fashion. Slice roll into ¼-inch-thick slices; separate into strips. Repeat with remaining basil.

8. Stir cornstarch mixture; add to wok. Cook and stir until sauce thickens and coats beans. (If cooking water has evaporated, add enough water to form thick sauce.)

9. Stir in green onions, basil and peanuts, if desired; mix well. Transfer to serving platter. Garnish as desired. *Makes 4 to 6 servings*

Step 2. Slicing mushroom caps into thin strips.

Step 7. Slicing basil roll into ¼-inch-thick strips.

Step 8. Cooking and stirring sauce until thickened.

Cauliflower and Potato Masala

Garam Masala*
   Cardamom pods
   2 teaspoons cumin seeds
   **2 teaspoons whole black
      peppercorns**
   1½ teaspoons coriander seeds
   1 teaspoon fennel seeds
   ¾ teaspoon whole cloves
   1 cinnamon stick, broken

   **1 head cauliflower (about 1¼
      pounds)**
   **8 ounces medium red skin
      potatoes**
   2 tablespoons vegetable oil
   **1 teaspoon minced garlic
      (page 116)**
   **1 teaspoon minced fresh ginger
      (page 130)**
   1 teaspoon salt
   1 teaspoon cumin seeds
   1 teaspoon ground coriander
   **1½ cups chopped tomatoes, fresh
      or canned**
   2 tablespoons chopped cilantro

*Also available at specialty stores or
Indian markets.

1. To prepare Garam Masala, remove seeds from cardamom pods to measure ½ teaspoon; discard pods.

2. Preheat oven to 250°F. Combine 2 teaspoons cumin, peppercorns, coriander, fennel, cloves, cardamom and cinnamon stick on pizza pan; bake 30 minutes, stirring occasionally. Transfer spices to clean coffee or spice mill or use mortar and pestle to pulverize. Store in covered glass jar for use in this and other Indian recipes.

3. To prepare cauliflower, cut leaves from cauliflower by slicing through stem between head and leaves with chef's knife; remove and discard leaves and stem. Cut around core with paring knife; remove and discard core.

4. To separate cauliflower into flowerets, break head into pieces, then cut into bite-sized pieces with paring knife.

5. Peel potatoes with vegetable peeler. Cut lengthwise into halves with chef's knife; cut each half lengthwise into 3 wedges.

6. Heat oil in large saucepan over medium-high heat. Add garlic, ginger, salt, 1 teaspoon cumin and coriander; cook and stir about 30 seconds or until fragrant.

7. Add tomatoes; cook and stir 1 minute. Add cauliflower and potatoes; mix well. Reduce heat to low; cover and cook about 30 minutes or until vegetables are tender.

8. Stir in ½ teaspoon Garam Masala; mix well. Pour into serving bowl; sprinkle with cilantro. Garnish as desired.

Makes 6 servings

Step 1. Removing seed from cardamon pod.

Step 3. Cutting leaves from cauliflower.

Step 4. Cutting floweret into bite-sized pieces.

Broccoli Timbales

1 pound fresh broccoli
3 eggs
1 cup heavy cream
1 tablespoon lemon juice
¼ teaspoon salt
   Dash ground black pepper
4 cups boiling water
   Chopped tomato and sliced
      green onion tops for garnish

1. Generously butter six 6-ounce ramekins or custard cups; set in 13×9-inch baking dish. Preheat oven to 375°F.

2. To prepare broccoli, trim leaves from broccoli stalks. Trim off tough ends of stalks. Cut broccoli into flowerets by removing each head to include small piece of stem; set aside.

3. Peel remaining broccoli stem pieces with vegetable peeler. Cut into 1-inch pieces; cut each piece in half lengthwise.

4. To cook broccoli, bring ½ inch of water in medium saucepan to a boil over high heat. Reduce heat to medium-low; add broccoli stem pieces. Cover; simmer about 10 minutes or until fork-tender. Transfer cooked stems with slotted spoon to food processor or blender. Add flowerets to same saucepan. Cover; simmer about 5 minutes or until flowerets turn bright green. Remove flowerets with slotted spoon to cutting board.

5. Add eggs to cooked stems in food processor; process until smooth. Add cream; pulse to blend. Add lemon juice, salt and pepper; pulse once.

6. Reserve 6 small flowerets for garnish. Chop remaining flowerets; add to food processor. Pulse several times to blend.

7. Divide mixture evenly among prepared ramekins. Add boiling water to dish so water comes halfway up sides of ramekins. Bake 25 to 30 minutes until knife inserted in center comes out clean. Top with reserved flowerets. Garnish, if desired. Let stand 5 minutes. Serve in ramekins. *Makes 6 servings*

Step 3. Cutting 1-inch stem piece in half lengthwise.

Step 4. Adding stem pieces to food processor.

Step 7. Adding boiling water to baking dish.

Cabbage Wedges with Tangy Hot Dressing

½ head red or green cabbage
    (about 1 pound)
1 slice bacon, cut crosswise into
    ¼-inch strips
2 teaspoons cornstarch
⅔ cup unsweetened apple juice
¼ cup cider or red wine vinegar
1 tablespoon brown sugar
½ teaspoon caraway seeds
1 green onion, thinly sliced

1. Discard any wilted or bruised outer leaves from cabbage. Cut cabbage half into 4 wedges with chef's knife. (To help keep wedges intact, do not cut core from each wedge.)

2. Cook bacon in large skillet over medium heat until crisp. Remove bacon with slotted spoon to paper towel; set aside. Meanwhile, dissolve cornstarch in apple juice in glass measuring cup. Stir in vinegar, brown sugar and caraway seeds; set aside. Add onion to hot drippings. Cook and stir until onion is soft but not brown.

3. Place cabbage wedges, flat sides down, in drippings mixture. Pour cornstarch mixture over cabbage wedges. Cook over medium heat 4 minutes. Carefully turn cabbage wedges over with spatula. Cook 6 minutes more or until cabbage is fork-tender and dressing is thickened.

4. Remove cabbage to cutting board with spatula; carefully cut core away from each wedge with utility knife. Transfer to warm serving dish. Pour hot dressing over cabbage wedges. Sprinkle with bacon pieces. Garnish as desired. Serve immediately.

Makes 4 servings

Step 1. Cutting cabbage into wedges.

Step 3. Testing doneness of cabbage.

Step 4. Cutting core from cooked cabbage.

Nutmeg & Honey Carrot Crescents

1 pound fresh carrots
⅓ cup water
2 tablespoons honey
¼ teaspoon grated nutmeg
2 tablespoons chopped walnuts
2 edible flowers, such as
**   snapdragons, for garnish**

1. Wash and peel carrots. To make carrot crescents, place 1 carrot on cutting board. Cut carrot in half lengthwise with utility knife. Place cut sides down. Hold carrot half flat to cutting board with one hand. Hold knife at a 45° angle, slanting it away from hand. Make ¼-inch-thick diagonal slices, beginning at large end of carrot. Repeat with remaining carrots.

2. Place carrot crescents and water in large saucepan; cover. Bring to a boil over high heat; reduce heat to medium-low. Simmer carrots about 8 minutes or until fork-tender.

3. Transfer carrots with slotted spoon to warm serving dish. Bring remaining liquid in saucepan to a boil until liquid is almost evaporated. Add honey and nutmeg; stir. Heat briefly and pour over carrots. Toss gently to coat. Sprinkle with walnuts. Garnish, if desired. Serve immediately.

Makes 4 servings

Step 1. Cutting carrots in half lengthwise.

Step 1. Cutting carrots into ¼-inch diagonal slices.

Step 2. Testing doneness of carrots.

Grilled Coriander Corn

4 ears fresh corn
3 tablespoons butter or
margarine, softened
1 teaspoon ground coriander
¼ teaspoon salt (optional)
⅛ teaspoon ground red pepper
Flat-leaf parsley and red chili
peppers for garnish

1. Pull outer husks from top to base of each corn; leave husks attached to ear. (If desired, remove 1 strip of husk from inner portion of each ear; reserve.)

2. Strip away silk from corn by hand.

3. Remove any remaining silk with dry vegetable brush. Trim any blemishes from corn.

4. Place corn in large bowl. Cover with cold water; soak 20 to 30 minutes.

5. Meanwhile, prepare barbecue grill for direct cooking.

6. Remove corn from water; pat kernels dry with paper towels. Combine butter, coriander, salt and ground red pepper in small bowl. Spread evenly with spatula over kernels.

7. Bring husks back up each ear of corn; secure at top with paper-covered metal twist-ties. (Or, use reserved strips of corn husk to tie knots at the top of each ear, if desired.)

8. Place corn on grid. Grill corn, on covered grill, over medium-hot coals 20 to 25 minutes or until corn is hot and tender, turning halfway through grilling time with tongs. Garnish, if desired. *Makes 4 servings*

Note: For ember cooking, prepare corn as recipe directs, but omit soaking in cold water. Wrap each ear securely in heavy-duty foil. Place directly on coals. Grill corn, in covered grill, on medium-hot coals 25 to 30 minutes or until corn is hot and tender, turning every 10 minutes with tongs.

Step 1. Pulling outer husk to base of corn.

Step 5. Briquets arranged in grill for direct cooking.

Step 6. Spreading butter mixture over kernels.

Fried Eggplant

1 medium eggplant (about
    1 pound)
1 teaspoon salt
6 ounces mozzarella cheese
½ teaspoon active dry yeast
1½ cups warm water
    (105°F to 115°F)
2 cups all-purpose flour, divided
⅛ teaspoon ground black pepper
4½ tablespoons olive oil, divided
2 tablespoons minced fresh basil
    or ½ teaspoon dried basil
    leaves, crushed
    Vegetable oil
1 egg white
    Lemon slices (optional)
    Fresh basil leaves for garnish

1. Rinse eggplant; cut crosswise into ¼-inch-thick slices. Place in large colander over bowl; sprinkle with salt. Drain 1 hour.

2. Cut cheese into ⅛-inch-thick slices. Trim cheese slices to size of eggplant slices. Wrap in plastic; set aside.

3. Sprinkle yeast over warm water in medium bowl; stir until dissolved. Whisk in 1½ cups flour and pepper until smooth. Let batter stand at room temperature 30 minutes.

4. Rinse eggplant and drain well; pat slices dry between paper towels. Heat 1½ tablespoons olive oil in large skillet over medium-high heat until hot; add eggplant slices in single layer without crowding to hot oil. Cook 2 minutes per side until slices are light brown. Remove with slotted spatula; drain on paper towels. Repeat with remaining olive oil and eggplant slices.

5. Sprinkle cheese slices with basil. Place each cheese slice between 2 eggplant slices; press firmly together. Spread remaining ½ cup flour on plate. Dip eggplant stacks in flour to coat lightly.

6. Heat 1½ inches vegetable oil in large saucepan to 350°F. Adjust heat to maintain temperature. Beat egg white in small bowl with electric mixer at high speed until stiff peaks form; fold into yeast batter. Dip eggplant stacks, 1 at a time, into batter; gently shake off excess. Fry stacks in oil, 3 at a time, 2 minutes per side until browned. Remove with slotted spatula; drain on paper towels. Serve hot with lemon slices. Garnish, if desired. *Makes 4 to 6 servings*

Step 1. Slicing eggplant.

Step 5. Placing cheese slices between eggplant slices.

Step 6. Frying eggplant stacks.

Herbed Mushroom Vegetable Medley

4 ounces button or crimini
    mushrooms
1 medium red or yellow bell
    pepper, cut into ¼-inch-wide
    strips
1 medium zucchini, cut crosswise
    into ¼-inch-thick slices
1 medium yellow squash, cut
    crosswise into ¼-inch-thick
    slices
3 tablespoons butter or
    margarine, melted
1 tablespoon chopped fresh
    thyme leaves *or* 1 teaspoon
    dried thyme leaves, crushed
1 tablespoon chopped fresh basil
    leaves *or* 1 teaspoon dried
    basil leaves, crushed
1 tablespoon chopped fresh chives
    or green onion tops
1 clove garlic, minced (page 116)
¼ teaspoon salt
¼ teaspoon ground black pepper

1. Prepare barbecue grill for direct cooking (technique on page 109).

2. To prepare mushrooms, brush dirt from mushrooms; clean by wiping with damp paper towel.

3. Cut thin slice from base of each mushroom stem with paring knife; discard. Thinly slice mushroom stems and caps.

4. Combine mushrooms, bell pepper, zucchini and squash in large bowl. Combine butter, thyme, basil, chives, garlic, salt and black pepper in small bowl. Pour over vegetable mixture; toss to coat well.

5. Transfer mixture to 20×14-inch sheet of heavy-duty foil. Using Drugstore Wrap technique, bring 2 long sides of foil together above mixture. Fold down in series of locked folds. Fold short ends up and over again; crimp closed to seal.

6. Place foil packet on grid. Grill packet, on covered grill, over medium coals 20 to 25 minutes or until vegetables are fork-tender. Open packet carefully to serve.

Makes 4 to 6 servings

Step 2. Wiping mushrooms with damp paper towel to clean.

Step 3. Cutting thin slice from base of mushroom stem.

Step 5. Wrapping vegetable mixture using Drugstore Wrap technique.

VEGETABLES & SIDE DISHES   261

Potato Pierogi

4 medium potatoes (about
    1½ pounds), peeled and
    quartered
⅓ cup milk
2 tablespoons butter or
    margarine
2 tablespoons chopped green
    onion
1 teaspoon salt, divided
½ teaspoon ground white pepper,
    divided
2¾ cups all-purpose flour
1 cup sour cream
1 egg
1 egg yolk
1 tablespoon vegetable oil
    Melted butter, cooked
    crumbled bacon or sour
    cream (optional)

1. To prepare filling, place potatoes in medium saucepan; cover with water. Bring to a boil over high heat. Reduce heat to medium. Simmer, uncovered, 20 minutes or until tender. Drain; return potatoes to saucepan.

2. Mash potatoes with potato masher. Stir in milk, butter, onion, ½ teaspoon salt and ¼ teaspoon pepper. (Potato mixture should be quite stiff.) Cool.

3. To prepare pierogi dough, combine flour, sour cream, egg, egg yolk, oil, and remaining ½ teaspoon salt and ¼ teaspoon pepper in medium bowl; mix well.

4. Turn out dough onto lightly floured surface. Knead dough 3 to 5 minutes or until soft and pliable, but not sticky (technique on page 190). Let rest, covered, 10 minutes.

5. Divide dough in half. Roll out each half into a 13-inch-diameter circle on lightly floured surface with lightly floured rolling pin. Cut out dough with 2½-inch-round cutter.

6. Place 1 rounded teaspoon potato filling in center of each dough circle. Moisten edges of circles with water and fold in half; press edges firmly to seal.

7. Bring 4 quarts lightly salted water to a boil in Dutch oven over high heat. Cook pierogi in batches 10 minutes. Remove with slotted spoon to serving dish.

8. Drizzle butter over pierogi, top with bacon or serve with sour cream, if desired. Garnish as desired. *Makes about 5 dozen pierogi*

Step 4. Kneading dough on floured surface.

Step 6. Pressing edge firmly to seal.

Step 7. Removing pierogi with slotted spoon.

Low-Fat Cajun Wedges

Russet potatoes
Nonstick cooking spray
**Cajun seasoning or other
  seasoning, such as paprika**
**Purple kale and fresh sage
  leaves for garnish**

1. Preheat oven to 400°F. To prepare potatoes, scrub potatoes under running water with soft vegetable brush; rinse. Dry well. *Do not peel.* Line baking sheet with foil and spray with cooking spray.

2. Cut potatoes in half lengthwise with chef's knife; then cut each half lengthwise into 3 wedges. Place potatoes, skin sides down, in single layer on prepared baking sheet.

3. Spray potatoes lightly with cooking spray and sprinkle with seasoning.

4. Bake 25 minutes or until browned and fork-tender. Garnish, if desired. Serve immediately.

Makes about 1 serving per potato

Step 2. Cutting potato halves into wedges.

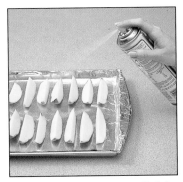

Step 3. Spraying potatoes lightly with cooking spray.

Low-Fat Potato Chips

Prepare as directed in step 1. Cut potatoes crosswise into thin slices with chef's knife or mandoline slicer. Place in single layer on prepared baking sheet; spray and season as directed in step 3. Bake 10 to 15 minutes until browned and crisp. Serve immediately.

Low-Fat Cottage Fries

Prepare as directed in step 1. Cut potatoes crosswise into ¼-inch-thick slices. Place in single layer on prepared baking sheet; spray and season as directed in step 3. Bake 15 to 20 minutes until browned and fork-tender. Serve immediately.

Low-Fat Potato Chips: Cutting potatoes into thin slices.

Spinach and Mushroom Stir-Fry

2 cloves garlic
1 red bell pepper
2 ounces fresh shiitake or button
    mushrooms*
10 ounces fresh spinach
2 tablespoons peanut oil
1 teaspoon minced fresh ginger
    (page 130)
¼ to ½ teaspoon red pepper flakes
1 teaspoon fish sauce

*Or, substitute ½ ounce dried Oriental mushrooms, soaked according to package directions.

1. To mince garlic, trim ends of garlic cloves. Slightly crush cloves under flat side of chef's knife blade (technique on page 116); peel away skin. Chop garlic with chef's knife until garlic is in uniform fine pieces.

2. To seed bell pepper, cut in half lengthwise. Scrape out stem, seeds and membrane with spoon, being careful not to cut through shell. Rinse out under running water; cut into 1-inch triangles.

3. To prepare mushrooms, brush dirt from mushrooms; clean by wiping with damp paper towel (technique on page 44). Cut thin piece from stem; discard. Cut into slices with utility knife.

4. Separate spinach into leaves. Swish in cold water. Repeat several times with fresh water to remove sand and grit. Pat dry with paper towels.

5. To remove stems from spinach leaves, fold each leaf in half, then pull stem toward top of leaf (technique on page 172). Discard stems.

6. Chop spinach coarsely with chef's knife.

7. Heat wok over high heat 1 minute or until hot. Drizzle oil into wok; heat 30 seconds. Add garlic, ginger and red pepper flakes; stir-fry 30 seconds. Add bell pepper and mushrooms; stir-fry 2 minutes. Add spinach and fish sauce; stir-fry 1 to 2 minutes or until spinach is wilted. Serve immediately.

Makes 4 servings

Step 2. Cutting bell pepper into 1-inch triangles.

Step 3. Cutting mushroom into slices.

Step 6. Chopping spinach coarsely.

Cheese-Stuffed Pattypans

**4 pattypan squash (about
    3 inches in diameter)
4 tablespoons butter or
    margarine
2 ribs celery, diced
½ cup chopped onion (page 68)
½ cup water
1 cup dry herb-seasoned stuffing
    mix
1 cup shredded sharp Cheddar
    cheese**

1. Preheat oven to 350°F. To prepare squash, wash and slice off each top, above scalloped edge, with utility knife; discard.

2. Scoop out seeds from center with spoon.

3. Place squash shells in large skillet. Pour ¼ inch of water into skillet; cover. Bring to a boil over high heat; reduce heat to medium-low. Simmer 5 minutes. Transfer squash shells, cut sides up, with slotted spoon to greased 8-inch square baking dish.

4. Heat butter in large skillet over medium-high heat until melted and bubbly. Cook and stir celery and onion in hot butter until tender. Add water, then stuffing mix. Stir to absorb water. Stir in cheese. Divide mixture evenly among squash shells.

5. Bake 20 to 30 minutes until squash shells are fork-tender and stuffing is lightly browned. Garnish as desired. Serve immediately. *Makes 4 servings*

Step 1. Slicing tops off squash.

Step 2. Scooping seeds from squash.

Step 4. Filling squash shells with cheese stuffing.

Stir-Fried Tofu and Vegetables

½ pound firm tofu cakes
1 medium yellow onion, peeled
1 medium zucchini (½ pound)
1 medium yellow squash
    (7 ounces)
1 small red bell pepper
4 ounces fresh snow peas
1 cup vegetable oil
8 medium button mushrooms,
    cleaned (page 44) and cut
    into thick slices
¼ cup water
1 tablespoon soy sauce
1 tablespoon tomato paste*
¼ teaspoon salt
⅛ teaspoon ground black pepper

*Leftover tomato paste may be transferred to small plastic bag and frozen.

1. Drain tofu on paper towels. Cut crosswise into ¼-inch-thick slices. Set aside.

2. Cut onion into 8 wedges with chef's knife; set aside. Cut zucchini and yellow squash crosswise into 1-inch-thick slices. Cut large squash slices into quartered chunks; set aside.

3. To seed bell pepper, cut pepper in half lengthwise with chef's knife. Scrape out stem, seeds and membrane with spoon, being careful not to cut through shell. Rinse out under cold running water. Cut pepper into ¼-inch-wide strips.

4. To destem snow peas, pinch off stem end from each pod, pulling strings down the pod to remove if present; set aside.

5. Heat oil in wok over medium-high heat about 4 minutes or until hot. Add tofu and fry about 3 minutes per side or until golden brown, turning once. Remove tofu with slotted spatula to baking sheet or large plate lined with paper towels; drain. Drain oil from wok, reserving 2 tablespoons.

6. Return reserved oil to wok. Heat over medium heat 30 seconds or until hot. Add onion and stir-fry 1 minute. Add zucchini, yellow squash and mushrooms; stir-fry 7 to 8 minutes until zucchini and yellow squash are crisp-tender.

7. Add red pepper, snow peas and water. Cook and stir 2 to 3 minutes until crisp-tender. Stir in soy sauce, tomato paste, salt and black pepper until well mixed. Add fried tofu; stir-fry until heated through and coated with sauce. Transfer to serving platter. Serve immediately. *Makes 4 servings*

Step 3. Scraping seeds and membrane from bell pepper.

Step 4. Destemming snow peas.

Step 6. Stir-frying zucchini, yellow squash and mushrooms.

VEGETABLES & SIDE DISHES   271

Zucchini Shanghai Style

4 dried mushrooms
Water
1 large tomato
½ cup chicken broth
2 tablespoons ketchup
2 teaspoons soy sauce
1 teaspoon dry sherry
¼ teaspoon sugar
⅛ teaspoon salt
1 teaspoon red wine vinegar
1 teaspoon cornstarch
2 tablespoons vegetable oil,
**   divided**
1 teaspoon minced fresh ginger
**   (page 130)**
1 clove garlic, minced (page 116)
1 green onion with top, finely
**   chopped**
1 pound zucchini, diagonally cut
**   into 1-inch pieces**
½ small yellow onion, cut into
**   wedges and separated**

1. Place mushrooms in small bowl; add enough warm water to cover mushrooms. Let stand 30 minutes. Drain, reserving ¼ cup liquid. Squeeze out excess water.

2. Cut stems off mushrooms; discard. Cut caps into thin slices.

3. To loosen skin from tomato, place in small saucepan of boiling water for 30 to 45 seconds. Rinse immediately under cold running water. Gently peel skin from tomato.

4. Cut tomato in half. Remove stem and seeds; discard. Coarsely chop; set aside.

5. Combine reserved ¼ cup mushroom liquid, chicken broth, ketchup, soy sauce, sherry, sugar, salt and vinegar in small bowl; set aside.

6. Combine cornstarch and 1 tablespoon water in small cup; mix well. Set aside.

7. Heat 1 tablespoon oil in wok over medium-high heat. Add ginger and garlic; stir-fry 10 seconds. Add mushrooms, tomato and green onion; stir-fry 1 minute. Stir in chicken broth mixture. Bring to a boil. Reduce heat to low; simmer 10 minutes, stirring occasionally. Remove from wok; set aside.

8. Add remaining 1 tablespoon oil to wok; heat over medium-high heat. Add zucchini and yellow onion; stir-fry 30 seconds. Add 3 tablespoons water; cover. Cook, stirring occasionally, until vegetables are crisp-tender, 3 to 4 minutes. Stir cornstarch mixture. Add to wok with mushroom mixture. Cook and stir until sauce boils and thickens.

Makes 4 to 6 servings

Step 3. Peeling tomato.

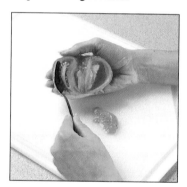

Step 4. Removing tomato seeds.

Chinese Vegetables

2 medium yellow onions, peeled
1 pound fresh broccoli*
8 ounces fresh snow peas *or*
    1 package (6 ounces) thawed
    frozen snow peas*
¾ cup water
1 tablespoon instant chicken
    bouillon granules
2 tablespoons vegetable oil
1 tablespoon minced fresh ginger
    (page 130)
8 ounces fresh spinach,* washed
    and coarsely chopped
    (page 266)
4 ribs celery,* diagonally cut into
    ½-inch pieces
8 green onions with tops,*
    diagonally cut into thin slices
    (page 116)

*Or, use sliced carrots, zucchini, green beans or green peppers in addition to, or in place of, the listed vegetables.

1. Cut yellow onions into eight wedges; separate layers.

2. Trim woody stems from broccoli; discard.

3. Cut broccoli tops into flowerets.

4. Cut larger flowerets and stalks into 2×¼-inch strips; set aside.

5. Trim snow peas and remove strings; set aside.

6. Combine water and bouillon granules in small bowl; mix well. Set aside.

7. Heat oil in wok or large skillet over high heat. Add yellow onions, larger pieces broccoli and ginger; stir-fry 1 minute. Add broccoli flowerets, snow peas, spinach, celery and green onions; toss lightly.

8. Add bouillon mixture; mix lightly until vegetables are well coated. Bring to a boil; cover. Cook until vegetables are crisp-tender, 2 to 3 minutes. *Makes 4 to 6 servings*

Step 3. Cutting broccoli into flowerets.

Step 4. Cutting larger flowerets and stalks into strips.

Step 5. Trimming snow peas.

Arroz Rojos

2 tablespoons vegetable oil
1 cup raw long-grain white rice
   (not converted)
½ cup finely chopped white onion
1 clove garlic, minced
½ teaspoon salt
½ teaspoon ground cumin
   Dash chili powder
2 large tomatoes, peeled, seeded,
   chopped (page 52)
1½ cups chicken broth
⅓ cup shelled fresh or thawed
   frozen peas
2 tablespoons chopped pimiento
   Red pepper arrows for garnish*

*To make red pepper arrows, cut a
½-inch-wide strip from a red pepper.
Make a V-shaped cut in strip at 1-inch
intervals.

1. Heat oil in medium skillet over medium heat until hot. Add rice. Cook and stir 2 minutes or until rice turns opaque.

2. Add onion; cook and stir 1 minute. Stir in garlic, salt, cumin and chili powder. Add tomatoes; cook and stir 2 minutes.

3. Stir in broth. Bring to a boil over high heat. Reduce heat to low. Cover and simmer 15 minutes or until rice is almost tender.

4. Stir in peas and chopped pimiento. Cover and cook 2 to 4 minutes until rice is tender and all liquid has been absorbed. Rice grains will be slightly firm and separate, rather than soft and sticky. Garnish, if desired.

Makes 4 to 6 servings

Step 1. Cooking rice until it turns opaque.

Step 2. Cooking tomatoes in rice mixture.

Step 4. Adding remaining ingredients to rice mixture.

Spätzle with Mushrooms

4 ounces shiitake or button mushrooms
3 tablespoons butter, divided
1¼ cups all-purpose flour
½ teaspoon salt
¼ teaspoon ground nutmeg
¾ cup milk
1 egg, lightly beaten
Flat-leaf parsley for garnish

1. To prepare mushrooms, wipe mushrooms clean with damp paper towel (technique on page 44). Cut thin piece from stem; discard. With utility knife, cut mushrooms into slices (technique on page 266).

2. Melt 1 tablespoon butter in large nonstick skillet over medium-high heat. Add mushrooms; cook and stir 5 minutes or until softened. Remove from heat.

3. To prepare spätzle, combine flour, salt and nutmeg in medium bowl. Combine milk and egg in small bowl; stir milk mixture into flour mixture.

4. Bring salted water in Dutch oven to a boil. Rest colander over Dutch oven; pour batter into colander. Press batter through holes with rubber spatula.

5. Stir spätzle to separate. Cook 5 minutes or until tender, yet firm (al dente). Drain spätzle.

6. Add remaining 2 tablespoons butter to skillet with mushrooms. Heat over medium heat until butter melts. Pour drained spätzle into skillet; toss with mushrooms and butter. Garnish, if desired. *Makes 4 servings*

Step 2. Cooking and stirring mushrooms until softened.

Step 4. Pressing batter through holes of colander.

Step 5. Stirring spätzle to separate.

Pad Thai

8 ounces flat rice noodles (⅛- to
    ¼-inch wide)
¼ cup water
3 tablespoons ketchup
3 tablespoons fish sauce
2 tablespoons packed brown
    sugar
1 tablespoon lime juice
1 jalapeño chili, seeded and finely
    chopped (page 75)
1 teaspoon curry powder
2 tablespoons peanut oil, divided
1 pound medium shrimp, peeled
    and deveined (page 30)
3 cloves garlic, minced (page 116)
3 eggs, lightly beaten
2 cups fresh bean sprouts, divided
⅔ cup roasted, skinless peanuts
    (salted or unsalted), chopped
3 green onions, thinly sliced
1 small carrot, shredded
¾ cup shredded red or green
    cabbage
½ cup cilantro, coarsely chopped
1 lime, cut into wedges

1. Place noodles in large bowl; cover with hot water. Let stand 10 to 30 minutes or until soft and pliable.

2. To prepare sauce, combine ¼ cup water, ketchup, fish sauce, sugar, lime juice, jalapeño and curry powder in medium bowl; set aside.

3. Heat wok or large skillet over high heat. Add 1 tablespoon oil and swirl to coat surface. Add shrimp; stir-fry 2 minutes or until shrimp turn pink and opaque. Transfer to bowl with slotted spoon.

4. Reduce heat to medium. Add remaining 1 tablespoon oil and heat 15 seconds. Add garlic; cook and stir 20 seconds or until golden. Add eggs; cook 2 minutes or just until set, turning and stirring every 30 seconds to scramble. Stir in sauce.

5. Increase heat to high. Add noodles; stir to coat with sauce. Cook 2 to 4 minutes, stirring often, until noodles are tender. (Add water, 1 tablespoon at a time, if sauce is absorbed and noodles are still dry.)

6. Add cooked shrimp, 1½ cups bean sprouts, peanuts and green onions; cook and stir 1 to 2 minutes or until heated through.

7. Transfer mixture to large serving platter. Pile remaining ½ cup sprouts, carrot, cabbage, cilantro and lime wedges around noodles. Squeeze lime over noodles before eating.

Makes 4 servings

Step 4. Stirring eggs to scramble.

Step 5. Stirring noodles to coat with sauce.

Cookies

Marshmallow Sandwich Cookies

2 cups all-purpose flour
½ cup unsweetened cocoa powder
2 teaspoons baking soda
¼ teaspoon salt
⅔ cup butter or margarine,
    softened
2 cups sugar, divided
¼ cup light corn syrup
1 large egg
1 teaspoon vanilla
24 large marshmallows

1. Preheat oven to 350°F.

2. Place flour, cocoa, baking soda and salt in medium bowl; stir to combine.

3. Beat butter and 1¼ cups sugar in large bowl with electric mixer at medium speed until light and fluffy, scraping down side of bowl once. Beat in corn syrup, egg and vanilla, scraping down side of bowl once. Gradually add flour mixture. Beat at low speed, scraping down side of bowl occasionally. Cover and refrigerate dough 15 minutes or until firm enough to roll into balls.

4. Place remaining ¾ cup sugar in shallow dish. Roll tablespoonfuls of dough into 1-inch balls; roll in sugar to coat. Place 3 inches apart on *ungreased* cookie sheets.

5. Bake 10 to 11 minutes or until set. Remove cookies with spatula to wire rack; cool completely.

6. To assemble sandwiches, place 1 marshmallow on flat side of 1 cookie on paper plate. Microwave at HIGH 12 seconds or until marshmallow is hot.

7. Immediately place another cookie, flat side down, over marshmallow; press together slightly. Repeat with remaining cookies and marshmallows.

8. Store tightly covered at room temperature. Do not freeze.

Makes 2 dozen sandwich cookies

Step 4. Rolling dough ball in sugar to coat.

Step 6. Placing marshmallow on cookie.

Step 7. Forming sandwich.

Belgian Tuile Cookies

½ cup butter, softened
½ cup sugar
1 large egg white (page 343)
1 teaspoon vanilla
¼ teaspoon salt
½ cup all-purpose flour
4 ounces bittersweet chocolate candy bar, chopped or semisweet chocolate chips

1. Preheat oven to 375°F. Grease cookie sheets; set aside.

2. Beat butter and sugar in large bowl with electric mixer at medium speed until light and fluffy, scraping down side of bowl once. Beat in egg white, vanilla and salt. Gradually add flour. Beat at low speed until well blended, scraping down side of bowl once.

3. Drop rounded teaspoonfuls of dough 4 inches apart onto prepared cookie sheets. (Bake only 4 cookies per sheet.) Flatten slightly with spatula.

4. Bake 6 to 8 minutes or until cookies are deep golden brown. Let cookies stand on cookie sheets 1 minute.

5. Working quickly, while cookies are still hot, drape cookies over a rolling pin or bottle so both sides hang down and form a saddle shape; cool completely.

6. Melt chocolate in small, heavy saucepan over low heat, stirring constantly.

7. Tilt saucepan to pool chocolate to one side; dip edge of each cookie into chocolate, turning cookie slowly to entirely edge with chocolate.

8. Transfer cookies to waxed paper; let stand at room temperature 1 hour or until set.

9. Store tightly covered at room temperature. Do not freeze.

Makes about 2½ dozen cookies

Step 3. Flattening dough slightly with spatula.

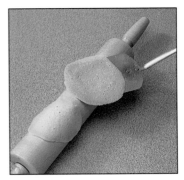

Step 5. Draping cookies over rolling pin.

Step 7. Coating edge of cookie with chocolate.

Czech Bear Paws (Medvědí Tlapičvky)

2 cups (about ½ pound whole) toasted ground hazelnuts (page 338)
2 cups all-purpose flour
1 tablespoon unsweetened cocoa powder
1 teaspoon ground cinnamon
½ teaspoon ground nutmeg
¼ teaspoon salt
1 cup plus 1 tablespoon butter, softened, divided
1 cup powdered sugar
1 large egg yolk (page 343)
½ cup chocolate chips
   Slivered almonds, cut into halves

1. Preheat oven to 350°F. Place hazelnuts, flour, cocoa, cinnamon, nutmeg and salt in medium bowl; stir to combine.

2. Beat 1 cup butter, powdered sugar and egg yolk in large bowl with electric mixer at medium speed until light and fluffy, scraping down side of bowl once. Gradually add flour mixture. Beat at low speed until soft dough forms, scraping down side of bowl once.

3. Grease 3 madeleine pans with remaining 1 tablespoon softened butter, 1 teaspoon per pan; dust with flour. (If only 1 madeleine pan is available, thoroughly wash, dry, regrease and flour after baking each batch. Cover remaining dough with plastic wrap; let stand at room temperature.)

4. Press level tablespoonfuls of dough in each prepared madeleine mold.

5. Bake 12 minutes or until lightly browned. Let cookies stand in pan 3 minutes. Carefully loosen cookies from pan with point of small knife. Invert pan on wire rack. Tap lightly to release cookies; cookies should be shell-side up. Cool completely.

6. Melt chocolate chips (technique on page 298). Cut off tiny corner of bag. Pipe scallop of melted chocolate on curved end of each cookie; place slivered almond halves on melted chocolate for claws. Let stand at room temperature 1 hour or until set.

7. Store tightly covered at room temperature. Do not freeze.

Makes about 3 dozen cookies

Step 3. Greasing madeleine pan.

Step 4. Pressing dough in mold.

Step 6. Placing slivered almond halves on chocolate.

Mexican Wedding Cookies

1 cup pecan pieces or halves
1 cup unsalted butter, softened
2 cups powdered sugar, divided
2 cups all-purpose flour, divided
2 teaspoons vanilla
¼ teaspoon salt

1. Place pecans in food processor. Process using on/off pulsing action until pecans are ground, but not pasty.

2. Beat butter and ½ cup powdered sugar in large bowl with electric mixer at medium speed until light and fluffy, scraping down side of bowl once. Gradually add 1 cup flour, vanilla and salt. Beat at low speed until well blended, scraping down side of bowl once. Stir in remaining flour and ground nuts with spoon.

3. Form dough into a ball; wrap in plastic wrap and refrigerate 1 hour or until firm.

4. Preheat oven to 350°F. Roll tablespoonfuls of dough into 1-inch balls; place 1 inch apart on *ungreased* cookie sheets.

5. Bake 12 to 15 minutes or until pale golden brown. Let cookies stand on cookie sheets 2 minutes.

6. Meanwhile, place 1 cup powdered sugar in 13×9-inch glass dish. Transfer hot cookies to dish.

7. Roll cookies in powdered sugar, coating well. Let cookies cool in sugar.

8. Sift remaining ½ cup powdered sugar over sugar-coated cookies before serving.

9. Store tightly covered at room temperature or freeze up to 1 month.

Makes about 4 dozen cookies

Step 3. Forming dough into a ball.

Step 6. Placing hot cookies in powdered sugar.

Step 7. Rolling cookies in powdered sugar.

Chocolate Madeleines

1 tablespoon butter, softened
1¼ cups cake flour or all-purpose
    flour
¼ cup unsweetened cocoa powder
¼ teaspoon salt
¼ teaspoon baking powder
1 cup granulated sugar
2 large eggs
¾ cup butter, melted and cooled
2 tablespoons almond-flavored
    liqueur or kirsch*
    Powdered sugar

*Kirsch is a brandy made from cherry juice and pits.

1. Preheat oven to 375°F. Grease 3 madeleine pans with softened butter, 1 teaspoon per pan; dust with flour. Set aside. (If only 1 madeleine pan is available, thoroughly wash, dry, regrease and flour after baking each batch. Cover remaining dough with plastic wrap; let stand at room temperature.)

2. Place flour, cocoa, salt and baking powder in medium bowl; stir to combine.

3. Beat granulated sugar and eggs in large bowl with electric mixer at medium speed 5 minutes or until mixture is light in color, thick and falls in wide ribbons from beaters, scraping down side of bowl once.

4. Beat in flour mixture at low speed until well blended, scraping down side of bowl once. Beat in melted butter and liqueur until just blended.

5. Spoon level tablespoonfuls of batter into each prepared madeleine mold. Bake 12 minutes or until puffed and golden brown.

6. Let cookies stand in pan 1 minute. Carefully loosen cookies from pan with point of small knife. Invert pan on wire rack. Tap lightly to release cookies; cookies should be shell-side up. Cool completely.

7. Dust with sifted powdered sugar.

8. Store tightly covered at room temperature up to 24 hours or freeze up to 3 months.

Makes about 3 dozen madeleines

Step 1. Greasing madeleine pan.

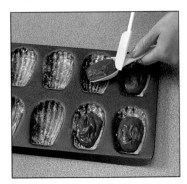

Step 5. Spooning tablespoonfuls of batter into madeleine mold.

Step 7. Dusting with powdered sugar.

Norwegian Wreaths (Berliner Kranser)

1 hard-cooked large egg yolk
1 large egg, separated (page 343)
½ cup butter, softened
½ cup powdered sugar
½ teaspoon vanilla
1¼ cups all-purpose flour, divided
    Coarse sugar crystals or
      crushed sugar cubes

1. Preheat oven to 350°F. Grease cookie sheets; set aside.

2. Beat cooked and raw egg yolks in medium bowl with electric mixer at medium speed until smooth.

3. Beat in butter, powdered sugar and vanilla, scraping down side of bowl once. Stir in 1 cup flour with spoon. Stir in remaining flour until stiff dough forms.

4. Place dough on sheet of waxed paper. Using waxed paper to hold dough, roll it back and forth to form a log; cut log into 18 equal pieces. Roll each piece of dough into 8-inch rope, tapering ends.

5. Shape ropes into wreaths; overlap ends and let extend out from wreath.

6. Place wreaths on prepared cookie sheets. Refrigerate 15 minutes or until firm.

7. Beat egg white with fork until foamy. Brush wreaths with egg white; sprinkle with sugar crystals. Bake 8 to 10 minutes or until light golden brown. Remove cookies with spatula to wire racks; cool completely.

8. Store tightly covered at room temperature or freeze up to 3 months.

Makes about 1½ dozen cookies

Step 2. Beating egg yolks until smooth.

Step 4. Rolling dough into 8-inch ropes.

Step 5. Shaping ropes into wreaths.

Mexican Sugar Cookies (Polvorones)

1 cup butter, softened
½ cup powdered sugar
2 tablespoons milk
1 teaspoon vanilla
1 teaspoon ground cinnamon, divided
1½ to 1¾ cups all-purpose flour
1 teaspoon baking powder
1 cup granulated sugar
1 square (1 ounce) semisweet chocolate, finely grated

1. Preheat oven to 325°F. Grease cookie sheets; set aside.

2. Beat butter, powdered sugar, milk, vanilla and ½ teaspoon cinnamon in large bowl with electric mixer at medium speed until light and fluffy, scraping down side of bowl once. Gradually add 1½ cups flour and baking powder. Beat at low speed until well blended, scraping down side of bowl once. Stir in additional flour with spoon if dough is too soft to shape.

3. Roll tablespoonfuls of dough into 1¼-inch balls; place 3 inches apart on prepared cookie sheets. Flatten each ball into 2-inch round with bottom of glass dipped in granulated sugar.

4. Bake 20 to 25 minutes or until edges are golden brown. Let stand on cookie sheets 3 to 4 minutes.

5. Meanwhile, combine granulated sugar, grated chocolate and remaining ½ teaspoon cinnamon in small bowl; stir to combine. Transfer cookies, one at a time, with spatula to sugar mixture; coat on both sides. Remove with spatula to wire racks; cool completely.

6. Store tightly covered at room temperature or freeze up to 3 months.

Makes about 2 dozen cookies

Step 2. Stirring in additional flour.

Step 3. Placing dough balls 3 inches apart on cookie sheet.

Step 5. Coating cookies with sugar mixture.

Molded Scotch Shortbread

1½ cups all-purpose flour
 ¼ teaspoon salt
 ¾ cup butter, softened
 ⅓ cup sugar
 1 large egg
    10-inch round ceramic
       shortbread mold

1. Preheat oven to temperature recommended by shortbread mold manufacturer. Place flour and salt in medium bowl; stir to combine.

2. Beat butter and sugar in large bowl with electric mixer at medium speed until light and fluffy, scraping down side of bowl once.

3. Beat in egg. Gradually add flour mixture. Beat at low speed until well blended, scraping down side of bowl once.

4. Spray shortbread mold with nonstick cooking spray. Press dough firmly in mold. Bake, cool and remove from mold according to manufacturer's directions.

5. If mold is not available, preheat oven to 350°F. Roll tablespoonfuls of dough into 1-inch balls; place 2 inches apart on *ungreased* cookie sheets. Press with fork to flatten.

6. Bake 18 to 20 minutes or until edges are lightly browned. Let cookies stand on cookie sheets 2 minutes. Remove cookies with spatula to wire racks; cool completely.

7. Store tightly covered at room temperature or freeze up to 3 months.
Makes 1 shortbread mold or 2 dozen cookies

Step 2. Scraping butter mixture from side of bowl.

Step 4. Pressing dough in mold.

Step 5. Pressing dough balls with fork to flatten.

Swiss Mocha Treats

**2 ounces imported Swiss
bittersweet chocolate candy
bar, broken**
**½ cup plus 2 tablespoons butter,
softened, divided**
**1 tablespoon instant espresso
powder**
1 teaspoon vanilla
1¾ cups all-purpose flour
½ teaspoon baking soda
½ teaspoon salt
¾ cup sugar
1 large egg
**3 ounces imported Swiss white
chocolate candy bar, broken**

1. Melt bittersweet chocolate and 2 tablespoons butter in small, heavy saucepan over low heat, stirring often. Add espresso powder; stir until dissolved. Remove from heat; stir in vanilla. Let cool to room temperature.

2. Place flour, baking soda and salt in medium bowl; stir to combine.

3. Beat remaining ½ cup butter and sugar in large bowl with mixer at medium speed until fluffy; scrape bowl once. Beat in bittersweet chocolate mixture and egg. Gradually add flour mixture. Beat at low speed until well blended; scrape bowl once. Cover; refrigerate 30 minutes or until firm.

4. Preheat oven to 375°F. Roll tablespoonfuls of dough into 1-inch balls; place 3 inches apart on *ungreased* cookie sheets. Flatten each ball into ½-inch-thick round with fork dipped in sugar.

5. Bake 9 to 10 minutes or until set. (Do not overbake or cookies will become dry.) Immediately remove cookies with spatula to wire racks; cool completely.

6. Place white chocolate in small resealable plastic freezer bag; seal bag. Microwave at MEDIUM (50% power) 1 minute. Turn bag over; microwave at MEDIUM 1 minute or until melted. Knead until chocolate is smooth.

7. Cut off tiny corner of bag; pipe or drizzle white chocolate onto cooled cookies. Let stand 30 minutes or until set.

8. Store tightly covered at room temperature or freeze up to 3 months.

Makes about 4 dozen cookies

Step 4. Rolling dough into 1-inch balls.

Step 6. Kneading bag until chocolate is smooth.

Step 7. Piping white chocolate onto cooled cookies.

Swedish Cookie Shells (Sandbakelser)

1 cup butter, softened
⅔ cup sugar
1 large egg white (page 343)
1 teaspoon vanilla
½ teaspoon almond extract
2 cups all-purpose flour, divided
¼ cup finely ground blanched
    almonds (page 304)

1. Beat butter and sugar in large bowl with electric mixer at medium speed until light and fluffy, scraping down side of bowl once. Beat in egg white, vanilla and almond extract until well blended, scraping down side of bowl once.

2. Gradually add 1½ cups flour and almonds. Beat at low speed until well blended, scraping down side of bowl once. Stir in remaining flour with spoon until soft dough forms. Form dough into 1-inch-thick square; wrap in plastic wrap and refrigerate until firm, 1 hour or overnight.

3. Preheat oven to 375°F. Grease sandbakelser tins. Press rounded teaspoonfuls of dough in tins or mini muffin pan cups.

4. Place tins on baking sheet. Bake 8 to 10 minutes or until cookie shells are lightly browned. Cool cookies in tins 1 minute.

5. Carefully loosen cookies from tins with point of small knife. Invert tins on wire racks. Tap lightly to release cookies; cookies should be shell-side up. Cool completely. Repeat with remaining dough; cool cookie tins between batches.

6. Serve cookies shell-side up. Store tightly covered at room temperature or freeze up to 3 months. *Makes about 10 dozen cookies*

Step 3. Pressing dough in sandbakelser tins.

Step 5. Loosening cookies from tins.

Classic Anise Biscotti

4 ounces whole blanched almonds (about ¾ cup)
2¼ cups all-purpose flour
1 teaspoon baking powder
¾ teaspoon salt
¾ cup sugar
½ cup unsalted butter, softened
3 large eggs
2 tablespoons brandy
2 teaspoons grated lemon peel
1 tablespoon whole anise seeds

1. Preheat oven to 375°F. To toast almonds, spread almonds on cookie sheet. Bake 6 to 8 minutes until toasted and light brown. Remove almonds with spoon to cutting board; cool. Coarsely chop almonds.

2. Combine flour, baking powder and salt in small bowl. Beat sugar and butter in medium bowl with electric mixer at medium speed until light and fluffy. Add eggs, 1 at a time, beating well after each addition and scraping side of bowl often. Stir in brandy and lemon peel. Add flour mixture gradually; stir until smooth. Stir in almonds and anise seeds. Cover and refrigerate dough 1 hour or until firm.

3. Preheat oven to 375°F. Grease large cookie sheet. Divide dough in half. Shape ½ of dough into 12×2-inch log on lightly floured surface. (Dough will be fairly soft.) Pat smooth with lightly floured fingertips. Repeat with remaining ½ of dough to form second log. Place logs on prepared cookie sheet.

4. Bake 20 to 25 minutes until logs are light golden brown. Remove cookie sheet from oven to wire rack; turn off oven. Cool logs completely.

5. Preheat oven to 350°F. Cut logs diagonally with serrated knife into ½-inch-thick slices. Place slices flat in single layer on 2 *ungreased* baking sheets.

6. Bake 8 minutes. Turn slices over; bake 10 to 12 minutes more until cut surfaces are light brown and cookies are dry. Remove cookies to wire racks; cool completely. Store cookies in airtight container up to 2 weeks.

Makes about 4 dozen cookies

Step 1. Chopping almonds.

Step 3. Shaping dough into logs.

Step 5. Slicing baked logs.

Bolivian Almond Cookies (Alfajores de Almendras)

4 cups natural almonds
1 cup all-purpose flour
¼ teaspoon salt
1 cup sugar
¾ cup butter, softened
1 teaspoon vanilla
½ teaspoon almond extract
2 large eggs
2 tablespoons milk
1 tablespoon grated lemon peel
1 cup sliced natural almonds

1. Place whole almonds in food processor. Process using on/off pulsing action until almonds are ground, but not pasty.

2. Preheat oven to 350°F. Grease cookie sheets; set aside.

3. Place ground almonds, flour and salt in medium bowl; stir to combine.

4. Beat sugar, butter, vanilla and almond extract in large bowl with electric mixer at medium speed until light and fluffy, scraping down side of bowl once. Beat in eggs and milk. Gradually add ½ of flour mixture. Beat at low speed until well blended, scraping down side of bowl once. Stir in lemon peel and remaining flour mixture with spoon.

5. Drop rounded teaspoonfuls of dough 2 inches apart onto prepared cookie sheets.

6. Flatten slightly with spoon; top with sliced almonds.

7. Bake 10 to 12 minutes or until edges are lightly browned. Remove cookies with spatula to wire racks; cool completely.

8. Store tightly covered at room temperature or freeze up to 3 months.

Makes about 3 dozen cookies

Step 1. Checking consistency of ground almonds.

Step 5. Dropping rounded teaspoonfuls of dough onto cookie sheet.

Step 6. Topping with sliced almonds.

Almond Milk Chocolate Chippers

½ cup slivered almonds
1¼ cups all-purpose flour
½ teaspoon baking soda
½ teaspoon salt
½ cup butter or margarine,
   softened
½ cup packed light brown sugar
⅓ cup granulated sugar
1 large egg
2 tablespoons almond-flavored
   liqueur
1 cup milk chocolate chips

1. Preheat oven to 350°F. To toast almonds, spread on baking sheet. Bake 8 to 10 minutes or until golden brown, stirring frequently. Remove almonds from pan and cool; set aside.

2. *Increase oven temperature to 375°F.*

3. Place flour, baking soda and salt in small bowl; stir to combine.

4. Beat butter, brown sugar and granulated sugar in large bowl with electric mixer at medium speed until light and fluffy, scraping down side of bowl once. Beat in egg until well blended. Beat in liqueur. Gradually add flour mixture. Beat at low speed until well blended, scraping down side of bowl once.

5. Stir in chips and almonds with mixing spoon.

6. Drop rounded teaspoonfuls of dough 2 inches apart onto *ungreased* cookie sheets.

7. Bake 9 to 10 minutes or until edges are golden brown. Let cookies stand on cookie sheets 2 minutes. Remove cookies with spatula to wire racks; cool completely.

8. Store tightly covered at room temperature or freeze up to 3 months.

Makes about 3 dozen cookies

Step 4. Scraping down side of bowl.

Step 6. Placing rounded teaspoonfuls of dough on cookie sheet.

Step 7. Removing cookies to wire rack.

Harvest Pumpkin Cookies

2 cups all-purpose flour
1 teaspoon baking powder
1 teaspoon ground cinnamon
½ teaspoon baking soda
½ teaspoon salt
½ teaspoon ground allspice
1 cup butter, softened
1 cup sugar
1 cup canned pumpkin
1 large egg
1 teaspoon vanilla
1 cup chopped pecans
1 cup dried cranberries (optional)
Pecan halves (about 36)

1. Preheat oven to 375°F.

2. Place flour, baking powder, cinnamon, baking soda, salt and allspice in medium bowl; stir to combine.

3. Beat butter and sugar in large bowl with electric mixer at medium speed until light and fluffy, scraping down side of bowl once. Beat in pumpkin, egg and vanilla. Gradually add flour mixture. Beat at low speed until well blended, scraping down side of bowl once. Stir in chopped pecans and cranberries with spoon.

4. Drop heaping tablespoonfuls of dough 2 inches apart onto *ungreased* cookie sheets. Flatten mounds slightly with back of spoon.

5. Press one pecan half into center of each mound. Bake 10 to 12 minutes or until golden brown.

6. Let cookies stand on cookie sheets 1 minute. Remove cookies with spatula to wire racks; cool completely.

7. Store tightly covered at room temperature or freeze up to 3 months.

Makes about 3 dozen cookies

Step 3. Stirring nuts and cranberries into dough.

Step 4. Dropping heaping tablespoonfuls of dough onto cookie sheet.

Step 5. Pressing pecan half into center of dough mound.

Oatmeal Candied Chippers

¾ **cup all-purpose flour**
¾ **teaspoon salt**
½ **teaspoon baking soda**
¾ **cup butter or margarine,**
    softened
¾ **cup granulated sugar**
¾ **cup packed light brown sugar**
3 **tablespoons milk**
1 **large egg**
2 **teaspoons vanilla**
3 **cups uncooked rolled oats**
1 **cup candy-coated semisweet**
    chocolate baking pieces

1. Preheat oven to 375°F. Grease cookie sheets; set aside.

2. Place flour, salt and baking soda in small bowl; stir to combine.

3. Beat butter, granulated sugar and brown sugar in large bowl with electric mixer at medium speed until light and fluffy, scraping down side of bowl. Add milk, egg and vanilla; beat well, scraping down side of bowl once. Add flour mixture. Beat at low speed, scraping down side of bowl once.

4. Stir in oats with mixing spoon. Stir in baking pieces.

5. Drop dough by tablespoonfuls 2 inches apart on prepared cookie sheets.*

6. Bake 10 to 11 minutes until edges are golden brown. Let cookies stand 2 minutes on cookie sheets. Remove cookies with spatula to wire racks; cool completely.

7. Store tightly covered at room temperature or freeze up to 3 months.

Makes about 4 dozen cookies

*Or, use a small ice cream scoop (#80) filled with dough and pressed against side of bowl to level.

Step 4. Stirring in oats.

Step 5. Placing dough on cookie sheet with ice cream scoop.

Step 6. Removing cookies to wire rack.

Florentine Cookies

¼ cup sliced blanched almonds
¼ cup walnuts
5 red candied cherries
1 tablespoon golden or dark
    raisins
1 tablespoon diced candied lemon
    peel
1 tablespoon crystallized ginger
¼ cup unsalted butter
¼ cup sugar
1 tablespoon heavy or whipping
    cream
3 tablespoons all-purpose flour
4 ounces semisweet chocolate

1. Finely chop almonds, walnuts, cherries, raisins, lemon peel and ginger; combine in small bowl. Set aside.

2. Preheat oven to 350°F. Grease 2 large cookie sheets.

3. Combine butter, sugar and cream in small, heavy saucepan. Cook, uncovered, over medium heat until sugar dissolves and mixture boils, stirring constantly. Cook and stir 1 minute more. Remove from heat. Stir in nut-fruit mixture. Add flour; mix well.

4. Spoon heaping teaspoonfuls of batter onto prepared cookie sheet, baking only 4 cookies per sheet to allow room for spreading. Repeat with remaining batter.

5. Bake cookies, 1 sheet at a time, 8 to 10 minutes until deep brown. Remove cookie sheet from oven to wire rack.

continued on page 314

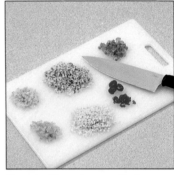

Step 1. Chopping candied cherries.

Step 3. Stirring nut-fruit mixture into butter mixture.

Step 4. Spooning batter onto cookie sheet.

Florentine Cookies, continued

6. If cookies have spread unevenly, push in edges with metal spatula to round out shape. Cool cookies 1 minute or until firm enough to remove from sheet, then quickly but carefully remove cookies with wide metal spatula to wire racks. Cool completely.

7. Repeat with remaining batter. (To prevent cookies from spreading too quickly, allow cookie sheets to cool before greasing and spooning batter onto sheets.)

8. Finely chop chocolate.

9. Bring water in bottom of double boiler just to a boil; remove from heat. Place chocolate in top of double boiler and place over water. Stir chocolate until melted; immediately remove from water. Let chocolate cool slightly.

10. Line large cookie sheet with waxed paper. Turn cookies over; spread chocolate on bottoms. Place cookies, chocolate side up, on prepared cookie sheet; let stand until chocolate is almost set.

11. Score chocolate in zig-zag pattern with tines of fork. Let stand until completely set or refrigerate until firm. Serve or store in airtight container in refrigerator. Garnish as desired.

Makes about 2 dozen cookies

Step 6. Shaping cookies with metal spatula.

Step 8. Chopping chocolate.

Step 11. Making zig-zag pattern in chocolate.

Gingerbread People

2¼ cups all-purpose flour
2 teaspoons ground cinnamon
2 teaspoons ground ginger
1 teaspoon baking powder
½ teaspoon salt
¼ teaspoon ground cloves
¼ teaspoon ground nutmeg
¾ cup butter, softened
½ cup packed light brown sugar
½ cup dark molasses
1 large egg
Red hot cinnamon candies (optional)
Icing (page 316)
Assorted food coloring (optional)
Assorted candies and decors for decorating

1. Place flour, cinnamon, ginger, baking powder, salt, cloves and nutmeg in large bowl; stir to combine.

2. Beat butter and brown sugar in large bowl with electric mixer at medium speed until light and fluffy, scraping down side of bowl once. Beat in molasses and egg. Gradually add flour mixture. Beat at low speed until well blended, scraping down side of bowl once.

3. Form dough into 3 discs; wrap in plastic wrap and refrigerate 1 hour or until firm.

4. Preheat oven to 350°F. Working with 1 disc at a time, unwrap dough and place on lightly floured surface. Roll out dough with lightly floured rolling pin to ³⁄₁₆-inch thickness.

5. Cut out gingerbread people with floured 5-inch cookie cutters.

6. Place cutouts on *ungreased* cookie sheets. Press red hot cinnamon candies into dough for eyes or coat buttons, if desired.

7. Gently press dough trimmings together; reroll and cut out more cookies. (Rerolled dough will produce slightly tougher cookies than first rolling.)

continued on page 316

Step 4. Rolling out dough to ³⁄₁₆-inch thickness.

Step 5. Cutting dough with floured cookie cutters.

Step 7. Pre... ...gh trimmings ...

Gingerbread People, *continued*

8. Bake about 12 minutes or until edges are golden brown. Let cookies stand on cookie sheets 1 minute. Remove cookies with spatula to wire racks; cool completely.

9. Prepare Icing. Icing may be divided into small bowls and tinted with food coloring to use for decorative piping, if desired.

10. Place each colored Icing in small resealable plastic freezer bag. Cut off tiny corner of bag.

11. Pipe Icing decoratively onto cooled cookies; press candies in Icing. Let stand at room temperature 20 minutes or until set.

12. Store tightly covered at room temperature or freeze up to 3 months.

Makes about 16 large cookies

*Icing**

1½ **cups sifted powdered sugar**
  2 **tablespoons milk plus additional, if needed**
½ **teaspoon vanilla**

*Prepared creamy or gel-type frostings in tubes may be substituted for Icing, if desired.

Place all ingredients in medium bowl; stir with spoon until thick, but spreadable. (If Icing is too thick, stir in 1 teaspoon additional milk.)

Step 10. Cutting off tiny corner of bag.

Step 11. Piping Icing onto cooled cookies.

Icing: Checking consistency of Icing.

Polish Fried Cookies (Chrusciki)

1 cup all-purpose flour
1 tablespoon granulated sugar
3 large egg yolks (page 343)
3 tablespoons sour cream
1 tablespoon vodka or whiskey
Vegetable oil for frying
2⅔ cups powdered sugar

1. Place flour and granulated sugar in medium bowl; stir to combine. Make well in center of flour mixture; add egg yolks, sour cream and vodka. Stir with spoon until soft dough forms.

2. Place dough on lightly floured surface; knead gently until dough is smooth. Form dough into 2 discs; wrap in plastic wrap and refrigerate until firm, 30 minutes or overnight.

3. Working with 1 disc at a time, unwrap dough and place on lightly floured surface. Roll out dough with lightly floured rolling pin to ⅛-inch-thick, 12×10-inch rectangle. Cut dough lengthwise in half; cut each half into 12 (1-inch-wide) strips.

4. Make 1-inch vertical slit down center of each strip. Insert one end of strip through slit to form twist; repeat with each strip.

5. Heat oil in large saucepan to 375°F. Place 6 strips at a time in hot oil.

6. Fry about 1 minute or until golden brown, turning cookies once with slotted spoon. Drain on paper towels.

7. Place ⅓ cup powdered sugar in small brown paper bag. Add 6 warm cookies at a time; close bag and shake until cookies are coated with sugar. Repeat with additional sugar and remaining cookies.

8. Cookies are best when served immediately, but can be stored in an airtight container 1 day.
Makes 4 dozen cookies

Step 5. Placing dough strips in hot oil.

Step 6. Turning cookies with slotted spoon.

Step 7. Shaking cookies in powdered sugar.

Linzer Sandwich Cookies

1⅓ cups all-purpose flour
¼ teaspoon baking powder
¼ teaspoon salt
¾ cup sugar
½ cup butter, softened
1 large egg
1 teaspoon vanilla
½ cup seedless raspberry jam

1. Place flour, baking powder and salt in small bowl; stir to combine.

2. Beat sugar and butter in medium bowl with electric mixer at medium speed until light and fluffy, scraping down side of bowl once. Beat in egg and vanilla. Gradually add flour mixture. Beat at low speed until dough forms, scraping down side of bowl once.

3. Form dough into 2 discs; wrap in plastic wrap and refrigerate 2 hours or until firm.

4. Preheat oven to 375°F. Working with 1 disc at a time, unwrap dough and place on lightly floured surface. Roll out dough with lightly floured rolling pin.

5. Cut dough into desired shapes with floured cookie cutters. Cut out even numbers of each shape. (If dough becomes soft, cover and refrigerate several minutes before continuing.)

6. Cut 1-inch centers out of half the cookies of each shape. Gently press dough trimmings together; reroll and cut out more cookies. Place cookies 1½ to 2 inches apart on *ungreased* cookie sheets.

7. Bake 7 to 9 minutes or until edges are lightly browned. Let cookies stand on cookie sheets 1 to 2 minutes. Remove cookies with spatula to wire racks; cool completely.

8. To assemble cookies, spread about 1 teaspoon jam on flat side of whole cookies, spreading almost to edges. Place matching cookies with holes, flat side down, on jam.

9. Store tightly covered at room temperature or freeze up to 3 months.

Makes about 2 dozen sandwich cookies

Step 5. Cutting dough with floured cookie cutters.

Step 6. Cutting 1-inch centers out of cookies.

Step 8. Spreading jam on whole cookies.

Chocolate-Raspberry Kolachy

2 squares (1 ounce each) semisweet chocolate, coarsely chopped
1½ cups all-purpose flour
¼ teaspoon baking soda
¼ teaspoon salt
½ cup butter or margarine, softened
3 ounces cream cheese or light cream cheese, softened
⅓ cup granulated sugar
1 teaspoon vanilla
¼ cup seedless raspberry jam
Powdered sugar

1. Preheat oven to 375°F. Lightly grease cookie sheets. Place chocolate in 1-cup glass measure. Microwave at HIGH 3 to 4 minutes or until chocolate is melted, stirring after 2 minutes; set aside.

2. Place flour, baking soda and salt in small bowl; stir. Beat butter and cream cheese in large bowl with electric mixer at medium speed until well blended, scraping down side of bowl occasionally. Beat in granulated sugar until light and fluffy, scraping down side of bowl once. Beat in vanilla and chocolate. Gradually add flour mixture. Beat at low speed, scraping down side of bowl once.

3. Divide dough in half; flatten each piece into a disc. Wrap in plastic wrap. Refrigerate about 2 hours or until firm.

4. Unwrap and roll out each piece of dough to ¼- to ⅛-inch thickness on well-floured surface with floured rolling pin. Cut out with 3-inch round biscuit cutter. Place 2 inches apart on cookie sheets. Place rounded ½ teaspoon jam in center of each circle.

5. Bring three edges of dough up over jam to form triangle; pinch edges together to seal, leaving center of triangle slightly open.

6. Bake 10 minutes or until set. Let cookies stand on cookie sheets 2 minutes. Remove cookies with spatula to wire racks; cool completely. Just before serving, sprinkle with powdered sugar.

7. Store tightly covered in refrigerator; let stand 30 minutes at room temperature before serving. Do not freeze.

Makes about 18 cookies

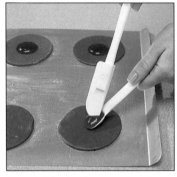
Step 4. Placing jam on dough.

Step 5. Shaping dough into triangle.

Moravian Spice Crisps

⅓ **cup shortening**
⅓ **cup packed brown sugar**
¼ **cup unsulfured molasses**
¼ **cup dark corn syrup**
1¾ **to 2 cups all-purpose flour**
2 **teaspoons ground ginger**
1 **teaspoon ground cinnamon**
½ **teaspoon ground cloves**
1¼ **teaspoons baking soda**
    Powdered sugar

1. Melt shortening in small saucepan over low heat. Remove from heat; stir in brown sugar, molasses and corn syrup. Set aside; cool.

2. Combine 1½ cups flour, spices and baking soda in large bowl. Beat in shortening mixture with electric mixer at medium speed; scrape bowl once. Gradually beat in additional flour until stiff dough forms; scrape bowl once.

3. Knead dough on lightly floured surface, adding more flour if too sticky. Form dough into 2 discs; wrap in plastic wrap and refrigerate 30 minutes or until firm.

4. Preheat oven to 350°F. Grease cookie sheets; set aside. Working with 1 disc at a time, unwrap dough and place on lightly floured surface. Roll out dough with lightly floured rolling pin to ¹⁄₁₆-inch thickness.

5. Cut dough with floured 2⅜-inch scalloped cookie cutter. (If dough becomes too soft, refrigerate several minutes before continuing.) Gently press dough trimmings together; reroll and cut out more cookies. (Rerolled dough will produce slightly tougher cookies than first rolling.) Place cookies ½ inch apart on prepared cookie sheets.

6. Bake 8 minutes or until firm and lightly browned. Remove cookies with spatula to wire racks; cool completely.

7. Place small strips of cardboard or parchment paper on cookies; dust with sifted powdered sugar. Carefully remove cardboard. Store tightly covered at room temperature or freeze up to 3 months.

Makes about 6 dozen cookies

Step 1. Stirring brown sugar, molasses and corn syrup.

Step 3. Kneading dough.

Tropical Coconut Squares

Base
- 1 cup butter, softened
- ½ cup granulated sugar
- 2 large egg yolks (page 343)
- ¼ teaspoon salt
- 2¼ cups all-purpose flour

Topping
- 3 tablespoons all-purpose flour
- ½ teaspoon baking powder
- 1½ cups packed light brown sugar
- 3 large eggs
- 1 teaspoon vanilla
- 1½ cups macadamia nuts
- 2 cups flaked coconut

1. Preheat oven to 350°F. Grease 15×10-inch jelly-roll pan; set aside.

2. For base, beat butter and granulated sugar in large bowl with electric mixer at medium speed until light and fluffy, scraping down side of bowl once. Beat in egg yolks and salt. Gradually add flour. Beat at low speed until well blended, scraping down side of bowl once.

3. Spread dough in prepared pan. Bake 16 to 18 minutes or until golden brown.

4. Meanwhile, for topping, place flour and baking powder in small bowl; stir to combine. Beat brown sugar and eggs in large bowl with electric mixer at medium speed 2 to 3 minutes or until very thick, scraping down side of bowl once. Beat in vanilla. Gradually add flour mixture. Beat at low speed until well blended, scraping down side of bowl once. Stir in nuts with spoon.

5. Spread batter evenly over hot crust; sprinkle evenly with coconut.

6. Return to oven; bake 20 to 22 minutes or until topping is golden brown and puffed.

7. Remove pan to wire rack; cool completely. Cut into about 2-inch squares.

8. Store squares tightly covered at room temperature or freeze up to 3 months.

Makes about 40 squares

Step 3. Spreading dough in prepared pan.

Step 5. Sprinkling batter with coconut.

Step 6. Baking until topping is golden brown.

Coconut Crowned Cappuccino Brownies

6 squares (1 ounce each) semisweet chocolate, coarsely chopped
1 tablespoon freeze dried coffee
1 tablespoon boiling water
¾ cup all-purpose flour
¾ teaspoon ground cinnamon
½ teaspoon baking powder
¼ teaspoon salt
½ cup sugar
¼ cup butter or margarine, softened
3 large eggs
¼ cup whipping cream
1 teaspoon vanilla
¾ cup flaked coconut, divided
½ cup semisweet chocolate chips, divided

1. Preheat oven to 350°F. Grease 8-inch square baking pan; set aside.

2. Melt chocolate squares in small, heavy saucepan over low heat, stirring constantly; set aside. Dissolve coffee in boiling water in small cup; set aside.

3. Place flour, cinnamon, baking powder and salt in small bowl; stir to combine.

4. Beat sugar and butter in large bowl with electric mixer at medium speed until light and fluffy, scraping down side of bowl once. Beat in 2 eggs, 1 at a time, scraping down side of bowl after each addition. Beat in chocolate mixture and coffee mixture until well combined. Add flour mixture. Beat at low speed until well blended, scraping down side of bowl once. Spread batter evenly into prepared baking pan.

5. For topping, combine cream, remaining 1 egg and vanilla in small bowl; mix well. Stir in ½ cup coconut and ¼ cup chips. Spread evenly over brownie base; sprinkle with remaining ¼ cup coconut and chips.

6. Bake 30 to 35 minutes or until coconut is browned and center is set. Remove pan to wire rack; cool completely. Cut into 2-inch squares.

7. Store tightly covered at room temperature or freeze up to 3 months.

Makes 16 brownies

Step 2. Stirring chocolate.

Step 5. Spreading topping over batter.

German Honey Bars (Lebkuchen)

2¾ cups all-purpose flour
2 teaspoons ground cinnamon
1 teaspoon baking powder
½ teaspoon baking soda
½ teaspoon salt
½ teaspoon ground cardamom
½ teaspoon ground ginger
½ cup honey
½ cup dark molasses
¾ cup packed brown sugar
3 tablespoons butter, melted
1 large egg
½ cup chopped toasted almonds (optional)
Glaze (recipe follows)

1. Preheat oven to 350°F. Grease 15×10-inch jelly-roll pan; set aside.

2. Place flour, cinnamon, baking powder, baking soda, salt, cardamom and ginger in medium bowl; stir to combine.

3. Combine honey and molasses in medium saucepan; bring to a boil over medium heat. Remove from heat; cool 10 minutes.

4. Stir brown sugar, butter and egg into honey mixture.

5. Place brown sugar mixture in large bowl. Gradually add flour mixture. Beat at low speed with electric mixer until dough forms, scraping down side of bowl once. Stir in almonds with spoon. (Dough will be slightly sticky.)

6. Spread dough evenly into prepared pan. Bake 20 to 22 minutes or until golden brown and set. Remove pan to wire rack; cool completely.

7. Prepare Glaze. Spread over cooled cookie. Let stand until set, about 30 minutes. Cut into 2×1-inch bars.

8. Store tightly covered at room temperature or freeze up to 3 months.

Makes about 6 dozen bars

Glaze

1¼ cups sifted powdered sugar
3 tablespoons fresh lemon juice
1 teaspoon grated lemon peel

Place all ingredients in medium bowl; stir with spoon until smooth.

Step 3. Bringing honey mixture to a boil.

Step 4. Stirring in brown sugar, butter and egg.

Step 7. Spreading Glaze over cooled cookie.

Luscious Lemon Bars

2 lemons
2 cups all-purpose flour
1 cup butter
½ cup powdered sugar
¼ teaspoon salt
1 cup granulated sugar
3 large eggs
⅓ cup fresh lemon juice
   Additional powdered sugar

1. Finely grate colored portion of lemon peel using bell grater or hand-held grater. Measure 4 teaspoons; set aside.

2. Preheat oven to 350°F. Grease 13×9-inch baking pan; set aside. Place 1 teaspoon lemon peel, flour, butter, ½ cup powdered sugar and salt in food processor. Process until mixture forms coarse crumbs.

3. Press mixture evenly in prepared pan. Bake 18 to 20 minutes or until golden brown.

4. Beat remaining 3 teaspoons lemon peel, granulated sugar, eggs and lemon juice in medium bowl with electric mixer at medium speed until well blended.

5. Pour mixture evenly over warm crust. Return to oven; bake 18 to 20 minutes longer or until center is set and edges are golden brown. Remove pan to wire rack; cool completely.

6. Dust with additional sifted powdered sugar; cut into about 2×1½-inch bars.

7. Store tightly covered at room temperature. Do not freeze.   *Makes 3 dozen bars*

Step 1. Grating lemon peel.

Step 3. Pressing crust mixture in 13×9-inch baking pan.

Step 5. Pouring lemon mixture over warm crust.

Chocolate Dipped Cinnamon Thins

1¼ cups all-purpose flour
1½ teaspoons ground cinnamon
¼ teaspoon salt
1 cup unsalted butter, softened
1 cup powdered sugar
1 large egg
1 teaspoon vanilla
4 ounces broken bittersweet
    chocolate candy bar

1. Place flour, cinnamon and salt in bowl; stir.

2. Beat butter in large bowl with electric mixer at medium speed until light and fluffy, scraping down side of bowl once. Add sugar; beat well. Add egg and vanilla; beat well, scraping down side of bowl once. Gradually add flour mixture. Beat at low speed, scraping down side of bowl occasionally.

3. Place dough on sheet of waxed paper. Using waxed paper to hold dough, roll it back and forth to form a log about 12 inches long and 2½ inches in diameter.

4. Securely wrap log in waxed paper. Refrigerate at least 2 hours or until firm. (Log may be frozen up to 3 months; thaw in refrigerator before baking.)

5. Preheat oven to 350°F. Cut log with long, sharp knife into ¼-inch slices. Place 2 inches apart on *ungreased* cookie sheets.

6. Bake 10 minutes or until set. Let cookies stand on cookie sheets 2 minutes. Remove cookies with spatula to wire racks; cool.

7. Melt chocolate in 1-cup glass measure set in bowl of very hot water, stirring twice. This will take about 10 minutes. Dip each cookie into chocolate, coating 1 inch up sides. Let excess chocolate drip back into cup.

8. Transfer to wire racks or waxed paper; let stand at room temperature about 40 minutes until chocolate is set.

9. Store between sheets of waxed paper at room temperature or in refrigerator. Do not freeze. *Makes about 2 dozen cookies*

Step 3. Forming a log.

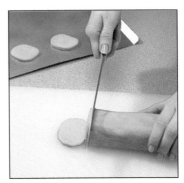

Step 5. Cutting dough into ¼-inch slices.

Step 7. Dipping cookies into melted chocolate.

Mint Chocolate Pinwheels

1¼ cups all-purpose flour
1 teaspoon baking powder
½ teaspoon salt
⅔ cup butter or margarine,
   softened
1 cup sugar
1 large egg
1 teaspoon vanilla
1 cup uncooked quick-cooking
   oats
1 cup mint chocolate chips

1. Place flour, baking powder and salt in small bowl; stir to combine.

2. Beat butter and sugar in large bowl with electric mixer at medium speed until light and fluffy, scraping down side of bowl once. Add egg and vanilla; beat well, scraping down side of bowl once. Gradually add flour mixture. Beat at low speed, scraping down side of bowl once. Stir in oats with mixing spoon.

3. Place chips in 1-cup glass measure. Microwave at HIGH about 2 minutes or until melted, stirring after 1½ minutes.

4. Divide cookie dough into halves. Add melted chocolate to one half; mix well.

5. Roll out each half of dough between 2 sheets of waxed paper into 15×10-inch rectangles. Remove waxed paper from top of each rectangle.

6. Invert chocolate dough over plain dough; remove waxed paper from chocolate dough. Using the waxed paper under the plain dough as a guide and starting at long side, tightly roll up dough jelly-roll style, removing waxed paper as you roll. Wrap dough in plastic wrap; refrigerate at least 2 hours or up to 24 hours.

7. Preheat oven to 350°F. Lightly grease cookie sheet. Unwrap log. With long, sharp knife, cut dough into ¼-inch slices. Place 3 inches apart on prepared cookie sheet.

8. Bake 10 to 12 minutes or until set. Remove cookies with spatula to wire racks; cool.

9. Store tightly covered at room temperature or freeze up to 3 months.

Makes about 3 dozen cookies

Step 6. Rolling up dough jelly-roll style.

Step 7. Cutting dough into ¼-inch slices.

Viennese Hazelnut Butter Thins

1 cup hazelnuts
1¼ cups powdered sugar
1 cup butter, softened
1 large egg
1 teaspoon vanilla
1¼ cups all-purpose flour
¼ teaspoon salt
1 cup semisweet chocolate chips

1. Preheat oven to 350°F. Spread hazelnuts in single layer on baking sheet. Bake 10 to 12 minutes or until toasted and skins begin to flake off; let cool slightly. Wrap nuts in heavy kitchen towel; rub to remove as much of the skins as possible. Process nuts in food processor until ground, but not pasty.

2. Beat powdered sugar and butter in medium bowl with electric mixer at medium speed until light and fluffy; scrape bowl once. Beat in egg and vanilla. Gradually add flour and salt. Beat in hazelnuts at low speed until well blended.

3. Place dough on sheet of waxed paper. Roll it back and forth to form a log 12 inches long and 2½ inches in diameter. Wrap in plastic wrap and refrigerate until firm, 2 hours or up to 48 hours.

4. Preheat oven to 350°F. Cut dough with knife crosswise into ¼-inch-thick slices. Place cookies 2 inches apart on *ungreased* cookie sheets.

5. Bake 10 to 12 minutes or until edges are very lightly browned. Let cookies stand on cookie sheets 1 minute. Remove cookies with spatula to wire racks; cool completely.

6. Place chocolate chips in 2-cup glass measure. Microwave at HIGH about 2 minutes, stirring once. Dip each cookie into chocolate, coating half way up sides. Let excess chocolate drip back into cup. Transfer cookies to waxed paper; let stand at room temperature 1 hour or until set.

7. Store tightly covered between sheets of waxed paper at room temperature or freeze up to 3 months.   *Makes about 3 dozen cookies*

Step 1. Rubbing hazelnuts gently to remove skins.

Step 3. Rolling dough in waxed paper to form a log.

Step 4. Cutting dough into ¼-inch-thick slices.

Desserts

Sweet Zucchini Spice Cake

3 cups grated peeled zucchini
   (about 1 pound)
1 cup ground walnuts
1 cup flaked coconut
4 large eggs
1 cup vegetable oil
2 tablespoons vanilla
2½ cups granulated sugar
  3 cups all-purpose flour
  2 teaspoons ground cinnamon
1½ teaspoons baking soda
  1 teaspoon baking powder
  1 teaspoon salt
   Pineapple Cream Cheese Icing
   (page 342)

1. Preheat oven to 350°F. Grease bottoms and sides of two 10-inch round cake pans with small amount of shortening.

2. Add 2 to 3 teaspoons flour to each pan. Gently tap side of pan to evenly coat bottom and side with flour. Invert pan and gently tap bottom to remove excess flour.

3. Combine zucchini, walnuts and coconut in medium bowl; set aside.

4. Beat together eggs, oil and vanilla in large bowl with electric mixer at medium speed until well blended. Beat in granulated sugar. Combine flour, cinnamon, baking soda, baking powder and salt in large bowl. Gradually add to egg mixture, mixing well after each addition. Stir in zucchini mixture. Pour evenly into prepared pans.

5. Bake 35 to 40 minutes or until wooden toothpick inserted in centers comes out clean. Cool layers in pans on wire racks 10 minutes. Loosen edge of cake with knife or flexible metal spatula. Using oven mitts or hot pads, place wire cooling rack on top of cake in pan. Turn cake and pan over so wire rack is on bottom. Gently shake cake to release from pan. Remove pan. Repeat with remaining cake layer. Cool layers completely.

continued on page 342

Step 1. Greasing the pan.

Step 2. Flouring the pan.

Step 5. Removing cake layer from pan.

Sweet Zucchini Spice Cake, continued

6. Gently brush loose crumbs off tops and sides of cake layers with pastry brush or hands.

7. Prepare Pineapple Cream Cheese Icing. Fill and frost cake with icing.

Makes one 2-layer cake

Pineapple Cream Cheese Icing

1 package (8 ounces) cream cheese
1 pound (about 4½ cups) powdered
    sugar
½ cup (1 stick) margarine, softened
1 can (8 ounces) crushed pineapple,
    drained

1. Place cream cheese on opened wrapper on cutting board. With utility knife, cut cream cheese lengthwise into ½-inch-wide slices. Then cut crosswise into ½-inch-square pieces. Let stand at room temperature until softened.

2. Sift powdered sugar into large bowl with sifter or fine-meshed sieve.

3. Beat together cream cheese and margarine in another large bowl with electric mixer at high speed until creamy. Blend in pineapple.

4. Gradually add powdered sugar, beating until frosting is smooth and of spreading consistency.

Step 6. Brushing off crumbs before icing.

Pineapple Cream Cheese Icing: Step 1. Softening cream cheese.

Pineapple Cream Cheese Icing: Step 2. Sifting powdered sugar.

Burnt Sugar Cake

1½ cups granulated sugar, divided
½ cup boiling water
2 large eggs
½ cup (1 stick) margarine,
  softened
1 teaspoon vanilla
2¼ cups all-purpose flour
1 tablespoon baking powder
1 teaspoon salt
1 cup milk
  Caramel Frosting (page 344)
  **Caramelized Sugar Shapes for
  garnish (page 344)**

1. To make sugar syrup, heat ½ cup granulated sugar in heavy 8-inch skillet over medium heat, stirring constantly, until sugar is melted and golden brown.

2. *Reduce heat to low.* Gradually stir boiling water into sugar mixture; continue cooking until sugar is dissolved, stirring constantly. Remove from heat; set aside.

3. Preheat oven to 375°F. Grease and flour two 8-inch round cake pans (technique on page 340).

4. To separate egg yolk from white, gently tap egg in center against a hard surface, such as side of bowl. Holding shell half in each hand, gently transfer yolk back and forth between 2 shell halves, allowing white to drip into medium bowl.

5. When all white has dripped into bowl, place yolk in another bowl. Transfer white to third bowl. Repeat separation process with remaining egg. (Egg whites must be free from any egg yolk to reach the proper volume when beaten.) Set aside egg yolks.

6. Beat egg whites with electric mixer at medium speed until foamy.

7. Gradually add ½ cup granulated sugar, beating at high speed until stiff peaks form; set aside.

8. Beat together margarine and remaining ½ cup granulated sugar in large bowl until light and fluffy. Beat in egg yolks. Blend in vanilla. Gradually add sugar syrup, mixing until well blended.

Step 1. Melting sugar.

Step 2. Adding water to sugar mixture.

continued on page 344

Burnt Sugar Cake, continued

9. Add combined flour, baking powder and salt to margarine mixture alternately with milk, beating well after each addition. Fold in egg white mixture. Pour batter evenly into prepared pans.

10. Bake 20 to 25 minutes or until wooden pick inserted in centers comes out clean. Cool layers in pans on wire racks 10 minutes.

11. Loosen edges of cakes with knife or flexible metal spatula. Using oven mitts or hot pads, place wire cooling rack on top of cake in pan. Turn cake over so wire rack is on bottom. Gently shake cake to release from pan. Remove pan. Repeat with remaining cake layer. Cool layers completely.

12. Gently brush loose crumbs off tops and sides of cake layers with pastry brush or hands.

13. To assemble, place one cake layer on cake plate. Tuck small strips of waxed paper under cake to keep plate clean while frosting cake. Prepare Caramel Frosting. Spread top of layer with frosting.

14. Top bottom layer with remaining cake layer. Frost top and side with remaining frosting. Remove waxed paper strips. Garnish, if desired.

Makes one 2-layer cake

Caramel Frosting

2 tablespoons margarine
⅔ cup packed brown sugar
⅛ teaspoon salt
⅓ cup evaporated milk
2½ cups powdered sugar
½ teaspoon vanilla

1. Melt margarine in 2-quart saucepan. Stir in brown sugar, salt and evaporated milk. Bring to a boil, stirring constantly. Remove from heat; cool to lukewarm.

2. Beat in powdered sugar with electric mixer at high speed until frosting is of spreading consistency. Blend in vanilla.

Caramelized Sugar Shapes: Heat ½ to ¾ cup granulated sugar in heavy 8-inch skillet over medium heat, stirring constantly, until sugar is melted and golden brown. Immediately drizzle into desired shapes on greased cookie sheet. Let stand until set. Carefully remove from cookie sheet.

Step 9. Folding in egg white mixture.

Step 11. Removing cake layer from pan.

Step 13. Spreading Caramel Frosting.

Lady Baltimore Cake

1¼ cups shortening
2¼ cups sugar
  2 teaspoons vanilla
3¼ cups all-purpose flour
4½ teaspoons baking powder
1½ teaspoons salt
1½ cups milk
  8 large egg whites* (page 343)
    Fruit Filling (page 348)
    Fluffy Frosting (page 348)

*Reserve 8 egg yolks, covered, in refrigerator for Fruit Filling.

1. Preheat oven to 350°F. Grease three 9-inch round cake pans with small amount of shortening.

2. Invert pan onto work surface. Place sheet of waxed paper over bottom of pan. Press around entire edge of pan to form crease in waxed paper. Cut along crease with scissors to form 9-inch circle. Repeat to make three circles. Place one circle in bottom of each pan.

3. Beat together shortening and sugar in large bowl with electric mixer at high speed until light and fluffy. Blend in vanilla.

4. Sift together flour, baking powder and salt. Add to sugar mixture alternately with milk, beating well after each addition.

5. Beat egg whites in separate bowl with electric mixer at high speed until stiff peaks form.

6. Fold egg whites into batter with rubber spatula by gently cutting down to bottom of bowl, scraping up side of bowl, then folding over top of mixture until evenly incorporated. Pour into prepared pans.

7. Bake 30 minutes or until wooden pick inserted in centers comes out clean. Cool layers in pans on wire racks 10 minutes. Loosen edge of cake with knife or flexible metal spatula. Using oven mitts or hot pads, place wire cooling rack on top of cake in pan. Turn cake and pan over so wire rack is on bottom. Gently shake cake to release from pan. Remove pan and peel off waxed paper. Repeat with remaining cake layers. Cool layers completely.

Step 2. Pressing around edge of pan to form crease.

Step 3. Beating together shortening and sugar.

Step 7. Removing cake layer from pan.

continued on page 348

8. Gently brush loose crumbs off tops and sides of cake layers with pastry brush or hands.

9. Prepare Fruit Filling. To assemble, spread two cake layers with filling; stack on cake plate. Top with remaining cake layer.

10. Prepare Fluffy Frosting. Frost cake with frosting.

Makes one 3-layer cake

Fruit Filling

½ cup (1 stick) butter or margarine
1 cup sugar
½ cup water
⅓ cup bourbon or brandy**
2 large eggs plus 8 reserved egg yolks
1 cup finely chopped raisins
¾ cup chopped pecans
½ cup chopped drained maraschino cherries
½ cup flaked coconut
¾ teaspoon vanilla

**Liquor may be omitted. Instead, increase water to ¾ cup and add 1 tablespoon rum extract with vanilla.

1. Melt butter in 2-quart saucepan. Stir in sugar, water and bourbon. Bring to a b   over medium-high heat, stirring   sionally to dissolve sugar.

    ?arate egg yolks from whites of   (te   nique on page 343).

    olks   th 8 reserved yolks

3. Stir small amount of hot mixture into egg yolks.

4. Add egg yolk mixture to remaining hot mixture in saucepan.

5. Cook and stir until thickened. (*Do not boil.*) Remove from heat.

6. Stir in raisins, pecans, cherries and coconut. Blend in vanilla. Cool completely.

Fluffy Frosting

1½ cups sugar
½ cup water
2 reserved egg whites***
2 teaspoons corn syrup *or* ¼ teaspoon cream of tartar
Dash of salt
1 teaspoon vanilla

***Use clean, uncracked eggs.

1. Combine sugar, water, egg whites, corn syrup and salt in top of double boiler. Beat with electric mixer at high speed 30 seconds.

2. Place on top of range; cook, stirring occasionally, over simmering water 7 minutes.

3. Remove from heat; add vanilla. Beat with electric mixer at high speed 3 minutes or until frosting is of spreading consistency.

Fruit Filling: Step 5. Cooking until thickened.

Fluffy Frosting: Step 1. Beating sugar mixture for 30 seconds.

Fluffy Frosting: Step 3. Beating to spreading consistency.

Banana Cake

2½ cups all-purpose flour
1 teaspoon salt
¾ teaspoon baking powder
¾ teaspoon baking soda
2 to 3 ripe bananas
⅔ cup shortening
1⅔ cups sugar
2 large eggs
⅔ cup buttermilk
⅔ cup chopped walnuts
   Vanilla Frosting (page 350)
   **Banana slices and fresh mint
      leaves for garnish**

1. Preheat oven to 375°F. Grease two 9-inch round cake pans with small amount of shortening. Add 2 to 3 teaspoons flour to each pan. Gently tap side of pan to evenly coat bottom and side with flour. Invert pan and gently tap bottom to remove excess flour.

2. Combine flour, salt, baking powder and baking soda in medium bowl; set aside.

3. Peel bananas and place in medium bowl. Mash with fork. Measure 1¼ cups; set aside.

4. Beat together shortening and sugar in large bowl with electric mixer at medium speed until light and fluffy. Add eggs, 1 at a time, beating well after each addition.

5. Stir in mashed bananas. Add flour mixture alternately with buttermilk, beating well after each addition. Stir in walnuts. Pour evenly into prepared pans.

6. Bake 30 to 35 minutes or until wooden pick inserted in centers comes out clean. Cool layers in pans on wire racks 10 minutes.

continued on page 350

Step 1. Flouring the pan.

Step 4. Adding eggs.

Banana Cake, continued

7. Loosen edge of cake with knife or flexible metal spatula. Using oven mitts or hot pads, place wire cooling rack on top of cake in pan. Turn cake and pan over so wire rack is on bottom. Gently shake cake to release from pan. Remove pan. Repeat with remaining cake layer. Cool layers completely.

8. Gently brush loose crumbs off tops and sides of cake layers with pastry brush or hands.

9. Prepare Vanilla Frosting. To assemble cake, place one layer on plate; spread with some of frosting. Cover with second cake layer.

10. Frost top and side of cake with frosting. Use flexible metal spatula to make surface as smooth as possible.

11. Pull cake comb around sides and top of cake for ridged effect. Garnish, if desired.   *Makes one 2-layer cake*

Vanilla Frosting

⅓ **cup plus 2 tablespoons all-purpose flour**
  Dash of salt
 1 cup milk
 ½ cup shortening
 ½ cup (1 stick) margarine, softened
1¼ **cups granulated sugar**
 1 teaspoon vanilla

1. Combine flour and salt in 2-quart saucepan. Gradually stir in milk until well blended. Cook over medium heat until thickened, stirring constantly. Cool.

2. Beat together shortening and margarine in large bowl with electric mixer at medium speed until creamy. Add sugar; beat until light and fluffy. Blend in vanilla. Add cooled flour mixture; beat until smooth.

Step 7. Removing cake layer from pan.

Step 11. Pulling cake comb across cake.

Zucchini Chocolate Cake

2 to 3 medium zucchini
½ cup (1 stick) margarine or butter, softened
½ cup vegetable oil
1⅔ cups sugar
2 large eggs
1 teaspoon vanilla
½ teaspoon chocolate flavoring
2½ cups all-purpose flour
¼ cup unsweetened cocoa
1 teaspoon baking soda
½ teaspoon salt
½ cup buttermilk
½ cup chopped nuts
1 cup (6 ounces) semisweet chocolate chips

1. Preheat oven to 325°F. Grease 13×9-inch baking pan with small amount of shortening.

2. Add 3 to 4 teaspoons flour to pan; gently tap sides of pan to evenly coat bottom and sides with flour. Invert pan and gently tap bottom to remove excess flour.

3. Shred zucchini using bell grater or hand-held grater; measure 2 cups. Set aside. (No need to peel zucchini before shredding.)

4. Beat together margarine, oil and sugar in large bowl with electric mixer at medium speed until well blended.

5. Add eggs, 1 at a time, beating well after each addition. Blend in vanilla and chocolate flavoring.

6. Combine flour, cocoa, baking soda and salt in medium bowl. Add to margarine mixture alternately with buttermilk, beating well after each addition. Stir in zucchini.

7. Pour into prepared pan. Sprinkle with nuts and chocolate chips.

8. Bake 55 minutes or until wooden pick inserted in center comes out clean; cool cake completely in pan on wire rack. Cut into squares. Frost with your favorite chocolate frosting, if desired.

Makes one 13×9-inch cake

Step 1. Greasing the pan.

Step 3. Shredding zucchini.

Step 7. Sprinkling nuts and chocolate chips over batter.

Blueberry Cake

1 lemon
½ cup (1 stick) butter, softened
⅔ cup sugar, divided
1 large egg
2½ teaspoons vanilla, divided
1½ cups all-purpose flour
1½ teaspoons baking powder
4 cups fresh blueberries
2 cups sour cream
2 large egg yolks (page 343)
¼ teaspoon ground cardamom
**Lemon peel and fresh mint
    leaves for garnish**

1. Preheat oven to 350°F. Grease 9-inch springform pan with small amount of shortening.

2. Finely grate colored portion of lemon peel using bell grater or hand-held grater. Measure ¼ teaspoon. Set aside.

3. Beat together butter and ⅓ cup sugar in large bowl with electric mixer at medium speed until light and fluffy. Blend in 1 egg and 1½ teaspoons vanilla.

4. Combine flour and baking powder in medium bowl. Add to butter mixture, mixing until well blended. Spread onto bottom of prepared pan; cover with blueberries.

5. Combine remaining ⅓ cup sugar, 1 teaspoon vanilla, sour cream, egg yolks, cardamom and grated lemon peel; pour over blueberries.

6. Bake 50 to 55 minutes or until set. *(Do not overbake.)* Cool 10 minutes. Loosen rim of pan. Cool cake completely before removing rim of pan. Garnish, if desired.

Makes one 9-inch cake

Step 4. Covering batter with blueberries.

Step 5. Pouring sour cream mixture over blueberries.

Step 6. Loosening rim of pan.

Buttermilk Pound Cake

3 cups sifted all-purpose flour
½ teaspoon baking powder
½ teaspoon baking soda
½ teaspoon salt
1 cup (2 sticks) butter or
   margarine, softened
2 cups superfine sugar*
2 large eggs
1 teaspoon vanilla
1 teaspoon lemon extract
1 cup buttermilk
1 orange for garnish
   Starfruit slices and strawberry
      slices for garnish

*Superfine sugar is more finely granulated than regular granulated sugar.

1. Preheat oven to 350°F. Grease two 9×5-inch loaf pans with small amount of shortening. Add 2 to 3 teaspoons flour to each pan. Gently tap sides of pan to evenly coat bottom and sides with flour. Invert pan and gently tap bottom to remove excess flour.

2. Combine flour, baking powder, baking soda and salt in medium bowl; set aside.

3. Beat together butter and sugar in large bowl with electric mixer at high speed until light and fluffy. Add eggs, 1 at a time, beating well after each addition. Blend in vanilla and lemon extract.

4. Add flour mixture alternately with buttermilk, beating well after each addition. Pour evenly into prepared pans.

5. Bake 35 to 40 minutes or until wooden pick inserted in centers comes out clean.

6. Remove thin strips of peel from orange using citrus zester. Reserve for garnish, if desired.

7. Cool loaves in pans on wire racks 10 minutes. Loosen edges; remove to racks to cool completely. Garnish, if desired.

Makes two 9×5-inch loaves

Step 1. Flouring the pan.

Step 3. Adding eggs.

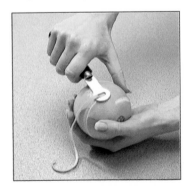
Step 6. Removing peel from orange.

Apple Upside-Down Cake

¼ cup (½ stick) plus 3 tablespoons
   butter, divided
½ cup packed brown sugar
½ teaspoon ground cinnamon
¼ teaspoon ground nutmeg
¼ teaspoon ground mace
3 McIntosh apples*
2 teaspoons lemon juice
1⅓ cups sifted cake flour
¾ cup granulated sugar
1¾ teaspoons baking powder
¼ teaspoon salt
½ cup milk
1 teaspoon vanilla
1 large egg, separated (page 343)

*Substitute any large cooking apples for
McIntosh apples.

1. Preheat oven to 375°F.

2. Melt ¼ cup butter in 8-inch square baking pan. Add brown sugar and spices; mix well.

3. Peel apples. Remove cores; discard.

4. Cut apples into rings. Arrange over brown sugar mixture in bottom of pan; sprinkle with lemon juice. Set aside.

5. Combine cake flour, granulated sugar, baking powder and salt in large bowl. Cut in remaining 3 tablespoons butter with pastry blender until mixture resembles coarse crumbs.

6. Add milk and vanilla; beat with electric mixer at low speed until dry ingredients are moistened. Continue beating 2 minutes at medium speed. Blend in egg yolk.

7. Clean beaters of electric mixer. Beat egg white in small bowl with electric mixer at high speed until stiff peaks form. Gently fold egg white into batter. Pour over apples in pan.

8. Bake 35 minutes or until wooden pick inserted in center comes out clean. Cool cake in pan on wire rack 5 minutes. Loosen edges and invert onto serving plate. *Let stand 1 minute before removing pan.* Serve warm.

Makes one 8-inch square cake

Step 3. Removing cores of apples.

Step 5. Cutting in butter.

Angel Food Cake

1¼ cups cake flour
1⅓ cups plus ½ cup sugar, divided
12 large egg whites (page 343)
1¼ teaspoons cream of tartar
 ¼ teaspoon salt
  1 teaspoon vanilla
 ¼ teaspoon almond extract
  Fresh strawberries for serving (optional)

1. Preheat oven to 350°F.

2. Sift together flour with ½ cup sugar four times.

3. Beat egg whites with cream of tartar, salt, vanilla and almond extract in large bowl with electric mixer at high speed until stiff peaks form.

4. Gradually add remaining 1⅓ cups sugar, beating well after each addition. Fold in flour mixture with rubber spatula by gently cutting down to bottom of bowl, scraping up side of bowl, then folding over top of mixture. Repeat until flour mixture is evenly incorporated.

5. Pour into ungreased 10-inch tube pan.

6. Bake 35 to 40 minutes or until cake springs back when lightly touched with finger.

7. Invert pan; place on top of clean, empty, heatproof bottle. Allow cake to cool completely in pan before removing from pan.

8. Serve with strawberries, if desired.

Makes one 10-inch tube cake

Step 2. Sifting together flour and sugar.

Step 4. Folding in flour mixture.

Step 6. Testing for doneness.

Apple Cheesecake

1 cup graham cracker crumbs
1 cup sugar, divided
1 teaspoon ground cinnamon, divided
3 tablespoons margarine, melted
2 packages (8 ounces each) cream cheese, softened
2 large eggs
½ teaspoon vanilla
2½ pounds apples, peeled and thinly sliced (4 cups)
½ cup chopped pecans

1. Preheat oven to 350°F.

2. Combine crumbs, 3 tablespoons sugar, ½ teaspoon cinnamon and margarine in small bowl; mix well. Press onto bottom and up side of 9-inch pie plate.

3. Bake crust 10 minutes.

4. Beat together cream cheese and ½ cup sugar in large bowl with electric mixer at medium speed until well blended. Add eggs, 1 at a time, beating well after each addition. Blend in vanilla; pour into crust.

5. Combine remaining sugar and ½ teaspoon cinnamon in large bowl. Add apples; toss gently to coat.

6. Spoon apple mixture over cream cheese mixture.

7. Sprinkle with pecans.

8. Bake 1 hour and 10 minutes or until set. Cool completely before serving. Store in refrigerator. *Makes one 9-inch cheesecake*

Step 2. Pressing crumb mixture onto bottom of pie plate.

Step 6. Spooning apple mixture over cream cheese mixture.

Step 7. Sprinkling with pecans.

Turtle Pecan Cheesecake

8 ounces chocolate or vanilla
   wafer cookies
¼ cup (½ stick) butter, melted
2½ packages (20 ounces total)
   cream cheese, softened
   (page 178)
1 cup sugar
4½ teaspoons all-purpose flour
¼ teaspoon salt
1 teaspoon vanilla
3 large eggs
2 tablespoons whipping cream
   Caramel Topping
   (recipe follows)
   Chocolate Topping
   (recipe follows)
1 cup chopped toasted pecans

1. Preheat oven to 450°F.

2. Place cookies in resealable plastic bag. Squeeze out excess air; seal bag. Roll over cookies with rolling pin until finely crushed.

3. Combine cookie crumbs and butter; press onto bottom of 9-inch springform pan.

4. Beat cream cheese in large bowl with electric mixer at medium speed until creamy. Add sugar, flour, salt and vanilla; mix well. Add eggs, 1 at a time, beating well after each addition. Blend in cream. Pour over crust. Bake 10 minutes.

5. *Reduce oven temperature to 200°F.* Continue baking 35 to 40 minutes or until set. Loosen rim of pan and remove; cool.

6. Prepare Caramel Topping and Chocolate Topping. Drizzle toppings over cheesecake; refrigerate. Sprinkle with pecans.

Makes one 9-inch cheesecake

Caramel Topping

½ (14-ounce) bag caramels
⅓ cup whipping cream

Combine ingredients in small saucepan; stir over low heat until smooth.

Chocolate Topping

4 ounces sweet baking chocolate
1 teaspoon butter
2 tablespoons whipping cream

Combine ingredients in small saucepan; stir over low heat until smooth.

Step 2. Crushing cookies with rolling pin.

Step 4. Adding eggs.

Step 6. Drizzling Chocolate Topping over cheesecake.

Raspberry Cheesecake Blossoms

**3 packages (10 ounces each)
frozen raspberries, in syrup,
thawed**
¼ cup butter, melted
8 sheets phyllo dough*
**1 package (8 ounces) cream
cheese, softened (page 178)**
½ cup cottage cheese
1 large egg
**½ cup plus 3 tablespoons sugar,
divided**
4 teaspoons lemon juice, divided
½ teaspoon vanilla
**Fresh raspberries and sliced
kiwifruit for garnish**

*Cover with plastic wrap, then a damp
kitchen towel to prevent dough from
drying out.

1. Drain thawed raspberries in fine-meshed sieve over 1-cup glass measure. Reserve syrup.

2. Preheat oven to 350°F. Grease 12 (2½-inch) muffin cups.

3. Brush melted butter onto 1 phyllo sheet. Cover with second phyllo sheet; brush with butter. Repeat with remaining sheets of phyllo.

4. Cut stack of phyllo dough in thirds lengthwise and then in fourths crosswise, to make a total of 12 squares. Gently fit each stacked square into prepared muffin cup.

5. Place cream cheese, cottage cheese, egg, 3 tablespoons sugar, 1 teaspoon lemon juice and vanilla in food processor or blender. Process until smooth. Divide mixture evenly among muffin cups.

6. Bake 10 to 15 minutes or until lightly browned. Carefully remove from muffin cups to wire racks to cool.

7. Bring reserved raspberry syrup to a boil in small saucepan over medium-high heat. Cook until reduced to ¾ cup, stirring occasionally.

8. Place thawed raspberries in food processor or blender. Process until smooth. Press through fine-meshed sieve with back of spoon to remove seeds.

9. Combine raspberry purée, reduced syrup, remaining ½ cup sugar and 3 teaspoons lemon juice in small bowl. Mix well.

10. To serve, spoon raspberry sauce onto 12 dessert plates. Place cheesecake blossom on each plate. Garnish, if desired.

Makes 12 servings

Step 1. Draining raspberries.

Step 3. Brushing butter onto phyllo.

Step 4. Fitting phyllo dough into muffin cups.

Topsy Turvy Apple Pie

Double Pie Crust
   2 cups all-purpose flour
   ½ teaspoon salt
   ¾ cup shortening
   5 tablespoons ice water

Apple Filling
   ¼ cup butter or margarine,
      softened
   ½ cup pecan halves
   ½ cup packed brown sugar
   4 large Granny Smith apples
   1 tablespoon lemon juice
   1 tablespoon all-purpose flour
   ½ cup granulated sugar
   1 teaspoon ground cinnamon
   1 teaspoon ground nutmeg
      Dash salt

1. Prepare Double Pie Crust following techniques on page 10. Cover dough with plastic wrap and refrigerate 30 minutes.

2. Spread butter evenly on bottom and up side of 9-inch pie plate. Press pecans, rounded side down, into butter. Pat brown sugar on pecans.

3. Preheat oven to 400°F. Roll out 1 disc of pie crust dough (technique on page 10). Place over brown sugar and pecans.

4. Peel apples. Remove cores; discard. Cut apples into slices.

5. Place apple slices in large bowl; sprinkle with lemon juice. Combine flour, granulated sugar, cinnamon, nutmeg and salt in small bowl. Add to apples; toss to coat.

6. Place apple mixture in pie crust; spread evenly to make top level.

7. Roll out top crust and place over filling (technique on page 10).

8. Trim edge leaving ½-inch overhang. Fold overhang under so crust is even with edge of pie plate. Press flat to seal. Flute, if desired. Pierce top crust with fork to allow steam to escape.

9. Bake 50 minutes. Remove from oven; cool 5 minutes on wire rack.

10. Place serving dish over warm pie plate. Invert both pie plate and serving dish so serving dish is on the bottom. Remove pie plate. Serve pie warm or at room temperature.

Makes 6 to 8 servings

Step 2. Patting brown sugar on pecans.

Step 4. Cutting apples into slices.

Step 10. Removing pie plate after inverting pie.

Mississippi Mist Pie

1 package (8 ounces) light cream cheese
6 to 8 limes
50 vanilla wafer cookies
5 tablespoons butter or margarine, melted
2 pints fresh strawberries
1 can (14 ounces) sweetened condensed milk
1 tablespoon green crème de menthe liqueur
Sweetened Whipped Cream (page 372)
Lime slices for garnish

1. Place light cream cheese on opened wrapper on cutting board. With utility knife, cut cream cheese lengthwise into ½-inch-wide slices. Then cut crosswise into ½-inch-square pieces. Let stand at room temperature until softened.

2. To juice limes, cut limes in half on cutting board.

3. Using citrus juicer, squeeze juice from limes into measuring cup or small bowl. Measure ½ cup lime juice; set aside.

4. Place cookies in food processor or blender container; process using on/off pulses until finely crushed.

5. Combine cookie crumbs and butter in medium bowl; mix well. Press firmly onto bottom and up side of 9-inch pie plate. Refrigerate until firm.

continued on page 372

Step 1. Softening cream cheese.

Step 3. Juicing limes.

Step 4. Processing cookies in food processor.

4. Hulling and slicing
strawberries

6. Reserve 3 strawberries for garnish. Cut green tops off remaining strawberries so that berries are no more than 1 inch tall. Arrange strawberries, cut ends down, on crust; refrigerate.

7. Beat cream cheese in large bowl with electric mixer at medium speed until smooth, scraping down side of bowl once. Add sweetened condensed milk; beat at medium speed until smooth. Add lime juice and liqueur; beat at low speed until well blended.

8. Pour into prepared crust, covering strawberries. Refrigerate at least 1 hour.

9. Prepare Sweetened Whipped Cream. Spoon into pastry bag fitted with star decorating tip. Pipe lattice design on top of pie.

10. Slice reserved strawberries. Garnish, if desired. *Makes 6 to 8 servings*

Sweetened Whipped Cream

1 cup whipping cream
3 tablespoons sugar
½ teaspoon vanilla

1. Chill large bowl and beaters thoroughly. Pour chilled whipping cream into chilled bowl and beat with electric mixer at high speed until soft peaks form. To test, lift beaters from whipping cream; mixture should have droopy, but definite, peaks.

2. Gradually add sugar and vanilla. Whip until stiff peaks form. To test, lift beaters from cream mixture; stiff peaks should remain on surface.

Step 6. Arranging strawberries on crust.

Step 9. Piping lattice design on top of pie.

Sweetened Whipped Cream: Step 2. Testing for stiff peaks.

Custard Rum Torte

6 large eggs
1¼ cups granulated sugar, divided
¾ teaspoon salt, divided
1¼ cups all-purpose flour
⅓ cup cornstarch
3½ cups milk
2 large egg yolks
2 tablespoons butter or
    margarine
2 teaspoons vanilla
2 pints fresh strawberries
6 tablespoons dark rum
4 cups heavy or whipping cream
    (2 pints)
¼ cup powdered sugar, sifted

1. Preheat oven to 350°F. Grease and flour 10-inch springform pan. Beat eggs in large bowl with electric mixer at high speed until foamy. Beat in ¾ cup granulated sugar, 2 tablespoons at a time, beating well after each addition. Beat 3 minutes more. Beat in ¼ teaspoon salt. Sift ⅓ of flour over egg mixture; fold in. Repeat until all flour has been incorporated.

2. Spread batter evenly into prepared springform pan. Bake 40 minutes or until wooden pick inserted in center comes out clean. Cool in pan on wire rack 10 minutes. Loosen cake from side of pan with knife or flexible metal spatula; remove side of pan. Remove cake from bottom of pan to wire rack. Cool completely. Clean pan.

3. For custard, combine remaining ½ cup granulated sugar, ½ teaspoon salt and cornstarch in large saucepan; mix. Stir in milk until smooth. Bring to a boil over medium heat, stirring frequently. Boil 3 minutes, stirring constantly; remove from heat. Whisk egg yolks in small bowl; gradually whisk in 1 cup hot milk mixture. Gradually whisk egg yolk mixture into remaining milk mixture in saucepan. Cook over low heat 1 minute, stirring constantly. Immediately pour custard into medium bowl. Cut butter into 6 pieces; add to custard and stir until melted. Stir in vanilla. Press waxed paper onto surface of custard; refrigerate. Cool completely.

4. Rinse and drain strawberries. Pat dry and reserve 8 whole strawberries; wrap in plastic wrap and refrigerate for garnish. Hull and thinly slice remaining strawberries

continued

Step 1. Sifting flour over egg mixture.

Step 3. Cooking and stirring custard until thickened.

Custard Rum Torte, *continued*

5. To cut cooled cake horizontally into 3 even layers, measure with ruler into 3 equal layers and mark with wooden picks. Cut through cake with thin serrated knife using wooden picks as guides.

6. To assemble, brush top of each layer with 2 tablespoons rum. Place one cake layer in bottom of cleaned springform pan. Spread evenly with ½ of custard. Arrange ½ of strawberry slices over custard in single layer. Top with second cake layer; spread with remaining custard and top with remaining strawberry slices. Place third cake layer on top. Cover and refrigerate at least 12 hours.

7. About 45 minutes before serving, beat cream with powdered sugar in large bowl with electric mixer at high speed until stiff. Spoon 2 cups whipped cream mixture into pastry bag fitted with large star tip; refrigerate.

8. Remove side of pan; place dessert on serving plate. (Do not remove bottom of pan.) Spread remaining whipped cream mixture evenly and smoothly on side and top of dessert.

9. Pipe reserved whipped cream mixture around top and bottom edges of dessert. Refrigerate 30 minutes before serving.

10. To serve, garnish with reserved whole strawberries. Cut dessert into slices. Refrigerate leftovers.

Makes 10 to 12 servings

Step 5. Cutting cake into 3 equal layers.

Step 6. Arranging strawberry slices on custard.

Step 9. Piping whipped cream garnish.

Crunchy Peach Cobbler

1 can (29 ounces) or 2 cans (16 ounces each) cling peach slices in syrup
⅓ cup plus 1 tablespoon granulated sugar, divided
1 tablespoon cornstarch
½ teaspoon vanilla
½ cup packed brown sugar
2 cups all-purpose flour, divided
⅓ cup uncooked rolled oats
¼ cup margarine or butter, melted
½ teaspoon ground cinnamon
½ teaspoon salt
½ cup shortening
4 to 5 tablespoons cold water
Sweetened Whipped Cream (page 372) for garnish

1. Drain peach slices in fine-meshed sieve over 2-cup glass measure. Reserve ¾ cup syrup.

2. Combine ⅓ cup granulated sugar and cornstarch in small saucepan. Slowly add reserved syrup. Stir well. Add vanilla. Cook over low heat, stirring constantly, until thickened. Set aside.

3. Combine brown sugar, ½ cup flour, oats, margarine and cinnamon in small bowl; stir until mixture forms coarse crumbs. Set aside.

4. Preheat oven to 350°F.

5. Combine remaining 1½ cups flour, 1 tablespoon granulated sugar and salt in small bowl. Cut in shortening with pastry blender or 2 knives until mixture forms pea-sized pieces.

6. Sprinkle water, 1 tablespoon at a time, over flour mixture. Toss lightly with fork until mixture holds together. Press together to form a ball.

7. Roll out dough into square ⅛ inch thick (technique on page 10). Cut into 10-inch square.

8. Fold dough in half, then in half again. Carefully place folded dough in center of 8×8-inch baking dish. Unfold and press onto bottom and about 1 inch up sides of dish.

9. Arrange peaches over crust. Pour sauce over peaches. Sprinkle with crumb topping.

10. Bake 45 minutes. Prepare Sweetened Whipped Cream. Serve warm or at room temperature with Sweetened Whipped Cream, if desired.

Makes about 6 servings

Step 1. Draining peaches.

Step 5. Cutting in shortening until mixture forms pea-sized pieces.

Step 8. Pressing dough onto bottom and up sides of dish.

Italian Ice

1 cup fruity white wine
1 cup water
1 cup sugar
1 cup lemon juice
2 egg whites* (page 343)
Fresh berries (optional)
Mint leaves for garnish

*Use clean, uncracked eggs.

1. Place wine and water in small saucepan; add sugar. Cook over medium-high heat until sugar has dissolved and syrup boils, stirring frequently. Cover; boil 1 minute. Uncover; adjust heat to maintain simmer. Simmer 10 minutes without stirring. Remove from heat. Refrigerate 1 hour or until syrup is completely cool.

2. Stir lemon juice into cooled syrup. Pour into 9-inch round cake pan. Freeze 1 hour.

3. Quickly stir mixture with fork breaking up ice crystals. Freeze 1 hour more or until firm but not solid. Meanwhile, place medium bowl in freezer to chill.

4. Beat egg whites in small bowl with electric mixer at high speed until stiff peaks form. Remove lemon ice mixture from cake pan to chilled bowl. Immediately beat ice with whisk or fork until smooth. Fold in egg whites; mix well. Spread egg mixture evenly into same cake pan.

5. Freeze 30 minutes. Immediately stir with fork; cover cake pan with foil. Freeze at least 3 hours or until firm.

6. To serve, scoop Italian Ice into fluted champagne glasses or dessert dishes. Serve with berries. Garnish with mint leaves, if desired. *Makes 4 servings*

Step 2. Pouring cooled syrup into cake pan.

Step 3. Breaking up ice crystals.

Step 4. Folding beaten egg whites into frozen mixture.

Index

METRIC CONVERSION CHART

VOLUME MEASUREMENTS (dry)

1/8 teaspoon = 0.5 mL
1/4 teaspoon = 1 mL
1/2 teaspoon = 2 mL
3/4 teaspoon = 4 mL
1 teaspoon = 5 mL
1 tablespoon = 15 mL
2 tablespoons = 30 mL
1/4 cup = 60 mL
1/3 cup = 75 mL
1/2 cup = 125 mL
2/3 cup = 150 mL
3/4 cup = 175 mL
1 cup = 250 mL
2 cups = 1 pint = 500 mL
3 cups = 750 mL
4 cups = 1 quart = 1 L

VOLUME MEASUREMENTS (fluid)

1 fluid ounce (2 tablespoons) = 30 mL
4 fluid ounces (1/2 cup) = 125 mL
8 fluid ounces (1 cup) = 250 mL
12 fluid ounces (1 1/2 cups) = 375 mL
16 fluid ounces (2 cups) = 500 mL

WEIGHTS (mass)

1/2 ounce = 15 g
1 ounce = 30 g
3 ounces = 90 g
4 ounces = 120 g
8 ounces = 225 g
10 ounces = 285 g
12 ounces = 360 g
16 ounces = 1 pound = 450 g

DIMENSIONS

1/16 inch = 2 mm
1/8 inch = 3 mm
1/4 inch = 6 mm
1/2 inch = 1.5 cm
3/4 inch = 2 cm
1 inch = 2.5 cm

OVEN TEMPERATURES

250°F = 120°C
275°F = 140°C
300°F = 150°C
325°F = 160°C
350°F = 180°C
375°F = 190°C
400°F = 200°C
425°F = 220°C
450°F = 230°C

BAKING PAN SIZES

Utensil	Size in Inches/Quarts	Metric Volume	Size in Centimeters
Baking or Cake Pan (square or rectangular)	8×8×2	2 L	20×20×5
	9×9×2	2.5 L	22×22×5
	12×8×2	3 L	30×20×5
	13×9×2	3.5 L	33×23×5
Loaf Pan	8×4×3	1.5 L	20×10×7
	9×5×3	2 L	23×13×7
Round Layer Cake Pan	8×1½	1.2 L	20×4
	9×1½	1.5 L	23×4
Pie Plate	8×1¼	750 mL	20×3
	9×1¼	1 L	23×3
Baking Dish or Casserole	1 quart	1 L	—
	1½ quart	1.5 L	—
	2 quart	2 L	—